THE
MAYFLOWER
MURDERER
And Other Forgotten Firsts in American History

THE MAYFLOWER MURDERER

And Other Forgotten Firsts in American History

Peter F. Stevens

William Morrow and Company, Inc.
New York

To my father, with wishes he were here
To my mother, with gratitude for her
faith

Copyright © 1993 by Peter F. Stevens

The following chapters have been previously published in similar form and content:
Chapter 17: Landmark Hero or Landmark Traitor?: Lambdin P. Milligan was adapted
from "The Saga of Lambdin P. Milligan," published in *Indiana Horizons* magazine,
Summer 1988.
Chapter 19: "As a Queen Should Go": Queen Emma's Landmark Trip was adapted from
"Queen Emma's Historic Voyage," published in *Honolulu Magazine,* October 1991.
Chapter 23: Avant-garde Aviatrix: Blanche Stuart Scott was adapted from "Avant-Garde
Aviatrix," published in *Indiana Horizons* magazine, Winter 1989.

It is the policy of William Morrow and Company, Inc., and its imprints and affiliates,
recognizing the importance of preserving what has been written, to print the books we
publish on acid-free paper, and we exert our best efforts to that end.

Library of Congress Cataloging-in-Publication Data

Stevens, Peter F.
    The Mayflower murderer and other forgotten firsts in American history / by Peter F.
Stevens.
        p.   cm.
    Includes bibliographical references and index.
    ISBN 0-688-11818-6
    1. United States—History—Miscellanea. 2. United States—Biography. I. Title.
E179.S84   1993
973—dc20   92-13925
                                                                          CIP

Printed in the United States of America

First Edition

1 2 3 4 5 6 7 8 9 10

BOOK DESIGN BY LISA STOKES

Contents

Part I

The New World and New Notions

1 Big, Bad John Billington: The Killer Pilgrim

In the woods near Plymouth a matchlock musket roared. A hunter's quarry crumpled to the forest floor. But the prey was not some wild turkey or other woodland animal. John Newcomen was on the ground, blood streaming from one of his shoulders.

Another man disappeared with his smoking musket into the forest. His name was John Billington, and he was about to become America's first murderer.

From the moment in 1620 that a thirty-year-old Londoner named John Billington, who had possibly come from Lincolnshire, led his wife, Elinor and their two young boys onto the *Mayflower* for the impending voyage to the New World, trouble traveled with the other passengers, the Pilgrims. Bradfords, Aldens, Brewsters, and the rest of the intrepid band sought a fresh start in America, where they intended to worship God without fear of persecution and to carve a community untainted by Europe's corruption and strife. But John Billington, a tough, foulmouthed miscreant, was to bring his own brand of strife to the settlement on the edge of the wilderness.

How Billington wangled his way onto the *Mayflower* is lost in history's murk, but from the onset of the vessel's legendary voyage, Pilgrim leader William Bradford grasped that Billington and his brood did not fit in with most of the other passengers. "They [the Billingtons] were an ill-conditioned lot and unfit for the company," Bradford later wrote. He contemptuously labeled them "one of the profanest families among them [the Pilgrims] and did not know how they had slipped aboard the ship."[1] According to a number of sources, Billington took part in an abortive mutiny aboard the *Mayflower*. By the time the Pilgrims, ravaged by scurvy and the other travails of the perilous Atlantic crossing, first saw the shores of Cape Cod, Billington had made, among his shipboard enemies, a formidable foe in a hard-nosed soldier named Myles Standish.

When the *Mayflower* dropped anchor off what later became Provincetown, Massachusetts, Standish and most of the other passengers may have wished that John Billington had been carried off by disease or had tumbled overboard during the voyage, along with his fractious family. And who could blame the Pilgrims if they harbored such dark thoughts? For one of the brawler's boys somehow got his hands on a musket, loaded it while dropping gunpowder below the ship's decks, and fired the weapon near his family's berth. Sparks ignited the gunpowder at his feet and spread perilously close to several nearby kegs of powder. Frantic passengers and sailors quelled the fire just before it reached the magazine. Francis Billington had nearly ended the "Pilgrims' progress" before it began. Adages such as "Like father, like son" and "The apple does not fall far from the tree" likely sprinkled the furious thoughts of the Pilgrims, almost blown to bits by the juvenile delinquent son of the company's bully.

John Billington thrashed his boy for the deed, but few onlookers likely believed the punishment would do little more than fill the air with the lad's howls. The Pilgrims must have suspected the Billingtons were to torment their neighbors as sorely on land as at sea.

Aboard the vessel that young Billington had nearly destroyed, the men gathered to sign a landmark American document, the Mayflower Compact. Each signer promised to work "for ye generall good of ye Colonie, unto which we promise all due submission and obedience."[2] Men such as William Bradford, William Brewster, John Alden, and Myles Standish meant to live by the lofty words of the pact, but the twenty-sixth of the forty-one signers had little intention of obeying anyone. Bradford later branded that twenty-sixth signer—John Billington—"a knave and so will live and die." Those words were to ring with chilling, portentous truth.

Billington, as did all the settlers, spent his first months in Plymouth battling for survival against starvation, disease, and the harsh New England winter of 1620–21. He and his family endured—to bedevil their neighbors.

As spring's thaw warmed the bodies and souls of the Pilgrims who had survived their first nightmarish winter in the New World, Billington's bullying began again, coupled with a streak of independence he manifested to lead his life as he, not his neighbors, saw fit. But by refusing to honor a summons for military duty, a critical civic obligation for all able-bodied men in a colony worried, with reason or not, that Indians could swoop down upon the settlers' thatched huts at any moment, Billington incensed even neighbors previously willing to overlook his cursing and his quarreling. The Pilgrims could not let his latest defiance go unpunished.

Billington was sentenced to be bound by his neck and heels, an excruciating punishment designed to make every muscle burn in agony. On April 4, 1621, Standish, undoubtedly eager to settle accounts with the bully, and several other men began binding Billington. Proving he could mete out punishment to others but could not abide it himself, he bellowed for mercy to the magistrates, headed by Governor John Carter. "Humbling himself and craving pardon,"[3] Billington convinced his neighbors to untie him; they must have hoped that his close brush with punishment had cowed him into obedience. They might as well have wished that New England's chill winters would grow balmy.

In May 1621 another of the Billington clan stirred an uproar throughout the settlement. This time the troublemaker was Billington's other son, aptly named John junior. The boy wandered into the woods beyond the cottages and did not return to the family's home, on the southern side of Plymouth. With the aid of the local Indian chief Massasoit, the Pilgrims learned that young Billington had been found by braves and was being cared for by Indians along Cape Cod. Ten of the Pilgrim men piled into a shallop—a coastal craft equipped with a sail and oars—in June and headed to Nauset to pick up the boy. When young Billington was handed back to the Pilgrims, some of the settlers probably

"Billington's Hovel." Nicknamed after John Billington, such a dwelling housed the Mayflower Murderer and his fractious family in early Plymouth.

figured that the Indians were glad to be rid of the troublesome youth. The search party was incensed that the boy's escapade had pulled them from farming and other labors essential to the colony's survival. What trouble would the bellicose Billingtons bring next?

Constant trouble was the answer. Throughout the 1620s John Billington ranted and railed against several of his neighbors, adding to his reputation as the black sheep of the village. But in a colony where every able-bodied man was an asset—no matter how surly and obnoxious his demeanor—most of the Pilgrims gritted their teeth at Billington's antics and blocked their ears, as best they could, against his mighty curses. According to one historian, the bully's passion was to hunt, and if so, every moment he spent in the forests away from the settlement was reason for his neighbors to give thanks to God.

In 1630 even Billington's many detractors must have felt a twinge of pity for him: His son John junior died, carried off by gangrene, an often mortal ailment in an era when anti-infectants were few. No one would ever know whether the namesake of the town bully would have followed in his father's dubious footsteps or would have found the path to salvation espoused by so many of the family's God-fearing neighbors. One suspects the doomed youth would have continued to embrace his father's loathsome legacy.

Perhaps looking for a way to vent his anger at the death of his boy, Billington somehow ran afoul of a new neighbor, John Newcomen. Either a fearless soul or unaware of Billington's reputation, Newcomen raised the bully's temper to a feverish pitch. Scholar Gleason L. Archer surmises that a quarrel started over a dispute about hunting; maybe Newcomen had stalked game in a spot Billington claimed as his private reserve. A number of concerned Pilgrims must have warned Newcomen to keep an eye over his shoulder, especially in the woods. If such advice was offered, Newcomen should have heeded it.

On a summer day in 1630 Newcomen strode into the woods outside Plymouth—and straight into the leveled musket of John Billington. Possibly the startled Newcomen froze for a moment, then lunged too late for the cover of a rock or tree. Billington's musket cracked, and the ball slammed Newcomen to the ground. As Newcomen's blood darkened pine needles and turf on the forest floor, Billington vanished in a haze of gunpowder smoke.

The bully had botched his crime. He apparently ambushed his victim too close to the village, for neighbors found Newcomen alive—and coherent enough to finger his assailant.

The stunned settlers stanched his gaping wound as best they could and carried him to the settlement. The horrifying news quickly spread through town: John Billington had shot John Newcomen! Men rushed to Billington's house, pushed past his wife, Elinor, and into the cottage, but he was still in the woods. A search party went after him but could not find him in the maze of trees, brush, and Indian trails he must have known so well from his hunting trips.

In the next day or two Billington swaggered back into the settlement. He undoubtedly believed that Newcomen was dead and nobody could pin the murder on John Billington—not without a witness. He must have blanched to learn that Newcomen was alive and talking, but as neighbors hauled the accused assailant to the lockup, on a hill overlooking the plantation's neat gardens and little cottages, he might have consoled himself with the fact that he was not yet a murderer. Not yet.

Despite the prayer vigils of the Pilgrims—and perhaps a silent prayer or two from the bully in the lockup—Newcomen died from his wound, probably felled by festering infection and its accompanying fever. The Thirteen Colonies' first murder victim had lost his struggle for life. His killer was about to fight for his own hide.

If Billington's accusers wondered whether he would plead for mercy, as he had nine years before, they were of no mind to listen to his entreaties. Billington's murder trial, the first such proceeding in American history, unfolded inside Plymouth's sturdy wooden meetinghouse, on the ground floor of the town's fort. Jurors returned their inevitable verdict to Bradford and the other magistrates: guilty "by plain and notorious evidence." Bradford wrote: "His [Billington's] fact was that he waylaid a young man, one John Newcomen, about a former quarrel and shot him with a gun whereof he [Newcomen] died."[4] John Billington was sentenced to hang; by English law, his executioners were also sanctioned to add the grisly punishment of drawing and quartering—to gut him and cut him into pieces after his hanging.

Sentence had been handed down upon the murderous bully, but Bradford and the other Pilgrims were apparently uncertain that they had the legal power to carry out an execution without assent from a higher authority. Some writers later asserted that Billington himself raised the legal dilemma, openly challenging during his trial his neighbors' authority to hang him. If so, the brawler displayed the cunning of today's death row inmates angling for legal loopholes to save their necks. He might also have bolstered his hopes with another thought: Plymouth could ill afford to kill an able-bodied man.

Bradford wrote to John Winthrop, the governor of the Massachusetts Bay Colony and a skilled attorney, for guidance in the Billington affair. With each day Billington avoided the noose, his yearning for a sentence commuted to a rigid form of probation seemingly increased.

Winthrop's reply, backed by other leaders of the colony, reached Bradford by August 1630. With the self-assurance of Old Testament judges, Winthrop and the others wrote that Billington "ought to die and the land be purged from blood."[5]

Sometime in August 1630 Billington's guards dragged him

inside the meetinghouse, and Bradford upheld the first death sentence in America. One wonders whether the convicted murderer maintained a cold-blooded killer's calm demeanor or whether the blood rushed from his face as the words "hanged by the neck" pealed to the beams of the meetinghouse. Given his groveling for mercy in 1621, one suspects the bully did not take his sentence with a stoic stare.

John Billington's date with the hangman arrived in September 1630. Despite the trouble he had wreaked upon his neighbors for a decade, the execution could not have been a pleasant event for the Pilgrims. After all, miscreant though he had been, he had been one of the original band of Mayflower Pilgrims to arrive on Plymouth's soil and had shouldered his fair share of the labors necessary to carve a settlement on the fringe of a wilderness. For better or worse, John Billington was part of the Pilgrims' adventure. Even Bradford, who had contemptuously dubbed Billington "a knave," admitted that the death sentence was "a matter of great sadness unto them [the Pilgrims]."[6]

His neighbors' sadness would not spare Billington from his fate. A young man lay in his grave because of the bully. With Elinor Billington, the couple's surviving son, Francis, and the rest of the village likely watching, John Billington, his hands bound, probably standing on a stool beneath a sturdy tree limb, waited for the noose's neck-crunching pull. If a hood was not draped across his face and head, he must have taken a final glance at Plymouth, as much his town as anyone in the crowd. Suddenly the noose snapped to taut attention and sent Billington thrashing into eternity.

Today memories of John Billington's terrible deed have faded. His name, however, is forever preserved by a lake west of Plymouth Plantation, which is called Billington's Sea. Some Americans tracing their bloodlines back to the *Mayflower* proclaim proudly their kinship to the Pilgrim lout. And on the Mayflower Compact, the hallowed names of Brewster, Mullins, Alden, Bradford, and Standish abide for posterity with the scrawl of America's first convicted murderer: big, bad John Billington.

2 The Penobscot Pirate: Dixie Bull

Rage certainly seethed in his heart and coursed through every limb. The French pinnace sailing beyond the dark blue horizon of Penobscot Bay was carrying off his business—"beaver coats, ruggs, blanketts, etc."[1]—stolen from his own ship, a coastal shallop, minutes before. But the outraged beaver trader, Dixie Bull, was not one to accept his losses with a resigned shrug of his shoulders. Thoughts of vengeance blazed within him. Vengeance he was to have, for Dixie Bull was about to become the first American to turn pirate.

Dixie Bull was not a ruffian born and bred. In England his family were reputable tradesmen, according to John Winthrop. Bull was living in London in early 1631, an apprentice skinner, or fur trader, when the siren's song of opportunity in the New World seduced him. The potential hazards of life in the wilds of New England daunted Bull little. Eager to make a mark for himself, he boarded a ship bound for Boston and landed at Winthrop's "city upon a hill" in the fall of 1631.

Bull did not linger long in Boston, the bold, likely urbane Londoner probably chafing beneath the stern tenets of Winthrop and the other Puritan "saints." By 1632 Bull was roaming the craggy shoreline and dense forests of Maine and setting himself up as a trader of beaver pelts. He owned a shallop. Bull became a familiar figure in the region's scattered trading posts, selling his pelts and buying supplies from his fellow traders; he also dealt with Indians and trappers to establish his business. The transplanted Londoner seemed well on his way to becoming a colonist of means and respectability, a man whose name appeared on a grant for a large tract of land in York, Maine.

Everything changed for Bull in June 1632. As his shallop plowed through the waters of Penobscot Bay, an armed pinnace swooped down upon his craft, and howling French raiders swarmed over the gunwales of the shallop. As Bull and his crew watched helplessly and feared for their lives, the Frenchmen looted his stock of blankets, biscuits, pelts, and everything else that was not nailed down, then sailed away. Some men would have considered themselves lucky to be alive after such an attack. Dixie Bull, however, was furious, churning with plans of retaliation upon the French raiders—or any French ship.

When Bull's friends in Maine's sparse settlements learned of his misfortune, they certainly understood his determination to retake his stolen supplies or to replenish them from some Frenchman's stores. A man of action, Bull quickly gathered some of his old crew and fifteen other locals, loaded his shallop with muskets and cutlasses, and sailed into local waters in search of French ships.

His hunt dragged on through the summer of 1632, his shallop sliding along the coastline, lookouts' eyes trained for a sudden appearance of a French sail to port, starboard, or broadside. But whenever vessels were sighted, they were always colonists' craft. Not one French vessel blundered within reach of Bull and his band. His frustration climbing with the passage of languid summer days, his chances of rescuing his ruined business evaporating, Bull formed another plan, one that was to stun his fellow colonists. The beaver trader decided to turn buccaneer. Any ship, French or friendly, he informed his crew, was fair game.

If any of his crewmen were horrified by their skipper's scheme, they must have feared Bull too much to resist him. In late summer and early fall of 1632 Bull's shallop boarded two or three New England ships and plundered them as shocked colonists gaped at the pirates—as American as their prey. Bull even shanghaied sturdy men from his victims' ranks, forcing the bewildered prisoners to turn pirate.

A shallop. Buccaneer Dixie Bull and his crew charted a
course into infamy in such a vessel in 1632.

His neighbors' ships were not the only quarry Bull had in his
sights. He steered his shallop into the waters off a trading post at
Pemaquid, Maine, and stormed the settlement. Apparently achiev-
ing total surprise, he encountered no resistance; he and his boys
carted off every item they could carry to their ship and began
pulling from the shoreline, probably slapping each others' backs
and shouting loud huzzahs to celebrate the raid's success, five
hundred pounds' worth of booty. Piracy, they surely thought, was
a profitable and easy venture.

The boisterous buccaneers had made a mistake: They had not
seized all of the traders' weapons. The merchants, as enraged as
Bull when his shallop had been plundered, ran to the shore with
muskets raised. Ragged shots rent the salt air. Bull's first mate
crashed to the deck. His blood gushing across the planks, his mates

wide-eyed with horror, he was the first American pirate to die in the line of his sorry duty.

Bull and his men had learned a harsh lesson: Piracy was not just easy loot but also a bloody trade. The first mate's death traumatized the crew, especially those who were shanghaied or lukewarm buccaneers. According to Captain Anthony Dicks, a Salem, Massachusetts, mariner held as a prisoner aboard the pirate shallop, the first mate's gory demise made some of the crew "afraid of the very rattling of the ropes."[2] But no matter how fearful some of Bull's men were, none had the temerity to mutiny against their captain, a situation indicating that their dread of Bull was still greater than their apprehensions of meeting the same grisly fate as their fallen first mate.

Thanks to Captain Dicks, whose brief account of his experiences at Bull's hands appeared in the journal of the Dorchester, Massachusetts, seafarer Roger Clap, a description of the strange shipboard life of Bull and his band survived. On most New England ships of the era, group prayer was part of the crews' daily routines; however, Dicks related that on Bull's shallop, the crew gathered each day to sing boisterous songs and hold bizarre conversations, both routines seemingly stereotypical pirate behavior.

Another familiar tenet of piracy was embraced wholeheartedly by Bull's men: a thirst for liquor. The crew's drinking posed a problem for Bull, and he disciplined those honoring too heavily the sentiment of "Yo-ho-ho, and a bottle of rum." Some of the seamen likely drank to forget the perilous circumstances in which they unwillingly found themselves; others doubtlessly filled the air with boasts of their illicit exploits. Bull's imposition of penalties against excessive drinking may have been hatched from his fear that ambitious or disgruntled crewmen might find in liquor the nerve to heave their captain over the side.

Drunkenness, settlers' muskets, and fears of mutiny were not the only problems weighing on Bull's mind: Word of Bull's treachery had reached Governor John Winthrop, in Boston. In response to Maine traders' pleas for help against the pirate, he ordered a pinnace bristling with cannon and twenty marines to pursue Bull. The vessel, delayed by bad weather, set sail from Boston in November 1632, according to historians Edward Rowe and George Francis Dow, and at Pemaquid, Maine, the site of one of Bull's depredations, joined four vessels from Piscataqua (present-day

Portsmouth, New Hampshire) ready to hunt down the pirate shallop.

Another historian, Jim McClain, asserts that the armed pinnace was not dispatched from Boston until May 1633 and was, of course, unable to find Bull and his buccaneers. McClain writes that the Puritans of Boston had sent a shallop to Piscataqua on a fact-finding mission about Bull. Meanwhile, according to McClain, four Piscataqua pinnaces and shallops and some forty men set out in pursuit of Bull, and upon reaching Pemaquid, the squadron sat off Pemaquid for about three weeks because of bad weather.

Bull either sensed or heard that America's first seagoing posse had assembled at Pemaquid to bring him and his crew to the gallows. Dicks wrote that Bull sent local authorities a letter describing his intention to give up piracy and sail south from New England waters and warning his enemies to stay away from him. According to Dicks, Bull requested that the Salem captain sail the pirates to Virginia, a colony derided by the Puritans as the home of whores and scoundrels, a perfect den, Winthrop and his ilk certainly thought, for the likes of Dixie Bull. Dicks bravely refused to help his captors and lived to tell his tale of captivity among the pirates. He asserted that while Bull knew New England's waters well, he seemingly lacked the navigational knowledge needed to sail a shallop to Virginia. Why else would he have asked a prisoner to take the helm of the pirate ship?

Despite Dicks's refusal to help the buccaneers, nature handed Bull an edge over the Colonial flotilla. For at least three weeks, wintry squalls and crashing waves forced the little fleet to ride anchor off Pemaquid.

The weather finally cleared, and the ships prowled the sea off Maine. But as the weeks passed, the search proved as fruitless as Bull's hunt for French targets: The buccaneer and his men had vanished into the briny mists.

Early in 1633 the searchers received the first scrap of news about Bull in months. Three deserters from his crew, presenting themselves as unwilling parties to Bull's misdeeds, claimed he had sailed his shallop into French waters and had joined England's, as well as New England's, sworn enemies. John Winthrop found the story plausible. If the deserters had indeed told the truth, Bull's joining the French was a strange irony, for the French had set the ex-beaver trader on his strange course, a course leading to piracy.

The Puritans who had outfitted the Boston-based pinnace were also dismayed by the unsuccessful expedition's bill: thirty-four pounds, seven shillings. The search ended, the officers and men surely weary of the search and perhaps disheartened that Bull was to escape the noose.

Or was he?

Roger Clap's words claimed otherwise. They claimed that Bull returned to England and met his fate at the end of a rope or some other violent way.

Dixie Bull's brief reign of terror had ended for his neighbors. His course had not been so bloody as those of other buccaneers to follow him into America's waters. After all, Captain Dicks had been captive to Bull and had survived to tell others of life aboard America's first pirate ship.

Few can dispute that Bull was a brazen adventurer, but he may also have been a man who just never anticipated that his raids would prod his fellow colonists into joint action against him.

Whatever the elusive, enigmatic Dixie Bull may have been, he holds a unique niche in our nation's annals: America's first buccaneer. If, as Clap wrote, Bull swung at the end of a rope, prayers from Pemaquid to Boston were answered. For Dixie Bull had been no Frenchman or Spaniard, an age-old enemy to the English-speaking world. He had been a *colonist*. In the eyes of his fellow settlers, no greater rogue had ever appeared in their midst. (Jim McClain found mention of Bull in London records of 1648, indicating that Bull finished his apprenticeship as a skinner and that he indeed escaped justice.)

3 In No Man's Shadow: Mistress Margaret Brent

O n January 21, 1648, astonishment probably creased every man's face inside the legislative Assembly of St. Mary's City (now St. Marys City), capital of Maryland. Jaws slack, eyes wide, the movers and shakers of the colony must have stared at a lone figure in their midst, a woman in her fifties. Clad in a well-cut dress and a sober coif, her appearance and her confident, almost haughty eyes earmarks of the gentlewoman born and bred, she had just delivered a demand to the men of the Assembly, an audacious demand guaranteed to leave virtually any man of 1648 speechless: Mistress Margaret Brent was demanding a vote in all Maryland's affairs. But only male settlers were accorded such a privilege in the colonies.

Margaret Brent, daughter of a British lord, owner of a Maryland plantation she had aptly named *Sisters* Freehold, was no ordinary settler—male or female. Every legislator knew just how potent a force the highborn woman was.

The saga of Margaret Brent was one of a woman refusing to bow to the social, cultural, and political chains constraining most women of her day. To many future historians, Margaret Brent of Maryland was America's first feminist.

*   *   *

Few settlers of eary America arrived with a "bluer" pedigree than Margaret Brent. She was born in 1601 in Gloucester, England, daughter of Richard Brent, lord of Admington and Lark Stoke. In her mother's veins reputedly ran the blood of an illustrious ancestor, King Edward III.

As one of thirteen children of Lord Admington, Margaret Brent surely learned that to be heard among a crowd, one had better learn how to assert oneself. She also learned that in a land where the Church of England held sway and where the seething tide of Puritanism was rising, Papists were compelled to retreat from public scrutiny or to thrust their jaws defiantly at foes and meet every insult and outrage with equal vehemence.

Little is known of Brent's early years. That she was well educated and versed in the ways and mores of the nobility did not alone explain her future eyeball-to-eyeball dealings with men unaccustomed to such behavior from any woman save a queen or a powerful lord's lady. Sometime during her formative years Mistress Brent discovered an affinity for that most male of English pursuits, the law. From the lofty words of the Magna Carta to arcane passages of English common law, she had tapped into the workings of the male world.

As religious strife between Great Britain's Catholics and Protestants waxed, the Brents were among those English who set their sights across the Atlantic. The family chose to cast their fates with those of the Catholics settling Maryland, the colony of Lord Baltimore, Cecilius Calvert. With her sister, Mary, and brothers, Giles and Fulke, Margaret Brent, at thirty-six unmarried, boarded a ship and set sail to a life far removed from any she had known. Her brothers notwithstanding, she had no man with whom to brave the dangers of the wild new land. But as time proved, she did not need a husband.

On November 22, 1638, the Brents reached St. Mary's City, the tiny settlement on a peninsula touched by the Potomac and the Patuxent rivers and by the waters of Chesapeake Bay. The so-called town filling Brent's eyes was no more than a smattering of houses, a little church, and two forts, St. Mary's and St. Inigoes; her eyes must have widened at her first sight of Indians.

Whatever qualms Brent had about her new surroundings dissipated as she and her family presented local authorities with a letter from Lord Baltimore granting the new arrivals land. Brent and her sister, Mary, were given seventy acres about a mile away from the town, and thanks to Baltimore, even if Margaret Brent married, the tract remained hers. To her new home, Brent rendered a name future feminists could applaud: Sisters Freehold.

Since landowners of the region were granted additional acreage for bringing new settlers to the colony, Margaret Brent paid the passage of five men and four women to earn a thousand acres. Soon, with Sisters Freehold and her other holdings, Mistress Brent established herself not only as a prominent local landowner but also as a growing voice in the colony's civic affairs.

Brent, her thirst for land and influence burgeoning, acquired a thousand acres on Kent Island, including a house, a mill, and livestock, from her brother Giles's repayment of a debt to her. Giles Brent was not the only male settler to owe debts to the budding land baroness: Maryland's early court records brimmed with Margaret Brent's suits to collect payment from local gents who had not been too proud to seek transactions with a woman but who likely found her legal efforts for recompense galling to the male ego. But ruffled male psyches seemed to matter little to the shrewd colonial businesswoman, whose financial successes aided her family's growing clout in Maryland, clout placing her brother Giles on the colony's Assembly and making him commander of the garrison of Kent Island.

Some historians claimed that much of the Brents' prominence came from an alleged marriage of the colony's governor, Leonard Calvert, Baltimore's brother, to Anne Brent, yet another Brent sister. However, while it is a reasonable theory, ironclad proof of such a marriage has yet to be unearthed.

Governor Calvert certainly had dealings with Margaret Brent, and one of their most intriguing ventures was their effort to educate the Piscataway Indian princess Mary Kitomaquund in the ways of the white man's world. And without Calvert's friendship and respect Margaret Brent might have found herself hard pressed to succeed in another undertaking certain to dismay many men: arguing her own legal cases in several instances, as well as functioning sometimes as other colonists' attorney, before Maryland's Provincial Court. The woman who strode into that courtroom with more legal knowledge lurking beneath her coif than many male lawyers was to be dubbed by some chroniclers as America's first woman lawyer.

What were Maryland's men to make of this "little woman" injecting herself into business and legal affairs and beating most male counterparts at the "game"? Many of her fellow settlers must have wondered against what traditionally male bastion Mistress Brent, so audacious even for a woman "to the manor born," would crash next. Governor Calvert's declining health was to furnish startling answers.

In May 1647 the ailing governor summoned Brent to his side and in front of witnesses who must have gaped with each word of the man's deathbed will, and perhaps startling even the formidable land baroness, named her executor of his will. Although he named a local luminary, Thomas Green, acting governor, the dying Calvert said to Brent: "Take all, pay all."[1] His words in effect bestowed upon her the responsibility for solving the colony's most critical problem: finding the means to pay soldiers on the verge of a mutiny that could shatter the colony.

The dilemma confronting Brent was one to make the slickest politician or hardest-eyed soldier blanch, the mistress of Sisters Freehold having inherited a more daunting task than did the new governor, Thomas Green. Two years before Calvert's death a revolt by the region's Puritans, Ingle's Rebellion, had forced the beleaguered Calvert to hire troops from Virginia to quell the Puritan menace. To the horror of the governor and the Brents, Giles Brent had been seized by the rebels and packed off to England as a captive; forced to suppress his concerns for Giles's welfare, Calvert had poured his energies into defeating the rebels and maintaining control of his colony. Shortly before his death he had finally put down the Puritan insurgents.

Although the Puritans were stalled for the moment in Maryland, the soldiers who had stymied the rebels posed a new menace to the colony. Calvert had offered his own lands and purse as collateral for the mercenaries' price tag, and to the future ire of his brother Lord Baltimore, he had also promised to dip into Baltimore's holdings if necessary to pay off the troops.

Giles Brent returned to the shores of the Chesapeake scant days after Calvert's death to find his sister at the center of the brewing furor between the grumbling soldiers and the colony. Knowing Calvert would likely have appointed him as executor of the will had he reached Maryland a little sooner, Giles Brent may well have wondered if his sister, capable as she was, was up to the formidable chore of holding grizzled soldiers at bay. The sight of those troops, in their steel helmets, cuirasses, blades, and muskets at the ready, was an ominous one to the colonists, a sight to fill even a sturdy man with dread.

If any of Maryland's men did worry about Margaret Brent's capacity to deal with the fractious soldiers, she quickly took steps to silence the doubters. She employed her knowledge of the law to gain control of not only Calvert's estate but also some of the colonial holdings of Maryland's proprietor, Lord Baltimore.

Even with her hands on the Calverts' colonial purse strings, Brent could not simply pay off the soldiers and be rid of them, for a new dilemma—no food to fill the furious troops' bellies—added to her woes. Painfully aware that impending starvation could thrust the soldiers to violence against the colony, she hurriedly bought corn from Virginia to ease the growling stomachs. Her expedient measure momentarily curbed any assaults by the troops. The purchase of grain, however, failed to solve the problem of paying the men.

Between 1647 and 1650 Brent's horses probably trotted the paths between Sisters Freehold and St. Mary's City blindfolded. Each time she gazed across her well-tended fields or upon the bustling little settlement on the edge of the shimmering Chesapeake, her mind and heart must have throbbed painfully with nightmarish thoughts of rapacious soldiers seizing her beloved manor and St. Mary's City. Perhaps she even lamented Calvert's decision to name her, not some man, as executor. But if such dark thoughts tormented her, she somehow repressed them and went about the tangled business of settling accounts with the troops.

Brent, doubtlessly after bouts of sleepless soul-searching, apparently concluded there was but one way to meet the soldiers' payroll. That way was to dip into the holdings of Lord Baltimore. As pragmatic a business gambit as her decision seemed, she must have known it would launch the powerful Baltimore into a rage. But whatever her fears or misgivings at rankling the mighty noble, she swallowed them, sold off some of his precious cattle, and paid off the fractious and probably startled troops. Ironically, many of the soldiers whom colonists had wanted to depart Maryland used their pay from Lord Baltimore's coffers to set up stakes in his colony.

Brent's action, undertaken with a resolve that few, if any, of her male neighbors could have surpassed, was a godsend for Governor Green and his Council members. Squaring accounts with the soldiers granted Maryland's leaders the opportunity to reestablish order in the colony—and they had a *woman* to thank largely for freedom from the specter of mutinous troops.

In the midst of the turbulence roiling Maryland in the late 1640s, Margaret Brent was emboldened to call in political markers for the thanks she believed the colony owed her. Little that Brent said or did probably shocked her male neighbors anymore, but if any still doubted that the mistress of Sisters Freehold viewed herself in decidedly different terms from most women of the era, she had a surprise in store.

Brent, nearing fifty and never having married—perhaps because men feared her or she loathed the prospect of any man seeking to bridle her life-style—rode into St. Mary's City on January 21, 1648, to the town hall. Passersby nodding politely to her could not have guessed that Margaret Brent was on a mission far different from any she had ever undertaken in the colony.

She walked into the town hall, adrenaline likely surging through every fiber of her being, and halted before the colony's Assembly. Inside the chamber even men who knew Brent well perhaps sensed she was about to unleash a verbal bombshell of some sort.

She spoke, and as her words rang through the room, jaws must have dropped. She fell silent and awaited the men's response to her demand for the right to vote in the Assembly: not only the right to vote but the right to two votes—one as a landowner, the other as the proprietor's attorney.

"The unmitigated gall!" some of the assemblymen perhaps cried. Although most admired Brent's abilities and accomplishments, they probably shook their heads in wonder. They must have certainly thought, even Mistress Margaret Brent must realize that women cannot vote!

The records of colonial Maryland tersely capture the Assembly's response to the uppity Margaret Brent: "The Govr. denied that the said . . . Brent should have any vote in the howse."[2]

The records also depict her reaction to the snub: "And the said . . . Brent protested against all proceedings in this present Assembly, unlessee shee may be pnt. and have vote as aforesd."[3]

An image of the diminutive Brent, eyes glimmering in anger

Bas-relief of Margaret Brent arguing for the vote in St. Mary's City, Maryland, on January 21, 1648.

and shoulders shaking, haranguing the men of the Assembly is not hard to envision. If, indeed, she turned her back on those men and stomped from the building, perhaps their rejection chilled her soul as much as the wintry air her limbs. But given her resilience and tenacity, she could not have been bowed by behavior of the Assembly. She had to know that she was the equal of any inside the hall and that while few of the assemblymen would likely make such an admission, in their hearts most knew it to be true.

Brent also endured the sting of another man's verbal slap, this one probably expected. Baltimore, livid over her sale of his cattle, ranted from England against the woman who had dared dip into his fortune to pay off the unruly soldiers. Maybe surprising Brent, the assemblymen of Maryland, having so heavy-handedly denied her the right to vote, leaped to her defense against Baltimore. They asserted:

> As for . . . Brent's undertaking and medling with your Lordship's estate here . . . it was better for the Collony's safety that

time in her hands than in any man's else in the whole Province after your Brother's death for the Soldiers would never have treated any others with that Civility and respect . . . she rather deserved favour and thanks from your Honour for her so much Concurring to the publick safety than to be justly liable to all those bitter invectives you have been pleased to Express against her.[4]

Despite the plaudits from the Assembly, the days of the Brents in Maryland were numbered. Baltimore, hard pressed politically in England since the Puritans, under Oliver Cromwell, had seized control of the government, not only mistrusted Margaret Brent but also may have worried that Giles Brent, an unabashed supporter of the Jesuits, whom the Puritans reviled, was a dangerous "friend" for any lord living in England. Giles Brent, heaping further concerns upon Baltimore's troubled state of mind, had married Margaret Brent's Indian ward, Mary Kitomaquund, a marriage the Brents' detractors could view as a naked grab for influence among the Piscataways. Although compelled by distance and by the Assembly's defense of Margaret Brent to accept the controversial sale of his cattle, Baltimore angrily decreed that under no circumstances were his deceased brother's holdings to end up in Brent hands. He had no intention of allowing Margaret Brent or her family to stroll before the Maryland Provincial Court in an attempt to parlay her role as Calvert's executor into owner of his assets through any legal machinations.

Margaret Brent and her siblings were not the sort to sit around and wait for fate to act upon them. They had departed Maryland by 1651 to begin life anew in Virginia. Leaving Sisters Freehold behind must have saddened and infuriated Margaret Brent, for unlike the home she had left in England, the Maryland estate was the product of *her* labors, not an ancestral abode passed through each generation. To the surprise of nobody who knew her, Brent soon became a "player" in Virginia's affairs; however, one suspects that the Virginia soil beneath her aging feet never felt so welcome as the acreage of Sisters Freehold. And so her imagination may have often traveled back to her Maryland manor until her death, which apparently occurred in 1671.

Long before Margaret Brent stepped in front of the Assembly in St. Mary's City, she had proved herself a woman of rare business acumen. Had her only legacy been that of a valiant pioneer of America's early days, that would have been tribute enough for most men of her day, let alone women. However, when Margaret Brent demanded the right to vote in *1648*, she sounded a note that through the centuries would swell slowly, too slowly for generations of the "fairer sex," into a chorus of voices that won American women the ballot.

Some historians charge that labeling Margaret Brent America's first feminist is hyperbole. The men of St. Mary's City, on the other hand, might have shaken their heads at such future skeptics and gravely said: "You obviously *don't know* Mistress Margaret. . . ."

4 "Thou Shalt Not Suffer a Witch to Live": The Strange Saga of Margaret Jones

Jeers erupted from hundreds of throats, rising into the warm June air. Guards led a gaunt woman up a gentle, grassy slope to the shadow of a sturdy elm. Her eyes, half shut against the sunlight after weeks in a dark cell, squinted at the noose dangling from one of the elm's limbs.

Then, as she had for weeks, she shrieked her innocence, but a new round of jeers drowned her voice. The Puritans of Boston did not want to hear her pleas for her life. They were on the town common to watch Massachusetts's first witch hang. Such was the probable scene of the last day in the life of Margaret Jones.

Nearly fifty-five years before the witchcraft trials earned infamy for Salem, Massachusetts, Margaret Jones was a midwife and a homespun healer in Charlestown, Massachusetts, her skills in preparing concoctions to ease her neighbors' ills well known in the little settlement across the Charles River from Boston. John Winthrop noted that among the ingredients she used in her potions and poultices were liquor, aniseed, and various herbs, nothing out of the ordinary for seventeenth-century dispensers of "physicke," or homemade medicines.

Little else is known of the woman besides the name of her husband, Thomas Jones. But one suspects that given her knowledge of potions and childbirth, knowledge not usually acquired in a few short years, Margaret Jones was likely a middle-aged woman, if not older.

Of her alleged misdeeds, an intriguing record remains. Sometime in the spring of 1648 Jones began arguing with several neighbors; although the actual reasons for the friction are uncertain, a contemporary of Jones's later wrote that after the quarrels, "some mischief befel such Neighbors in their Creatures, or the like."[1] Even worse for Jones, according to Winthrop, her medicines were allegedly causing terrible reactions—nausea, deafness, pains—in her patients; he also claimed that a mere touch of the woman's fingers brought on reactions similar to those of her potions. Making matters worse, Jones warned some of her ailing patients that if they stopped taking her "physicke," they would never recover. Her warning may well have been genuine concern on her part; neighbors interpreted her words as a threat.

When her former friends' suspicious glares confronted her, Jones must have begun to worry. She understood what her neighbors were thinking: the sudden spate of accidents and ailments afflicting Charlestown's settlers and even their animals had all the earmarks of witchcraft to seventeenth-century minds. And what more logical suspect for a sorceress than a cantankerous woman well versed in the use of plants, potions, liquids, and powders that could be turned from medical purposes to satanic arts?

John Hale, a twelve-year-old boy who was to become a minister, wrote later in his life that Jones's alarmed neighbors gathered "some things supposed to be bewitched, or have a charm upon them" and burned the items. Jones "came to the fire and seemed concerned,"[2] the implication being that a witch was perturbed that her victims were using a "white magic" ritual to combat her "black magic."

What this incident meant fuels all sorts of speculation. If the items burned by Jones's neighbors included objects actually lifted from her home, she had grounds to be concerned; either someone had sneaked into her house to remove the objects or a few neighbors had pushed their way into the house to remove the objects. Assuming that among the items may have been some of Jones's herbs and potions, one could further explain her concern as her little practice was going up in smoke. Fear of witchcraft, a tangible, blood-chilling matter in Old England and New England alike, could easily have driven Puritans to an invasion of the Joneses' house. To have burned "bewitched" or "charmed" objects proved that the people of Charlestown feared Margaret Jones.

Jones's husband, Thomas, was also under suspicion for complicity in his wife's suspected spells. Word that a couple was allegedly practicing witchcraft soon reached across the river to terrify the souls of Boston with imaginings of Satan and his servants on the loose in Massachusetts. On Bendall's Dock, in Cole's Inn, along the shore of the Mill Pond, colonists must have shuddered with each mention of the Joneses.

John Winthrop and Boston's other leaders knew they had to take speedy action to determine whether the talk of witchcraft was the by-product of neighborhood feuds or was truly evidence of devilish deeds. Sometime in the middle of May 1648 the General Court of the colony sent men to Charlestown to seize Margaret and Thomas Jones. The guards loaded the pair into a boat—no bridge as yet connected Charlestown and Boston—and shoved off for the latter town. With each stroke of oars pulling the couple toward Boston, the husband and wife must have felt that they were the ones in the throes of some spell, one with a deadly, irreversible outcome.

Once the boat ground to a halt on the Boston side of the river, the Joneses were escorted to the local prison, set along a path appropriately named Prison Lane (today Boston's courthouse sits on the site), and were shoved into dark, fetid cells to ponder a nightmarish ordeal to come.

The Joneses' cells, especially Margaret's, were to be a laboratory for the authorities. They intended to subject the Charlestown couple to a common witch-hunting practice known as watching; the court's order for the witch test reached the jailers on May 18, 1648.

If Margaret Jones had any idea of what "watching" meant, the blood must have drained from her face, for her captors walked into her cell with ropes at the ready and hauled her to the center of the room, where a stool or a table was placed. Then the men gruffly offered her a choice: She could sit of her own will on the filthy floor with her legs crossed or be tightly bound in that position. One look at the grim faces probably convinced her to choose the first option. For the next twenty-four hours she was to sit cross-legged without food or sleep.

GOV. JOHN WINTHROP
1588-1649   SCHOOL OF VAN DYKE

Governor John Winthrop of Massachusetts was one of the judges who sentenced the colony's first convicted witch, Margaret Jones, to the noose.

Throughout the watching, her cell's door was purposely left ajar or had a small hole cut into the wood. The opening was to let in Jones's "imp," a witch's "familiar." Many seventeenth-century witch-hunters believed that a witch's imp came to its mistress or master once every twenty-four hours, usually under cover of night, after helping carry out a witch's malevolent curses upon his or her victims and before heading out again to help unleash its witch's latest spells. Imps, witch-hunters believed, could appear in many guises, from men, women, and children to cats, toads, and other animals.

Hour after hour passed in Jones's cell, her limbs alternately numb and painful as she sat cross-legged. Her watchers were either inside the cell or just outside the door, waiting for her imp but unsure what infernal manner of specter or beast might appear in the room.

Suddenly a scene straight from the most deeply rooted nightmares of any Puritan erupted inside the cell of Margaret Jones. Her imp materialized—in the form of a ghostly child. Or so Winthrop believed. He wrote: "In the prison, in the clear day-light, there was seen in her [Jones's] arms, she sitting on the floor, and her clothes up, etc., a little child, which ran from her into another room, and the officer following it, it was vanished. The like child was seen in two other places . . . and one maid that saw it, fell sick upon it, and was cured by the said Margaret."[3]

The scene is virtually beyond comprehension to today's sensibilities. What rational explanation could account for Winthrop's vivid words, words seemingly more appropriate to an Edgar Allan Poe than to a sober-minded leader? Any answer, if it exists at all, lies in the collective mind of seventeenth-century New Englanders. For many of the era, belief in devils and witches was literal. Scholars and psychiatrists can offer a dizzying range of explanations—from Puritan paranoia to religious zealotry to mass hysteria—to account for seventeenth-century witch trials, but the fact that Winthrop and many otherwise sane settlers believed that Jones's imp had appeared was a ruinous development for her.

Because witch-hunters believed that witches suckled their imps, Jones's jailers stripped her and subjected her body to a search (sometimes women conducted such searches of female witches). The rough hands poking and prodding Jones's flesh were seeking one sign above all others on her body—a "witch's teat," for feeding the imp. According to Winthrop, the searchers found the sign: "She had an apparent teat in her secret parts as fresh as if it had been newly sucked, and after it had been scanned upon a forced search, that was withered and another began in the opposite side."[4]

To suspicious Puritans, such overwhelming physical signs of Jones's witchcraft were the hardest possible evidence of her crimes. Her day in court, when she was to face the magistrates and a jury, was imminent; for the first time in Boston's annals, a colonist was to stand trial for witchcraft.

Thomas Jones proved luckier than his wife. He apparently passed his captors' watching, never to face trial for sorcery.

Not everyone in the community believed Jones a witch. One

of her friends, Alice Stratton, steadfastly professed Jones's innocence and visited her in the prison with a Bible. An onlooker
recorded how one day in the cell both women were racked by sobs
over the terrible turn Jones's life had taken.

In late May or in June 1648 Margaret Jones, probably man-
acled, was hauled before the General Court, which from 1632 to
1659 met in Boston's First Church. She faced not only the evidence
of her "imp" and her "witch's teat" but also neighbors' damning
testimony of her evil potions and other alleged spells in what
sounded like people jumping at the chance to rid themselves of a
fractious, nonconformist neighbor once and for all.

Sitting in judgment of Jones was a who's who of early Massachusetts's foremost leaders: Thomas Dudley; John Endecott;
Richard Bellingham; Richard Saltonstall; Increase Nowell; Simon
Bradstreet (see Chapter Seven); William Pynchon; William Hibbins; and, of course, John Winthrop. Ironically, William Hibbins's
wife, Ann, was to be hanged for witchcraft in 1656.

We can picture those men, their faces twitching in anger and
even fear as the strange story of Jones's imp, the description of
her witch's marks, and her neighbors' vivid testimony painted as
damning a portrait as would depict any suspected New England
witch to follow Jones to the prisoner's bar. Winthrop's journal
proves how much the legal deck was stacked against the unfortunate Jones:

The evidence against her was,

1. that she was found to have such a malignant touch, as many
persons (men, women, and children) whom she stroked or
touched with any affection or displeasure, or, etc, were taken
with deafness, or vomiting, or other violent pains or sickness.

2. she practicing physic, and her medicines being such things
as aniseed, liquors, etc., yet had extraordinary violent effects.

3. she would use to tell such as would not make use of her
physic, that they would never be healed, and accordingly their
diseases and hurts continued, with relapse against the ordinary course, and beyond the apprehension of all physicians
and surgeons.

4. some things she could tell of (as secret speeches) which she had *no ordinary means* to come to the knowledge of.[5]

Winthrop's remaining commentary about the trial deals in depth with Jones's imp and her witch's teat.

Practicing evil physic, foretelling the future, bearing the physical marks of a witch, employing an imp—the so-called evidence left little room for doubt in the minds of most townspeople. But Margaret Jones stood before her hard-eyed accusers and vociferously denied all charges of witchcraft, haranguing the court. Her denials were to no avail; the stern judges viewed her cries of innocence as bald-faced lies from a malevolent woman seeking desperately to escape a noose. Winthrop, annoyed that Jones had the gall to plead innocent, wrote: "Her behaviour at her trial was very intemperate, lying notoriously and railing upon the jury and witnesses."[6]

Her "railing" was futile. Her neighbors found her guilty.

As the judges imposed the death sentence, perhaps she slouched hopelessly against the prisoner's bar or continued screaming her outrage. Neither pity from her accusers nor a miracle from her God would she have. A rope beckoned for the first—but not the last—of Massachusetts's convicted witches. The day of her death was set for June 15, 1648.

A few hours before Margaret Jones was taken to face the noose, some of her neighbors, including twelve-year-old John Hale, jammed into her cell and begged her to admit her witchcraft to save her immortal soul from the fires of hell. The doomed woman remained steady in her professed innocence despite the badgering of her visitors, her head perhaps shaking at people with no qualms about stretching her neck but with concern for dispatching her into the hereafter with the stain of crimes she denied. Hale recorded the sad scene inside the cell: " . . . she constantly professed herself innocent of that crime [witchcraft]. Then one prayed her to consider if God did not bring this punishment upon her for some other crime; and asked if she had not been guilty of stealing many years ago. She answered she had stolen something; but it was long since, and she had repented of it, and there was grace enough in Christ to pardon that long ago."[7]

There was not grace enough in most Puritans' hearts to consider the possibility that the woman still shouting her innocence was telling the truth. She was hauled from the prison and hanged somewhere in Boston; although no record of the exact site of the execution was made, two logical possibilities for the spot are Boston Common and Boston Neck, the latter the site of a public gallows later in the seventeenth century.

When the noose finally "turned off"—a Puritan term for death by hanging—Margaret Jones, many onlookers felt relieved that Satan had been stymied in their little colony. But they were wrong. The shadow of alleged witchcraft was to creep across New England and stoke the flames of the witchcraft hysteria in Salem in 1692.

A few postscripts to the strange, sad saga of Margaret Jones: Her husband, Thomas, was released from prison and wisely decided to flee the town. He boarded a ship, the *Welcome,* riding anchor off Charlestown; no sooner had Jones set foot on the vessel, wrote Winthrop, than it began to founder. The *Welcome*'s alarmed captain, well aware that Jones's wife had perished as a convicted witch, pleaded for authorities to remove Thomas Jones from the ship. Winthrop and other leaders were happy to oblige the panic-stricken shipmaster. Once Jones was hauled from the *Welcome,* he was heard of no more.

At least one person continued to profess Margaret Jones's innocence even after the hanging. Alice Stratton charged that her friend had "died wrongfully" and that Jones's blood was upon the the magistrates' hands. Winthrop and company, a thin-skinned lot in the face of criticism, cast baleful eyes at Stratton and were soon hard at work seeking signs that she was a witch. After all, one can imagine the town's leaders surmising, who would befriend a known witch except another witch? But to the certain disappointment of the men hoping to muzzle Stratton's accusations through the threat of the noose, the search yielded no damning evidence that the court could pin on Stratton. She fortunately escaped the same fate as her luckless friend.

Margaret Jones's brief but fiery foray on early America's stage had ended, but her legacy, though not her name, endured each time a New Englander convicted of witchcraft stood hopelessly with a noose fastened around her or his neck. Of Jones's guilt, Winthrop never evinced the slightest doubt; however, in John Hale's thoughts, a sense of uncertainty that she was a witch seemingly lingered, the grown Hale wondering if what he had seen at twelve had been as black and white as Winthrop believed. Unlike Winthrop, whose journal depicted the distraught Jones as the seeming embodiment of a witch, Hale, at least, recorded Jones's unwavering assertion that "as for witchcraft she was wholly free from it—and so she said unto her death."[8]

As would many convicted witches who followed her to a rope.

5 Four for Freedom: America's First Abolitionists

In a modest Germantown, Pennsylvania, house on the wintry day of February 18, 1688, one sound, a quill's rasp across paper, was heard. But what a sound as four solemn Mennonite men picked up the quill in turn and gravely signed a letter. The grating quill was America's opening salvo against the "peculiar institution" slavery.

Nearly one hundred years before Abraham Lincoln affixed his signature to the Emancipation Proclamation, Francis Daniel Pastorius, Gerhard Hendericks, and Dirck and Abraham Op den Graeff blanched at the heart-searing sight of blacks in bondage and set their outrage to words. "Have these poor negers as much right to fight for their freedom as you have to keep them slaves?"[1] asked America's first abolitionist tract. As the four signers soon learned, few American colonists cared to probe the disturbing answers to the grim question.

The four Mennonites had probably thought little about slavery before arriving in Pennsylvania in the 1680s, for the terrible institution was not practiced in Germany and the Netherlands. But one historian later speculated that a nightmarish episode possibly endured by Pastorius, the Op den Graeffs, or Hendericks during the Atlantic crossing shoved the shade of slavery into their minds. Shortly after a ship laden with Pennsylvania-bound settlers began its voyage, another vessel appeared on the horizon. Horror gripped the colonists and crew alike. The strange vessel was a Turkish raider.

As the Turkish ship surged toward the settlers' vessel, dread turned to panic for the Mennonites, their minds reeling with images of rape, torture, and Eastern slave bazaars. Desperate prayers surely rang above the decks of the colonists' ship.

Their pleas were answered, their captain somehow outrunning the Turks. However, the memories of those horrible minutes on the sea haunted the lucky passengers. The introduction of the four Mennonites' 1688 petition read: "How fearful and fainthearted are many on sea when they see a strange vessel, being afraid it should be a Turk, and they should be taken and sold for Slaves into Turkey."[2] The four had learned a harsh lesson, one they recalled each time they saw men, women, and children in chains.

Who were the four men destined to write America's first antislavery petition, to become the country's first abolitionists? History sheds more light on Francis Daniel Pastorius than on the Op den Graeffs and Hendericks. Born into a wealthy, cultured, and politically connected family in Sommerhausen, Germany, in 1651, Pastorius grew to be a son cast much in the image of his father, Melchior Pastorius, a man of voracious intellect, political savvy, and deeply held Lutheran beliefs.

Following in his father's footsteps, Pastorius, a pale, quiet youth with a large nose, pored over philosophy, religion, and law at some of Germany's and Switzerland's finest universities, mastered at least six languages, and earned his law degree in 1676. But setting up shop in some office clogged with legal tomes and briefs did not fire the fancy of the young attorney. Serenaded by wanderlust's notes, he craved to experience the seething world beyond the orderly life of a German barrister.

Pastorius, unable to suppress his desire to see the world, closed his office in Frankfurt in 1680 and hit Europe's highways as a tutor to spoiled, indolent young noblemen whose parents probably hoped that Pastorius's love of learning would rub off on youths more interested in cards, fencing, wine, and women than in books. On blue bloods' payrolls, Pastorius traveled with his charges through England, France, and Holland, feeding his appetite for different places, different views, and different ways of life.

Traveling across northern Europe did not satisfy the yearnings of Pastorius's soul for some higher meaning to his life. As he strolled amid great cities' awe-inspiring architecture and streets teeming with all manner of people, he reflected less upon the man-made glories of Europe than upon the poverty and the religious strife everywhere around him. His thoughts turned inward, to God.

His disturbing introspection led him to criticism of his frivolous, troublesome pupils. In his letters he harangued his charges' gaudy garb, their silly patter, their dancing, and all the costly excesses of rich, lazy lords. Despairing that such youths would ever find salvation, he inevitably decided he could no longer abide their antics. For the sake of his mind and his immortal soul, he believed, he must find another path through life.

With so much despair among Europe's poor, with nobles of no mind to pay attention to the masses' misery, and with religious discord raging throughout the Continent, the erstwhile lawyer longed for a haven from discord. He remembered having spent some exhilarating hours in Frankfurt speaking with friends of an Englishman named William Penn. They had discussed Penn's colony, Pennsylvania, where Quakers and Mennonites were founding a society based on tenets of tolerance and respect for God's word. Pastorius's eyes turned westward—to the untamed New World. There, in Penn's settlement, the disenchanted Pastorius hoped, he could find a life to ease his troubled soul.

In April 1683 spokesmen for a band of Frankfurt Quakers offered the restless lawyer a proposition that must have seemed a divine message to him: They asked him to travel to Pennsylvania as their agent to purchase land for a German settlement in America. He wasted little time in leaping at the offer.

Leaving Europe's woes behind posed little problem for Pastorius, but as he prepared to board ship, the realization that he was likely never to lay eyes on his family, especially his father, suddenly struck him. The lawyer's words fairly choking with emotion, his eyes probably misting, the son said to old Melchior Pastorius: "If therefore we see one another no more on this side of the grave, we shall meet in Heaven."[3]

Pastorius set sail to his great adventure in the spring of 1683. The Atlantic crossing was a nightmare of inadequate portions of rancid food and of days and nights among scurvy-riddled passengers packed into the ship's fetid hold. When the vessel finally docked off Philadelphia on August 20, 1683, the lawyer gave thanks to his God for sparing him on the grueling voyage. Then he viewed his new home for the first time.

What he found upon setting foot in Penn's town, nestled between the Schuylkill and Delaware rivers, were eighty or so houses arrayed along a neatly devised grid of streets seemingly shouting the settlers' determination to lead orderly lives in their corner of the wilderness. He met Penn, and the pair struck up a lifelong friendship based on kindred intellects; Pastorius was slated to serve in the founder's inner circle. As agent of the Frankfurt Company Pastorius purchased fifteen thousand acres from Penn, the tract sitting northwest of Philadelphia.

At first Pastorius and his six servants lived in a riverfront cave, his dank habitat worlds away from the lodgings he had once known with his blue-blooded pupils. He and his staff eventually erected a rude shelter, generously called a "house" in his journal, on a lot on modern-day Front Street. The dwelling, thirty feet long and fifteen wide, half underground, with oiled paper serving as windows, was little more than a ramshackle dugout; however, Pastorius, proving that he was not cowed by his squalid new surroundings, placed a small sign on one of the greasy windows. "It is a little house," the placard read, "but it welcomes the good. For sinners, no admission."[4] Penn reportedly chuckled at the words—one of the few times Philadelphians ever saw their taciturn leader crack a smile.

Pastorius lived in Philadelphia for about two years, but he directed his energies to establishing a thriving settlement northwest of the town, an outpost slated to become Germantown. Although Pastorius's efforts on behalf of the Frankfurt Company led many historians to pronounce him the founder of Germantown, the assertion is apparently inaccurate: A handful of Dutch settlers had started the settlement on five thousand acres they had purchased before Pastorius arrived among them. Some scholars were to claim that because the town's original settlers were Dutch, even the name Germantown proved a misnomer. However, other chroniclers pointed out that the first inhabitants hailed from Krefeld, a weavers' town slightly north of Düsseldorf, a town that was part of Dutchman William of Orange's realm but arguably a German rather than a Dutch town.

While Pastorius was not the actual founder of Germantown,

he certainly played a major role in the town's layout, helping design the neat street patterns and division of lots. "So far as concerns our newly founded city, Germanopolis," he wrote in November 1684, "it is situated upon a rich black soil, surrounded by numerous pleasant springs. The main street is sixty feet wide, and the cross-street is forty, and each family has a farmyard of three acres in size."[5] To Pastorius, the site was a veritable Eden, full of grassy patures for cattle and dotted with soaring stands of oaks, walnuts, and chestnut trees. About a two-hour walk from Philadelphia, Germantown was close to the hub of Penn's settlement but far enough away to escape the drunken sailors, traders, and even loose women who were already shaping their colonial version of Sodom and Gomorrah in the midst of outraged Quakers who were striving to live in a godly fashion but were hard pressed to prevent worldlier sorts from indulging in all the vices.

Not long before Pastorius had embarked for his Eden, he had met two brothers, Abraham and Dirck Op den Graeff, longing to start life anew in Pennsylvania. The brothers packed their families and a few belongings onto a ship six weeks after Pastorius's departure and followed him to the settlement between the Delaware and the Schuylkill. Little had the brothers and Pastorius imagined at their first meeting that they were to strike their new land's opening blow against slavery.

The Op den Graeffs were not cut from the same intellectual cloth as Pastorius, but the brothers were intelligent, hardworking men, who were masters of a valuable trade, linen weaving. With them came a third brother, Hermann, also a weaver. The arrival of the three craftsmen delighted Pastorius because in his vision of a vibrant and commercially successful Germantown, he felt that the town's future lay in the production of linen cloth. In large part because of the Op den Graeffs' looms, Germantown was to become one of the young colony's textile centers, Abraham Op den Graeff's skill in his trade such that his cloth was in demand by the Pennsylvania Provincial Council.

Earning a living, growing enough food to sustain their families, and leading lives of tolerance and religious reflection were concerns enough for any Friends scraping for survival in a new land teeming with not only opportunities but also dangers: Indians, disease, and, of course, the ever-present threat of starvation. The Op den Graeffs shouldered their New World burdens and still found time to plunge into the civic affairs of the little community. Their influence among their fellow Mennonites was second only to that of Pastorius, the ex-lawyer and the weavers all proving key figures in the incorporation of Germantown in 1689.

Gerhard Hendericks, the other Mennonite whose name emblazoned the antislavery petition, boarded the *Francis and Mary* with his wife, his daughter, and a male servant in 1685 and reached Germantown on October 12 of that year. On a two-hundred-acre lot he began his new life.

The lives of Hendericks, the Op den Graeffs, and Pastorius were largely existences of sobriety in conduct and dress, the settlers honoring God, family, and honest labor above all other concerns. The men of Germantown eschewed oaths of any sort, did not believe in the baptism of infants, refused any mode of military duty, and offered passive resistance toward foes. Such beliefs had spawned persecution of Quaker sects in Europe, where militarism and conformity to established religion—Anglican, Lutheran, Calvinist, or Catholic—were usually the norms. Puritans and other colonists, proving that some old ways still flourished in the new land, loathed the "radical" beliefs of the Quakers, so called because they supposedly "quaked" with religious rapture during their services; in Massachusetts, Puritans had executed six Quakers.

Despite the hostility of their colonial neighbors, people such as Pastorius, Hendericks, and the Op den Graeffs were unshakable in their determination to plant lasting religious and communal roots in the New World. The men, women, and children in their plain dress were in Pennsylvania to stay.

Thankful to have found a corner of the world where they could live their lives as they deemed fit, Pastorius, Hendericks, and the Op den Graeffs came to the belief that the colonies should be a haven of freedom and tolerance for all men. And all men, in the view of the four from Germantown, included the New World's most wretched souls of all: slaves.

How, the four reasoned, could the Quakers and the Mennonites strive to deal fairly with the Indians, whom Pastorius admired for their honesty, pleasant nature, and kindness, yet turn from the plight of blacks in chains?

By February 1688 the four men could no longer ignore the sickening sight of slavery. One can imagine them, wearing well-cut but drably hued waistcoats and brimmed hats, gathered at a

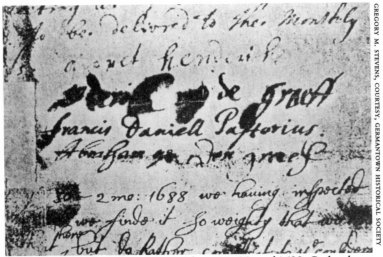

The four signatures on the antislavery petition of 1688: Gerhard Hendricks, Dirck op den Graeff, Francis Daniel Pastorius, and Abraham op den Graeff.

table in a Germantown home and rubbing their hands near a hearth's crackling fire. The men's faces assuredly grim, they must have discussed the evil of slavery far into the night. Pastorius, the lawyer once accustomed to devising well-rendered briefs, was probably the one whose quill shaped the thoughts of each man into inky reality upon paper. And with each stroke and flourish of his quill was born America's first petition against slavery.

Their eyes shining perhaps with pride and passion, the four men must have carefully perused the tract:

> These are the reasons why we are against the traffic of men-body, as followeth: Is there any that would be done or handled at this manner? viz., to be sold or made a slave for all the time of his life? . . . the most part of such negers are brought hither against their will and consent. . . . There is a saying, that we should do to all men like as we will be done ourselves; making no difference of what generation, descent, or colour they are. . . . But to bring men hither, or to rob and sell them against their will, we stand against. . . . Ah! Do consider well this thing, you who do it, if you would be done at this manner—and if it is done according to Christianity! . . . Pray,

what thing in the world can be done worse towards us than if men should rob or steal us away and sell us for slaves to strange countries; separating husbands from their wives and children. . . . therefore, we contradict, and are against this traffic of men-body. . . . And such men [slaves] ought to be delivered out of the hands of the robbers, and set free.

Or, have these poor negers not as much right to fight for their freedom, as you have to keep them slaves?[6]

The first to dip the quill into the black ink and sign at the bottom of the letter was Gerhard Hendericks, the last of the four to have arrived in Germantown. Dirck Op den Graeff, Pastorius, and Abraham Op den Graeff followed suit.

They were probably unaware that with their heartfelt sentences and their signatures they had fired the first written shots against slavery in America. The four men, however, surely sensed their tract's moral importance.

To Dirck Op den Graeff fell the honor of ferrying the landmark letter to the monthly meeting of Quakers at the house of Richard Worrell, in Dublin, Pennsylvania, on February 30, 1688. That the presentation of the petition caused an immediate stir among the Friends was evident in the notes of the gathering: "At our monthly meeting at Dublin . . . we having inspected ye matter above mentioned & considered it we finde it so weighty that we think it not Expedient for us to meddle with it here, but do Rather comitt it to ye consideration of ye Quarterly meeting, ye tennor of it being nearly related to ye truth, on behalfe of ye monthly meeting."[7]

In effect, the Quakers assembled at Worrell's house were unnerved by the letter, grasping not only its unassailable morality but also the explosive potential of its words. They opted to pass the petition at the Friends' quarterly meeting, in Philadelphia. There the local movers and shakers of the sect could decide how to handle the lofty sentiments of the four men from Germantown.

When the petition was read at the meeting in Philadelphia on April 4, 1688, Quakers again blanched at the call to arms against slavery, an accepted, if abominable, practice in the colonies. The prospect of haranguing other settlers over the buying and selling of slaves performing the harshest labor on plantations and docks was a menacing notion for the Friends, already reviled by many settlers in the colonies. Plain-speaking Quakers simply had no plain answer for the antislavery tract, except to defer any action to the yearly gathering of Friends at Burlington. Most certainly accepted the assertions of the four from Germantown but seemingly wished that Pastorius and company had suppressed the urge to promulgate their inflammatory views on paper.

Pastorius, Hendericks, and the Op den Graeffs probably welcomed the fact that their letter would stir debate at the yearly meeting. But the reluctance of fellow Friends to close ranks with the four men must have dismayed Pastorius and company. The pangs of conscience that the petition was churning in Quakers lingered in Philadelphia Friends' description of the letter as "a thing of too great a weight."[8] The weight was to descend upon the Burlington meeting, where the Friends would make or break the colonies' first stand against slavery.

On July 5, 1688, the Friends at Burlington listened with troubled attention to every word of the controversial petition. Then they pondered the grave document, examined their consciences, and rendered judgment: "A paper being here presented by some German Friends Concerning the Lawfulness and Unlawfulness of buying and Keeping of Negroes, It was adjudged not to be so proper for this Meeting to give a Positive Judgement in the case, It having so General a Relation to many other Parts, and, therefore, at present they forebear it."[9] The waffling of the Friends probably mirrored their trepidation about the antagonism the tract could spark from slaveowners.

Despite the defeat, the four Germantown men had captured in their missive the essence of the best America was to represent—the land of the *free*—long before the Declaration of Independence, the Constitution, and the Emancipation Proclamation. Long before John Adams, William Lloyd Garrison, Harriet Beecher Stowe, Frederick Douglass, and John Brown raised their eloquent, often incendiary voices against the "peculiar institution," the four Pennsylvanians were the first Americans to glare into the hideous face of slavery and to proclaim: "we . . . are against the traffic of men-body . . . ." Today their words should be required reading for all Americans.

Two of the men, Pastorius and Abraham Op den Graeff, lived at least long enough to see their letter bear its first political fruit, for in 1711, twenty-three years after the four men had penned their signatures to their antislavery petition, the Quakers, no longer able to ignore the "too great a weight," publicly condemned slavery. Between the first lines of the Germantown letter and the Quakers' official denunciation of slavery, the abolitionist movement stirred.

The immortal nineteenth-century poet John Greenleaf Whittier composed a poem entitled "The Pennsylvania Pilgrim," a glowing paean to Pastorius. The poem's final lines could justifiably pay homage not only to its subject but also to three other men—Gerhard Hendericks and Abraham and Dirck Op den Graeff. Wrote Whittier: "The world forgets, but the wise angels know."

How fitting that Abraham Lincoln bore the same first name as one of the signers of America's first protest against slavery.

Part II

Vices and Voices from the Wilderness

6 Mrs. Butterworth's Kitchen: The Counterfeiter's Lair

Something was amiss in the kitchen of Mary Butterworth. As the woman in her thirties hunched over a table littered with scraps of muslin and paper, she appeared the very picture of an industrious housewife of tiny Rehoboth, a village straddling the boundary of Massachusetts and Rhode Island in 1715, but as her hands reached for a nearby flatiron, her eyes likely twinkled with malicious glee. A smirk may have creased her lips. For Mary Butterworth, on the surface a prim and proper colonial woman, was not engrossed in some household chore. She was hard at work on another task: the turning out of counterfeit bills.

With flatiron, muslin, paper, and crow's quill pens, the Rehoboth wife was about to unleash a flood of masterfully rendered bogus bills upon New England and become not only the first woman counterfeiter in America's annals but also, perhaps, the most clever American practitioner of forgery, the forbidden art.

Where Mary Butterworth acquired her talent for forgery is anybody's guess, as much a mystery as the physical appearance of this colonial criminal. Her father, named Peck, ran the Sign of the Black Horse, a Rehoboth inn frequented by travelers heading north to Boston or south to Providence and Newport. As a girl Mary Peck saw all manner of men wrapping their hands wearily around mugs of foaming flip, mulled cider, or heavy ale, but if she learned the counterfeiter's trade from some miscreant holing up in her father's tavern, only she knew.

Learning such traditional women's work as sewing and quilting, Butterworth honed a keen eye and nimble fingers that were to serve her well in her forgeries. When she came of age, she married a prosperous Rehoboth housewright named John Butterworth, Jr., and apparently stuck to her household tasks for the first years of her marriage. By 1715 she and her husband had seven children.

The roles of wife and mother, however, so grueling for most women of the era, did not tax the full energy of Mary Butterworth. Although her husband was a successful tradesman outside his home, Mary was the ruler of his roost, running the household with methodical efficiency. Around the little town John Butterworth was called "Mary's husband,"[1] a telling sobriquet in a culture in which men held the upper hand over women in virtually every aspect of daily life.

Mary's husband must have gaped at his wife in 1715, for strong-willed Mary Butterworth added a new task to her daily routine—forgery. She turned her kitchen into a counterfeiter's laboratory, experimenting with various modes of duplicating colonial bills, bills of credit, one hand ladling her family's dinner into trenchers, the other perhaps mixing ink to print her fledgling forgeries.

From the onset of her scheme to print bogus bills in her kitchen, Butterworth refused to consider copper plates, the counterfeiter's usual method of producing bills, for her operation. She knew that such plates were the most damning evidence of the counterfeiter's craft, and if a sheriff or a constable found plates in her house, she had a possible ticket for an ear cropping, every bit as bloody and painful as it sounded, or a trip to the gallows. But without some sort of plates, she could not reproduce a bill well enough to fool a child, let alone some crafty tradesman or merchant.

Sometime in 1715 Butterworth found an ingenious solution to her problem, one with several steps that highlighted her household skills. She began her forgery by wetting a piece of muslin. She carefully pressed the moist muslin atop a legal bill of credit and dragged a flatiron firmly across the cloth and the bill. Like

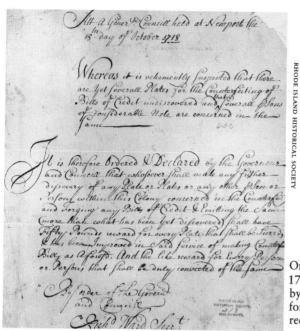

On the trail of Mary Butterworth: a 1718 notice of a £50 reward offered by the government of Rhode Island for every counterfeit plate or bill recovered

some magician's trick, the bill's image materialized on the muslin. Butterworth had her plate—not copper, but muslin.

Next, beneath the still-damp muslin, Butterworth slipped a piece of paper cut to the exact dimensions of the legal bill. She grabbed her flatiron again and pressed it once more against the muslin. Then she removed the wet cloth. A smile of triumph undoubtedly lit her face, for the image of the bill was plainly visible on the paper.

Butterworth's task, however, was hardly complete. The bill's image, while evident, was too faint to pass as real money. She picked up a crow's quill pen, which her brother Israel had cut to a razor-thin point; she dipped it into a vial of printer's ink and meticulously began outlining the bill's every word and number to their proper height, width, and tint. She fought any urge to rush her job, for one errant scratch of her quill could catch the eye of New Englanders who knew every inch of a genuine bill of credit.

Finally, the bleary-eyed housewife laid down her quill and squinted at her handiwork. Butterworth's bill was ready.

She scooped up her muslin plate and tossed it into the kitchen hearth, where flames consumed the evidence of her crime in a few sharp hisses. Mary Butterworth, "probably the first of her sex to practice the art [counterfeiting] in the New World,"[2] was in business.

As with any budding entrepreneur, legitimate or criminal, Butterworth needed a way to move her product. She chose a variation upon a time-honored business theme—traveling salesmen. Offering to sell her handmade bills at half of the forgeries' printed values to family and other locals she knew and trusted, she soon built a bona fide counterfeiting ring. Three of her brothers—Israel, Stephen, and Nicholas Peck—were the ring's "board," with Mary, of course, as "CEO." Other gang members included two young Irish immigrants named Noble who were employed by John Butterworth as carpenters; two men named Chafee; and Nicholas Camp and his sister, neighbors to the Butterworths. Underscoring Mary Butterworth's cunning, she also enlisted Daniel Hunt, a deputy sheriff, and, allegedly, *Judge* Daniel Smith, of the local court, not to mention many of her fellow worshipers at the Rehoboth Congregational Meetinghouse.

Her daring band of accomplices traveled the roads of New England and passed Butterworth's forged bills with ease. In her kitchen Mary fashioned her muslin plates and churned out stacks of five- and three-pound Rhode Island notes; five-pound Connecticut bills; five- and three-pound Massachusetts bills. The instant she was done with a muslin plate, she flung it into the flames.

Mary was soon hard-pressed to keep up with her gang's demands for more bills, and in the venerable tradition of New England, she began to train an apprentice forger, Hannah Peck, the wife of her brother Nicholas. Hannah Peck turned out to be a real find for the gang, for she quickly learned to forge bills nearly as expertly as those crafted by her mentor in the Butterworths' kitchen.

What had compelled Mary Butterworth to turn forger and to form a counterfeiting gang? Several of her neighbors alluded to her innate love of money, which even her husband, well-to-do compared with most locals, could not satisfy. But greed was seemingly not her sole motive. Although Rehoboth needed a new meetinghouse, the town lacked funds to build the structure. With her husband slated to be one of the project's contractors if building ever got under way, Mary began counterfeiting at about the same time workers put their saws to lumber. Soon the workers were drawing their pay—in "Butterworth bills." By the time the new meetinghouse was finished in 1719, Mary Butterworth's talents had undoubtedly footed much, if not all, of the new edifice in what appeared a classic case of greed advancing "God's good," an appalling notion to any religious-minded colonist. Except in Rehoboth, the counterfeiters' den.

For seven years Mary Butterworth's kitchen was the secret headquarters of a booming colonial cottage industry. Butterworth bills changed hands in New England's shops, docks, common markets, and inns. Although colonial authorities eventually realized to their dismay that someone was passing skillfully counterfeited bills, constables had no luck tracing who had printed the bills or passed them.

The rising number of counterfeit bills circulating throughout Rhode Island led worried legislators to recall a legally issued series of five-pound notes. The authorities logically suspected the counterfeiters' den was underneath their noses, but no one in his or her right mind suspected that the forger was a woman.

Nothing, it seemed, could go wrong for New England's queen of counterfeiting, could unmask the criminal secret hidden in the Rehoboth kitchen. Nothing until one of her gang, Arthur Noble, rode cockily into Newport, Rhode Island, on July 19, 1723.

Noble, one of the Irish carpenters hired by John Butterworth, had served both his bosses, husband and wife, well. A high-spirited young man, the Irishman could not resist a chance to watch a colonial gala, a mass hanging just outside Newport, where twenty-six pirates were to be strung up on gallows erected at Bull Point. Noble cantered into town with excitement pounding in his heart—and with a wad of Butterworth's bills bulging in his purse.

On July 19, 1723, the day after a huge crowd had clogged Bull Point to gawk at the condemned buccaneers and cheer as they twitched from their nooses beneath the summer sky, Newport still buzzed with excited chatter of the pirates' last moments. The taverns were full of locals and outsiders alike, tossing down drafts of liquor, recounting the previous day's events, laughing, cursing, and, in short, carousing as much as Newport's constables allowed.

As Arthur Noble strolled through the town's streets, he spied three young Rehoboth women. Boys being boys, he convinced the women to join him for drinks and dinner at a nearby tavern. The Irishman and his guests were soon laughing and flirting at one of the inn's tables, and when Elizabeth Weir, probably the innkeeper's wife, sidled up to Noble's table to collect the tab for the party, he handed her a forged bill.

Weir was apparently familiar with counterfeit bills, for she quickly summoned the constables. For Noble the party was over. He was soon sitting in a local cell.

Either from fear of Mary Butterworth or from some vague honor code among thieves, the Irishman kept his mouth shut, protecting his boss and his fellow gang members. But the constables found a trail leading to another of Butterworth's minions, Nicholas Camp, and seized him.

Camp, lacking Noble's nerve, began squealing. Before he was through talking, he had told Governor Samuel Cranston everything: the gang's names, the counterfeiting ring's full scope of operations, and the ringleader's identity. The governor's eyes must have widened as the "stoolie" sang his tale of the woman who had bedeviled New England's authorities for seven years.

Mary Butterworth's day of reckoning unfolded on August 15, 1723. Warrants in hand, three deputy sheriffs surprised her and several gang members in her home, and as her neighbors watched in astonishment, the sheriffs hauled the counterfeiter and at least one accomplice to waiting cells in Bristol, Rhode Island.

In the face of incessant interrogations by the sheriffs, Butterworth refused to break, maintaining a stony silence about her forgeries and her helpers. Her friends' lips were as tight as their boss's, and frustrated authorities were forced to release the gang on a lack of evidence. Butterworth, however, was held in her cell; Rhode Island's leaders were determined to convict her through physical evidence of her crime.

Pieces of that evidence were in the authorities' hands, for in Butterworth's kitchen, sheriffs had found many of the tools of her illicit trade: her flatiron, her pens, scraps of paper and muslin. Butterworth could explain that most of the evidence was household items; if any forged bills were actually found in her home, she could claim that someone must have paid her unwitting husband with counterfeits. The only evidence that could guarantee a conviction was a counterfeiter's plate. And probably fighting to restrain a sense of smug satisfaction, Mary Butterworth knew her enemies would never find her illicit plates—not even if they combed the ashes of her hearth for years to come. All she had to do was to wait out the authorities.

Their hands tied by the absence of Butterworth's plates, Butterworth's jailers bowed to the inevitable. The queen of counterfeiters walked, a free woman after the "Court of Assize & General Goal & Delivery" at Bristol, Rhode Island, released her for a lack of evidence.

For years after Butterworth's release, local sheriffs kept the counterfeiter under tight surveillance, but she was not one to tempt fate twice. The only things she cooked up in her kitchen for the rest of her life were meals. If ever she had the urge to reach again for flatiron, quills, muslin, and paper, she gritted her teeth, pushed aside the thought, and reached instead for a broom or the handle of a churn.

Mary Butterworth died in 1775 at the age of ninety-one, and as she drew her final breath, perhaps a faint smile lingered on her lips for a moment at memories of how she had cheated merchants, sheriffs, politicians, and the hangman. In that last moment she perhaps took satisfaction in having outfoxed *men* and in having slipped the social shackles of her sex to carve out a career—even if it was as a counterfeiter.

Two fitting bits of irony to Mary Butterworth's saga were that a woman's, not a man's, sharp eyes—those of Elizabeth Weir—had found the trail to Butterworth's kitchen and that Mary Butterworth had cooked up her bold scheme in that same kitchen, the very symbol of many colonial housewives' bondage. One suspects that the ironies were not lost on America's first female forger.

7 The Pioneer Poetess: Anne Bradstreet

She was exhausted but could not stop. Wintry gusts rattled the diamond-shaped windowpanes of her clapboarded house. With her free hand she pulled a shawl closely around her shoulders, then nudged her chair a few more inches toward the hearth, where a winter fire blazed with more noise than effect against the drafts. Upstairs her bed, piled high with thick coverlets, beckoned. Still, she stayed huddled over sheafs of paper and dipped her quill in a vial of ink. She had no choice, for her creative juices were flowing, and they would ebb only when the Puritan woman's head began bobbing toward sleep.

If we could peek through a window to the past, we might well find such a scene at the home of Anne Bradstreet, America's first published poetess.

Anne Bradstreet was born in or near Northampton, England, in 1612. Her father, Thomas Dudley, a staunch Puritan and a veteran of the army of "good Queen Bess," Elizabeth I, had made the acquaintance of a noble, the earl of Lincoln, who favored Putian beliefs. Dudley went to work for the earl as the steward of Lincoln's estate, including Sempringham Manor, and the Dudley children grew up in the rarefied surroundings of royalty, a life-style most hardworking Puritans could only gape at as they passed such dwellings as the earl's castle.

Young Anne Bradstreet was instilled with strict Puritan tenets of worship, but as she strolled through the earl's lush gardens, she gained an awareness of the beauty of nature that she was to carry with her all her life. To the Puritan girl, beauty in all its forms became important. She later admitted that in her youth she had been vain, leading one to smile at the image of a sober-minded Puritan lass unable to resist primping herself in any available mirror.

Along with her interest in her appearance, Anne Dudley was consumed by another passion: a love of learning. Her father's growing wealth allowed him to hire tutors for his daughter, and the earl gave the girl free rein in his library.

Lincoln's library was undoubtedly a revelation to Dudley, for amid the shelves of books she found not only Puritan works but also the collected wisdom of the ages: history, science, philosophy, and poetry. She read all she could lay hands on, but all must have paled to her budding intellect alongside the graceful stanzas of such poets as Edmund Spenser and perhaps even Shakespeare. The steward's daughter was soon as well read as the spoiled offspring of many nobles.

When Dudley turned sixteen, she caught the heart of twenty-five-year-old Simon Bradstreet, her father's assistant steward. If her later writings are any barometer, she fell head over heels in love with him from the start of their courtship. And why not? The son of a minister, Bradstreet held a master's degree from prestigious Emmanuel College and was a young man of ambition; he was also a man undaunted by a woman of high intellect in an era when "wifely concerns" were the only realm open to most of the "fairer sex." Simon Bradstreet and Anne Dudley were married in 1628, and their love was to endure over four decades of incredible hardship.

One of the first hints of personal hardships to come was Anne Bradstreet's bout against one of the era's dread diseases, smallpox, in the first year of her marriage. She survived, but the affliction probably left pockmarks upon her face. That the illness left scars upon her young psyche was undeniable: She was to write that during her suffering she prayed for forgiveness of her vanity and that God cured her. Her use of the word "vanity" hints that she may have seen the disfiguring disease as a warning against too much pride in one's physical charms.

Anne Bradstreet's world changed forever when civil and religious strife racking England grew worse after Charles I gained the crown in 1625. There was ever-increasing antipathy from the Church of England toward the Puritans, who eschewed the state church's ceremonies and symbols as smacking of Catholicism. By 1630 Puritan leaders were alarmed by assaults upon some of their ministers and by Charles's dissolution of three Parliaments, signaling that the land was on the brink of civil war. The time had come, many Puritans decided, to pull up stakes and find their New Canaan, a promised land where, like Israel's tribes of old, the Puritans could worship in their own way. In 1630, with her husband, her parents, and other members of her family, Anne Bradstreet stood upon the deck of the *Arbella,* flagship of a four-vessel fleet laden with Puritan passengers led by John Winthrop. As she stared at the slowly vanishing docks and cottages of Southampton, she must have known that she was never to glimpse England again, that the memories of her life amid the earl's gardens, the Lincolnshire countryside, and precious volumes of his library were all she had against the frightening uncertainties of the New World. Leaving behind all she had known was a shock to the refined Puritan wife, merely eighteen, a shock she alluded to in her future work.

In May 1630, seventy-two days after the *Arbella* slipped away from Southampton, Bradstreet and her fellow passengers crowded the gunwales for their first look at the New Canaan. Many praised God for their deliverance; others were too weary or sick from scurvy and other ailments to care.

At first the springtime splendors of the land, with its wild strawberries, dense, fragrant stands of pines, and warming sunshine, heartened the new arrivals. But one glance at the gaunt colonists who had survived the previous winter in Salem and in Charlestown filled the hearts and souls of Winthrop's band with dread. Later Bradstreet recalled her fear that God had cast her and the others into a hellish wilderness. How she must have longed for England's tidy gardens and civilization in the first days after setting foot on Massachusetts soil.

The Bradstreets' first New England winter thrust them into the same frantic struggle for survival that they had seen in May in the sickly faces of their predecessors to the colony. In their house in Cambridge, near present-day Harvard Square, the family shivered alongside smoldering fires, never able to chase bone-numbing cold; the Bradstreets and Dudleys survived, Thomas Dudley recorded, on clams, mussels, acorns, and any other scrap of food they foraged with freezing fingers.

Anne Bradstreet may not have realized at the time that the harsh new life in New England was to stoke her creative flame, for she was preoccupied with lasting long enough to see the spring of 1631, not to mention battling a severe case of culture shock. Slowly her Puritan upbringing gave her the faith to accept her plight as God's will.

The Bradstreets survived the winter of 1630–31, and well educated and better heeled than most of their neighbors, Simon Bradstreet and Thomas Dudley surged to the front rank of the fledgling colony's political affairs as the decade unfolded. The 1630s also brought children to the Bradstreets, their first, Samuel, born in 1633.

For Anne Bradstreet, who had often cried from fear that she was never to conceive, her family was the center of her life, as was true of any God-fearing Puritan mother. She gave birth to her daughter Dorothy in 1634, but as was often the case in the seventeenth century, the aftermath of labor nearly killed the new mother when she suffered an illness diagnosed as consumption, a catchall for a variety of the era's maladies. She lived, but the illness was a portent of ailments to come.

By the time the Bradstreets and their four children settled permanently in Merrimack (now North Andover) in 1643 or 1644, the Puritan wife's health was not only holding up well enough to let her run her household with all the skill a husband could want but also allowing her to continue another labor she had begun soon after her arrival in the colony. This labor was one of love, a link to past days spent blissfully in Lincoln's library. Anne Bradstreet, who had tried her hand at verse as early as the age of nineteen, was writing poetry in Merrimack. A poet's voice, muted at first, meant only for her family, had been stirring in the wilds of the Massachusetts Bay Colony. America's first woman poet was at work.

In 1650 Anne Bradstreet, her jaw likely dropping, her eyes widening, discovered that she was a published poet. The Reverend

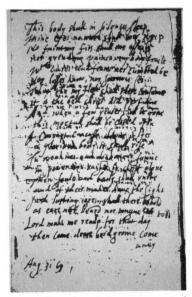

GREGORY M. STEVENS

Anne Bradstreet's final poem, "As Weary Pilgrim," the only existing poem entirely in her own handwriting. *We are grateful to the Stevens Memorial Library of North Andover, Massachusetts, owner of the Anne Bradstreet manuscript, for permission to reproduce "As Weary Pilgrim."*

John Woodbridge, her brother-in-law, had gathered some of her poems and had them run off by a London printer named the Sign of the Bible. The first printed verses by an American woman were long-windedly entitled *The Tenth Muse Lately Sprung Up in America. Or Severall Poems, Compiled with Great Variety of Wit and Learning, Full of Delight. . . . By a Gentlewoman in Those Parts.*

To many on both sides of the Atlantic, the existence of such a book caused more astonishment than the volume's poems. A *colonial woman* had summoned the colossal nerve—gall, some undoubtedly said—to present her jottings for publication!

Actually Bradstreet did not know what her brother-in-law had done until the book was printed. He acknowledged her ignorance of his scheme and wrote of his concern that she might be peeved at him for having spirited away her work without her approval. Of course, he probably thought Puritan decorum would have compelled the poetess to quash his brainstorm of submitting her work to a printer.

The name of the "gentlewoman" was not mentioned with the book's title. Her identity came to light in the preface; readers in Old and New England learned that the "Tenth Muse" was Anne Bradstreet.

The book's introduction also noted that the poetess was not a woman who allowed her children to go hungry, her garden untended, her laundry unwashed as she wondered whether a couplet or a meter rang sweetly to the ear. Instead she was a woman who picked up her quill only after her household tasks were done, a woman who sacrificed a few hours of sleep, not her family's welfare, on the altar of her muse. The introduction's depiction of her as a prim and proper Puritan housewife appears the likely work of Bradstreet's "agent," John Woodbridge, intended to defuse any questions that seventeenth-century minds might raise about the moral character of any woman allegedly taking time from her household duties to write poetry, to some minds a frivolous pastime, to others a vocation of men.

Bradstreet's reaction to the publication of her poems was probably a mix of pride and of regret that the poems in print were her early work, written before she was thirty. As she later proved, the entries in *The Tenth Muse* were the efforts of a poetess in bloom, but one without a unique voice—yet. Her first volume reflected the influences of other writers, including several French poets and Sir Walter Raleigh; her early poems were often derivative, reflecting the knowledge she had accrued in the earl's library rather than the experiences, novel to the mind-set of her readers back in England, of a gentlewoman starting life over in a wilderness teeming with natural wonders, endless hardships, and death. "A Dialogue Between Old England and New" was the only poem in *The Tenth Muse* that gave readers a true glimpse of the voice developing within the soul of Anne Bradstreet. The voice was to be that of America's pioneer poetess.

As a poetess Bradstreet hit her stride in the 1650s and 1660s. Whenever she sat at her writing table and dipped her quill into ink, she drew upon her experiences to pen vivid, often surprising insights into the mind of a Puritan housewife.

Bradstreet devoted much of her most memorable work to her husband, Simon, who often left his wife and children behind while traveling to Boston on political business. In the early 1660s he sailed for England to plead for the favor of the new king, Charles II, who had received scanty support from the colonists at his restoration to the throne in 1660. Despite fears that her husband might perish on the long voyage or that the king might toss him into a rank cell in the Tower of London, Anne Bradstreet showed

her backbone by running her household with Puritan precision
and by continuing to compose verse. Her ardor for Simon shone
especially in her work entitled "To My Dear and Loving Husband":

> *If ever two were one, than surely we.*
> *If ever man were loved by wife, then thee.*
> *If ever wife was happy in a man,*
> *Compare with me ye women if you can.*[1]

Again and again her love for her husband blazed—by Puritan
standards of propriety—in many of her verses: in "A Letter to
Her Husband, Absent upon Publick Employment"; "As Loving
Hind"; and other poems from the quill of the remarkable Puritan
woman.

Anne Bradstreet wrote also of the joys and the sorrows of
giving birth and of rearing children, her "eight birds hatcht in one
nest."[2] Some of her most poignant work ruminates on the deaths
of several of her grandchildren and on the death of a daughter-in-
law who perished during childbirth, a particularly heart-wrench-
ing event for Bradstreet, who had nearly gone to the grave during
her daughter Dorothy's birth.

With a soul-searching honesty welcome in poets of any era,
Anne Bradstreet not only examined marital life but also hinted at
thoughts most Puritans kept under tight rein: thoughts of her
sexuality. Here she was on tricky turf, for one misstep could earn
censure from shocked neighbors. Still, she admitted in an essay
that as a teenager in England she had entertained sexual thoughts
sinful to many right-thinking Puritans. Perhaps the sight of Simon
Bradstreet striding about the earl of Lincoln's estate had conjured
such lust in the teenaged heart of the future poetess.

As Anne Bradstreet's work matured in the 1650s and 60s, it
reflected a poet seeking life's truths in religion, love, family, marriage, and death. The themes were hardly novel to lovers of verse,
but her voice, chiming with increasing grace and a better technical
grasp than her first poems had displayed, rose from a unique setting: the American wilderness.

From that setting came the work that many labeled her mas-
terpiece, "Contemplations." It was an ambitious effort linking
Bradstreet's religious reflections and nature. Maybe, like the later
American writer Henry David Thoreau, of Walden Pond fame,

Bradstreet found inspiration from her own Walden, some wooded glen or lush meadow or sun-splashed pond of the Merrimack countryside. Whatever the source of her inspiration for "Contemplations," her masterwork was that of a poet confident enough of her ability to craft a piece featuring seven-line stanzas and ending with an alexandrine, a twelve-syllable line of verse. Critics may argue that her workmanship seems callow alongside most European poets of the day, but in the wilds of New England during the mid-seventeenth century a unique poetess was at work.

That Bradstreet was able to write meritorious poetry amid the rigors of pioneer life was the true measure of her talent and her dedication to her craft. Her health always tenuous, the demands of raising eight children taxing, so often left alone by her husband to fend with the incessant demands of running the Bradstreet household and to face the natural dangers of New England, she somehow juggled her dual roles as housewife and poetess. Where did she find the time for verse?

In 1666 Bradstreet's house, where she had so successfully performed her balancing of family duties and poetry's call, burned to the ground. The ashes of the Bradstreets' eight hundred or so books, a huge collection by colonial standards, smoldered in the blaze's aftermath; some of the poetess's verses had surely vanished with her family's library. If so, some of the finest words she had ever set to paper were likely lost to posterity. Thankfully much of her work did survive the calamity.

In 1678 a second collection of Bradstreet's work, *Several Poems Compiled with Great Variety of Wit and Learning,* was printed in Boston. The book's scope and its technique surpassed her first effort and proved that Bradstreet, having honed her skills with the passage of years, was a poetess who had inhaled deeply of life and had infused her work with a wide range of emotions and experiences rooted in both the Old and the New World. Even her sternest Puritan neighbors might have understood if the poetess had beamed with pride upon the publication of *Several Poems.* But such fleeting pleasure was denied her.

Anne Bradstreet was never to see her second book. In the fall of 1672 she was stricken again with some form of consumption. She was about sixty years old, buffeted by the burdens of her life in New England, and apparently sensed that she was not to slip the grasp of her newest illness. According to the anguished memory of her son Simon, she wasted away, her body racked, one of her arms grotesquely swollen. Finally the light passed from her eyes. The doomed poetess had welcomed death in her final stanzas:

> *Lord make me ready for that day*
> *then Come deare bridgrome Come away.*[3]

We do not know what Anne Bradstreet looked like or the exact spot of her Merrimack grave. Seven of her children survived her, and her husband, Simon, lived into his nineties. One of her sons, Dudley, was suspected of witchcraft, but the charges were dropped. Roughly two centuries after her death one of her descendants carved a niche for himself among America's literary luminaries; his name was Oliver Wendell Holmes.

At least Anne Bradstreet left us some of her poems, a wonderful glimpse into the mind, heart, and soul of an extraordinary woman. To those who think that New England's Puritans were all dour souls for whom "love" and "joy" were alien words, a session with the first American woman who saw her poetry in print is in order. Anne Bradstreet will still surprise readers.

8 A Bard in Bondage: Phillis Wheatley

Susannah Wheatley spied a little girl. The child, shivering, frail body covered by only a rag, slumped on the auction block of Boston's slave market on a day in 1761. Perhaps the girl raised her downcast eyes long enough to see the throng of white men and women eyeing the blacks on the block as if at a cattle auction. If she did, she may have glimpsed the face of Susannah Wheatley peering at her, the woman likely wearing a prim bonnet and fine yet sensible garb, probably alongside a man in a tricornered hat.

Something in the girl's wretched appearance melted Susannah Wheatley's heart. The woman was at the market in search of a personal servant, but when she and her husband decided to purchase the child, the couple were to gain far more than that for which they bargained. The little slave girl soon on her way to the Wheatleys' comfortable house, on busy King Street, had a special gift that glimmered all too briefly in Boston and beyond. She was destined to become America's first black woman to see her poetry in print.

Except for the child's age, seven or eight, the Wheatleys knew little about their newest slave. They could not fathom the trauma of a black child kidnapped from her family and her home, probably

Senegal, to a world beyond her comprehension. Weak and weary, she bore the physical signs of her gruesome voyage on a slaver. The emotional scars were hidden in her young heart.

The Wheatleys named the child Phillis. She could not yet comprehend that from the moment the couple had bought her, she was far luckier than the other slaves chained in the ship's hold with her: The Wheatleys had no intentions of mistreating the little slave. Susannah Wheatley was preoccupied with Phillis's fragile health, and as the days passed, Mrs. Wheatley, her husband, John, and their teenage twins, Mary and Nathaniel, began regarding the frail African as if she were an adopted child, not a slave. The twins taught Phillis to read and write English and discovered something sure to startle almost any white of the era: The Black girl soaked up her lessons the way a sponge absorbs water. Within sixteen months of her arrival in the house on King Street the young slave had an amazing grasp of her new tongue.

The Wheatleys, honored members of the Old South Meeting-house, nestled on the corner of Marlborough and Milk streets, fed not only Phillis's mind but also her soul with the tenets of the Congregationalist faith, the religious and social cornerstones of Boston's birth. To the family's utter delight, she grabbed at Christianity with the same eagerness she showed at the sight of any book. More often than not the volume she pored over was the Good Book. And as she studied her Bible, she had likely begun to grasp that this family, white slaveowners though they were, had saved her from a wretched fate she sensed more than understood yet and had given her a religion she found wondrous and comforting.

The preferential treatment the Wheatleys lavished upon the girl must have galled the family's other servants, who, even if they liked the newcomer, could not have been thrilled that Mrs. Wheatley gave the girl a room of her own. The young slave also ate her meals with the family, undoubtedly causing the other servants to gape at first, not to mention white guests at the Wheatleys' supper table. To the further astonishment of the Wheatleys' servants, the girl's only chores were scarcely more taxing than those of Mary and Nathaniel Wheatley.

By the time Phillis Wheatley was in her mid-teens, the family realized they had something of a prodigy on their hands. She had begun composing verse, poetry redolent of her voracious reading of the Bible and classical works, and she especially loved the work of Alexander Pope, the great English poet who had died in 1744.

In 1767 the thirteen-year-old slave penned her first poem of note: "To the University of Cambridge [Harvard]." Considering her tender age, her thirty-two-line stab at blank verse was surprisingly well crafted, her handwriting rendered in strokes as firm and well formed as those of many white children at Boston's Latin School.

"To the University" was a diatribe of sorts against the nemesis of neighborhoods past and present—rowdy college students. The slave from King Street admonished the boys of Harvard Yard to behave themselves and expounded on themes to remain the linchpins of her future verse: Christianity, personal virtue, and education. One cannot help speculating that the young slave had seen the high-spirited Harvard men in action and had perhaps winced as a target of some students' puerile banter on the cobbles of Boston.

Interestingly she referred to herself in the poem as an "Ethiop." Her reference to her race seemingly indicated that despite her preferential status in the Wheatley household, she was conscious of her true status—a slave.

Her quill soon poured words into poems with titles such as "On Friendship" and "On Atheism." In 1769 "On the Death of Mr. Snider [Seider], Murder'd by Richardson" reflected the sixteen- or seventeen-year-old slave's acute awareness of the stormy events pushing locals toward outright rebellion against the British. Her poem was inspired by the tragic death of a youth named Christopher Seider, cut down by a Tory customs official named Richardson. Many eulogized the unfortunate Seider as the first patriot martyr.

Maybe Wheatley viewed Seider's funeral procession, two thousand or more strong, six boys lugging the coffin to interment in the shadow of a liberty tree. If she attended the somber ceremony, she heard Samuel Adams's vitriolic denunciation of Richardson; in her poem's title, she unabashedly used the word "murder'd." As events were to prove, a spark of patriotism was flaring within the teenage slave.

For Wheatley in March 1770, "murder" surely proved too tame a word to describe what happened a short distance from her owners' front stoop. The crack of redcoat muskets rent the cold night air, and five Bostonians crumpled dead or dying to the snow-shrouded cobblestones of King Street. Unless her always question-able health prevented her from setting foot in the snow outside the Wheatleys' house, she certainly saw the bloody site where the slain had fallen during the Boston Massacre. On that cold March evening the roar of muskets and the screams of the victims must have drowned out, for at least a few grim hours, the gentle whispers of Phillis Wheatley's muse.

Another event in 1770, in September—the death of the famed preacher George Whitefield, who had been in the vanguard of New England's Great Awakening several decades earlier—set Whea-tley's quill scraping upon paper with words mined from her soul's depths. To the young poetess, Whitefield had been far more than a beacon of her religious faith. Unlike many of his contemporaries of the collar, Whitefield had preached that God's salvation was for blacks as well as whites. The young slave's admiration of the de-ceased reverend burned for all to see in the title of her tribute to him: "An Elegiac Poem on the Death of that Celebrated Divine, and Eminent Servant of Jesus Christ, the Late Reverend and Pious George Whitefield." Her elegiac's lines, her competent prosody put her on the poetical map—from Boston to London. She signed her work "Phillis, a Servant girl of 17 years of Age, Belonging to Mr. J. Wheatley... but 9 years in this Country from Africa."

With John Wheatley undoubtedly bankrolling the poetess, the elegiac was printed on broadsides and sold through an advertise-ment in the *Massachusetts Spy*. Soon local readers were wagging their heads and tongues in astonishment at the notion that a black slave girl had written verse. Her poem was printed in Newport, New York, and Philadelphia, winning admirers from the ranks of merchants, tradesmen, and intellectuals. At the dinner tables of notable Bostonians, the poetic slave was suddenly in demand, many locals eager for a firsthand look at the black girl courted by her muse on King Street. The fawnings of her newfound fans were apparently not heady enough to fool her into thinking that prom-inent Bostonians now saw her as a near equal, for she always insisted that hosts seat her at a separate table from the rest of their diners. Between bites of Indian pudding and other staples of co-lonial repasts, she obviously sensed that to complimentary white hosts, she was part celebrity, part curiosity. She also knew she was something else: a poetess.

As Wheatley continued to sharpen her verse, her fragile health, probably strained by asthma, spurred her solicitous owners to send her to the fresh air of the countryside in the spring of 1772, hoping that the change of locale would spare her from maladies afflicting Bostonians. During her stay in the country (in colonial Boston the country could have been somewhere within eye's view of the town), however, she returned to Boston on Sundays to attend services with the Wheatleys at the Old South Meetinghouse.

Whether sitting in her room on King Street or in the warm sunshine of some country meadow, Wheatley fed her bottomless appetite for knowledge by studying Greek mythology, geography, astronomy, and, of course, classical and neoclassical poetry. But foremost on her mind was probably not the work of other poets but a project she had begun near winter's onset in 1772: Phillis Wheatley was gathering her poems into a book.

When she was finished, John Wheatley did not walk into the office of a local printer with his slave's manuscript in hand. Instead he sent London bookseller Archibald Bell her poems, a cover letter, and a fact sheet emphasizing her race.

Bell was a man with high and mighty friends, including the countess of Huntingdon, a fervent foe of slavery. In January 1773 Bell showed Wheatley's manuscript to the countess, who had read the slave's tribute to Whitefield and had helped get it into print in England. Wheatley's work so enthralled the noblewoman that she was determined to see the manuscript in print.

The countess and her allies were equally resolute to head off a question sure to erupt from readers on both sides of the Atlantic: Was the poetess really a black slave?

To silence any cries of fraud, Bell wrote to the Wheatleys with a request that they send a drawing of their servant to appear in the book. The Wheatleys sent Bell not only the drawing, sketched by another slave, Scipio Moorhead, but also a letter signed by eighteen of Boston's most influential men, including John Hancock, whose boldly inked name was to become a legend on another document, the Declaration of Independence. "To the Publick," the letter dispatched to prove that the poems were the work of Phillis Wheatley, asserted:

WE whose Names are under-written, do assure the World, that the Poems specified in the following Page, were (as we

verily believe) written by Phillis, a young Negro Girl, who
was but a few Years since, brought an uncultivated Barbarian
from *Africa,* and had ever since been, and now is, under the
Disadvantage of serving as a Slave in a Family in this Town.
She has been examined by some of the best Judges, and is
thought qualified to write them.[1]

The letter was to run in Bell's publication of Wheatley's poems.

Bell's communication to the Wheatleys had contained another
request. The countess of Huntingdon, proving that her lofty antislavery views were probably matched by her ego, had reportedly
requested the author to dedicate the book to none other than the
countess herself. Wheatley's dedication did so.

When "To the Publick" and Moorhead's sketch arrived at
Bell's office, at 8 Aldgate Street, London, Bell must have taken a
long look at the image of the slave commended by the eighteen
names gracing the letter. What he saw was the face of a black
woman in her twenties with grave, lovely features beneath a ruffled
bonnet from which her curls peeked. Her slender left hand rested
against her chin, giving her the aspect of someone immersed in
thought, a poetess listening to her muse.

As Bell began putting the book together, John and Susannah
Wheatley made a decision that changed forever the life of their
servant. The poet's health was still spotty, and upon a physician's
counsel that ocean air might do her tortured lungs some good, the
Wheatleys informed her that she was to accompany their son,
Nathaniel, on a business trip to London. Once again she was to
cross the Atlantic. This time, however, she would not be packed,
chained, sobbing, and screaming, into the crowded hold of a slave
ship.

Phillis Wheatley arrived in London in June 1773 and discovered an alien, wonderful world where she was received by many
nobles and intellectuals with fanfare overwhelming for any important white, let alone a slave. For someone who had likely viewed
Boston's customhouse and its white-steepled churches as grand
structures, the Tower of London, the city's palaces, its bridges, its
cathedrals, and its sprawling expanse along the Thames must have
made Boston seem a puny colonial backwater. At home she had
earned the esteem of merchants, jurists, and clerics; in England
who could have blamed the young slave if her head was momen-

tarily turned by the sights and the highborn, especially the countess of Huntingdon, telling her how wonderful her poems were?

Another American abroad in July 1773 made a special point to speak with the poetess, fast becoming the toast of London's antislavery bigwigs. And if Wheatley longed for a chat with a man with few of the affectations she must have encountered among her blue-blooded admirers, this visitor was that man; his name was Benjamin Franklin.

One can only imagine the actual conversation between the nearly seventy-year-old Franklin, a man who knew his way around the political, economic, scientific, and literary fast tracks of the colonies and of England, and the slave poet of Boston. It is not hard to picture a twinkle behind Franklin's spectacles as he gazed at the lovely young woman sitting across from him and likely discussed Pope, Milton, the writer's trade, and perhaps even slavery with her. That he left an indelible impact upon Wheatley was later evidenced by her second book, never to reach print, with its dedication to Franklin.

Wheatley's whirl through London society was such that she may eventually have won an audience at the court of George III, but after five glorious weeks in England she received chilling news: Susannah Wheatley had taken seriously ill.

Wasting no time, the poet boarded a ship for Boston and left behind her new circle of friends and admirers. She was never to see them again.

She set eyes on Boston's familiar brick buildings, its white spires, and its busy docks in October 1773 and rushed back to the house on King Street with prayers that her mistress had not died while her slave was at sea. To the poetess's momentary relief, Susannah Wheatley was still alive.

In January 1774 something from London followed the poet across the Atlantic, something that must have sent her heart soaring and lifted the spirits of Susannah Wheatley. The young slave's hands perhaps trembling, she held copies of a volume entitled *Poems on Various Subjects, Religious and Moral*. Her work, on high-grade paper, featuring her portrait, was the first book of poems by a black American woman. Whites soon to pay two shillings or so for the slender volume would purchase a work penned by a *slave*.

Wheatley's book had numerous reprintings in America, and

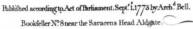

The African Muse at work: Portrait of Phillis Wheatley, slave poetess
AMERICAN ANTIQUARIAN SOCIETY

many readers marveled at Boston's black muse. They included the likes of a mariner named John Paul Jones, who wrote a letter expressing his admiration for Wheatley. Yet other readers were enraged or dumbfounded at the thought that a black—any black— was capable of writing poetry and refused to believe that the book was anything more than some sort of chicanery. Even the testimony of the eighteen noteworthy men in "To the Publick" was not enough to sway some skeptics.

With a swiftness the poetess could have likened to the Greek tragedies she had read, her triumph was soon tinged with sorrow. Susannah Wheatley died in March 1774.

For Phillis Wheatley, the loss of the woman who had been almost as much mother and friend as mistress was incalculable. The woman so concerned for the health of the frail little girl on the auction block in 1761 was no longer to rush to her aid every time she coughed or sniffled and to encourage her whenever words trickled rather than rushed from her quill.

The unraveling of Phillis Wheatley's world, a slow, painful process, began with her mistress's final breath on that gloomy

March day. Within a few years of Mrs. Wheatley's death, her husband, the man who had sent the slave's poems to London, and Mary Wheatley, who had helped teach the young slave to read and write, were also dead. John Wheatley had freed the poetess before his death, but even her manumission likely helped little to ease her grieving heart.

Another emotion, patriotism, soon claimed much of Wheatley's attention. Despite some fond recollections of England, she was swept up in the outbreak of the Revolution. Shortly after the Battle of Bunker Hill, on June 17, 1775, Wheatley fled from Boston to Providence, Rhode Island, but even if the fray's fury, which had littered the grassy slope with more than a thousand redcoat casualties at a cost of about four hundred rebels, had spurred her flight, the colonies' quest for independence also sent words spewing with patriotic zeal from her quill.

Wheatley sent a letter and a poem to General George Washington in October 1775. While she was probably aware that the Virginian was a slaveowner who was still opposed to blacks serving in his ragtag army, a stand that did not prevent blacks from fighting in the rebels' ranks, she might have sensed that he would still read her words to him. She was right.

Washington not only read the poem but loved it. What leader would not have preened over such verse? Wheatley's lines were an unabashed tribute to him and his mission to lead the colonies to liberty, correctly envisioning a man—perhaps the only man— capable of guiding the colonials to ultimate victory over King George's crack regiments.

In February 1776 Washington wrote a reply to Wheatley and told her that he wanted to publish her poem but was concerned that doing so would make him appear a pompous man. Thomas Paine, the editor of the *Pennsylvania Magazine,* had no such compunction: He ran Wheatley's poem, along with her letter to Washington, in the April 1776 issue of the publication and referred to Wheatley as "the famous Phillis Wheatley, the African Poetess."

Seeing her work in *the* Thomas Paine's magazine must have kindled memories of those heady days in 1773, when her book had won her admirers from the countess of Huntingdon to Benjamin Franklin. Now, having earned the gratitude of Washington, she accepted his invitation to meet with him at his headquarters in Cambridge, Massachusetts, in 1776 and was accorded the utmost civility from the man she had styled "Generalissimo of the armies of North America." The modest fanfare she enjoyed at the camp was to be the last such response to her work.

By 1778 Wheatley was back in Boston, whose citizens were never again to hear the harsh crunch of redcoats' boots upon the city's streets. She was a free woman, but the lot of an ex-slave, even an accomplished and well-known poetess, was not easy.

Wheatley must have thought a new and wonderful chapter in her life was opening in the spring of 1778, for she had met John Peters, a handsome, extremely intelligent man who, like her, was a manumitted slave. He dressed as a man of means, carried a cane, and worked as a grocer. But storekeeping was hardly the stuff of Peters's ambitions: He studied law and actually worked in that field for a while, a laudable and virtually unheard-of accomplishment for a black man in eighteenth-century America.

Peters and Wheatley married in April 1778, Wheatley seemingly having found a man whose looks and intelligence compared with hers, a man who could fill the void left in her life by the deaths of three Wheatleys. However, from the start of the couple's union, life was a struggle. Many whites in Boston apparently resented Peters's ambition, viewing him as an upstart blind to his proper "place" in the town's social order. Nathaniel Wheatley reputedly disliked John Peters and broke off his relationship with Phillis. How distant the days when Nathaniel and Mary Wheatley had taught a little slave to read and write must have seemed for Mrs. Peters.

When Peters was reportedly jailed for failure to pay his debts, a common enough ordeal for many men, white or black, of the day, Phillis Peters took a job at a local boardinghouse to support her children (she had three; two died at early ages). Among strange, perhaps rough men likely casting lewd glances and words at her, the poetess, whose former mistress had never subjected her to taxing housework, faced, in all likelihood, filthy floors, brimming chamber pots, and rancid bedding in the boardinghouse. Her health inevitably eroded from the physical and emotional strains.

Despite the tolls of her difficult marriage, the demands of motherhood, money worries, and failing health, Wheatley still sought her muse. Her compositions occasionally appeared in broadsides or pamphlet form, but her attempts to find a publisher for her second book failed, including an advertisement in the October 30, 1779, issue of the Boston *Evening Post & General Advertiser.*

In September 1784 Phillis Wheatley's by-line appeared for the final time. Her poem's theme was one she had experienced—the death of a baby.

The *Massachusetts Centinel* ran a small announcement on December 8, 1784: "Last Lord's day died, Mrs. Phillis Peters, aged 31, known to the literary world by her celebrated miscellaneous Poems." In an unmarked grave were buried the remains of the slave-poetess and one of her children.

By the time of Wheatley's death critics' doubts that she had actually written the poetry bearing her name had been largely dispelled. Her poems were indeed her own, but denunciations lingered unfairly. Thomas Jefferson, a slaveowner and allegedly the lover of a slave, Sally Hemings, conceded that Wheatley's work was indeed hers, but he claimed that her poems were unworthy of serious criticism. Such an ardent admirer of French thinkers, Jefferson should have listened to perhaps the greatest French intellectual of all, Voltaire, who had recognized the unique voice of a slave whose soul, if not her body, was hers and hers alone.

Part III

Recipes and Rebels

9 A Taste of Heaven: Dr. Baker's Chocolate Factory

Something was in the air. People on their daily rounds along the roads of Dorchester and Milton Village, Massachusetts, turned their noses toward the Neponset River and sniffed the spring breeze. "Chocolate!" the passersby likely murmured, eyes aglow in delight, mouths watering.

The year was 1765. The heavenly scent drifted from a sawmill on the banks of the river, within eyeshot of Boston. Inside the mill an Irishman watched two millstones grinding fragrant cocoa and sounding a call to a culinary revolution that was to capture the palate of America.

In the fall of 1764 John Hannon arrived in Milton Village without a shilling in his pocket. His stomach probably rumbled with hunger, and his clothes were surely shabby. He was looking for work, for a chance to make a life for himself.

Aside from his likely vagabond appearance, something else about him must have troubled the industrious local Yankees who sent wary glances at the stranger: Whenever the man opened his mouth, his words spilled out in an Irish brogue. To colonists whose hearts still beat with the anti-Irish prejudices of their Puritan ancestors, an Irishman in their midst was reason for concern.

Hannon was probably lamenting the day he had left the "ould

sod" of Ireland. He had, however, something to offer Americans. The Irishman knew how to make chocolate, the sweet nectar that had become a choice beverage to colonists but had to be imported and laboriously ground with mortar and pestle or cumbersome "hand mills."

One of the locals, Dr. James Baker, met Hannon somewhere in Milton, chatted with him, and realized that if the stranger really knew how to start up a chocolate mill, profit beckoned anyone willing to gamble on bankrolling him. Baker, a Harvard graduate who had practiced medicine and had run a Dorchester store, was apparently a restless sort, looking for his golden opportunity. He decided to take a chance on the man with the brogue.

Hannon did not need a large space to set up shop, but he did need waterpower to grind large loads of cocoa beans. In the spring of 1765 Baker found his partner an ideal site, a sawmill perched alongside the Neponset River. Hannon soon was ready to begin grinding beans between two enormous round millstones. Praying that the Irishman had been telling the truth about his chocolate-making expertise, Baker likely waited with a racing heart and sweaty palms.

Spun by the Neponset's flow, set to one third the speed used to grind corn, the top stone lurched into motion. Then Hannon poured cocoa beans into a hole cut through the center of the top stone, the bottom stone started whirling, and the motion of both stones pulverized the beans into a dense, syrupy liquid. The hot liquid was collected in a kettle and poured into molds to cool and form chocolate cakes, which were actually more like bricks. John Hannon was no lying braggart; he had delivered the goods. In the first grating strains of the two millstones, America's first true chocolate factory and a financial dynasty had been born on the banks of the Neponset. The dynasty, however, was not to bear the name Hannon.

Hannon and Baker were not the first Americans to make chocolate, for in Providence, Rhode Island, in 1752, Obadiah Brown had built a water-powered chocolate mill and had churned out four hundred pounds of the stuff for Newport merchants. But Brown's venture had been a mere drop in the kettle and, unlike the future course of Baker and Hannon's plant, had been short-lived, the reason that the Baker plant won acclaim as America's first real chocolate concern. (Most texts on the matter flatly call

The old Baker Chocolate Factory, perched on the banks of the Neponset River, Dorchester, Massachusetts

Baker's plant the first.) Hannon and Baker were in the chocolate business for the long haul.

With the exceptions of the lucky passersby who caught a whiff of chocolate from the sawmill, Americans had no idea that a cure for chocolate lovers sore-armed from grinding cocoa beans with mortar and pestle or hand mills was in the offing. The Harvard man and the Irish immigrant were to bring smiles to the faces of the Thirteen Colonies' "chocoholics."

Soon after the first chocolate droplets cooled, Baker and Hannon were selling their hard cakes to sweet-toothed neighbors. The exact nature of the partnership between the Yankee and the Irish immigrant is hard to define, but at the beginning of their venture, Hannon was apparently the "hands-on" person and Baker the financer. The pair's first chocolate was fittingly sold under Hannon's name, advertised in handbills to lure chocolate buffs to sample the partners' aromatic cakes, intended to be scraped by customers and boiled with water to make cups of cocoa.

The locals obliged Hannon and Baker in increasing numbers.

To meet the rising demand from patrons, the duo moved their operation in 1768 to a fulling (cloth) mill on the Dorchester side of the Neponset, renting the space from Baker's brother-in-law, Edward Preston. In coming years Baker came to regret bringing Preston within sight of the chocolate plant, for Preston was to show he knew a good thing when he saw it—and was ready to capitalize on it.

Baker, who had first recognized that good thing, opened a second chocolate factory in 1772. It is unclear whether a rift had developed between the partners or whether they simply expanded the operation to meet customers' frenzied thirst for hot chocolate. What was certain was that Baker had obviously learned much of the Irishman's craft, for the new mill ground at least 895 pounds of chocolate in 1773.

Whatever Baker's reason for having opened the second plant, he had made a lucky decision: Flames engulfed Hannon's factory in 1775. The loss of the entire operation had been precluded by the establishment of Baker's plant.

Hannon rented space in a nearby snuff mill and was soon back in production. Presumably he guarded his cakes from any tobacco residue wafting into his plant from the adjacent snuff maker, and his wares continued to sell.

Flames of another sort, those of the Revolutionary War, soon blazed near the mills. While musketry and cannonades rose above nearby Boston, Hannon and Baker fought to keep their business afloat. Dependent upon West Indies cocoa beans, the chocolate makers ran shipments of beans through the gauntlet of British warships prowling the Atlantic coastline. They must have agonized each day that an expected shipment was late, and they surely grimaced if customers wanted to pay for chocolate with Continental currency scarcely worth the paper upon which it was printed. Luckily for the two entrepreneurs, the war shifted to other theaters after General Washington's cannon on Dorchester Heights, and undoubtedly within view of the two anxious chocolate makers, sent Lord William Howe, his redcoats, and the Royal Navy scampering forever from Boston. Hannon and Baker could get back to business without worrying about "lobsterbacks" ransacking or torching the chocolate mills.

The British were gone locally, but Hannon and Baker still had to run beans from the Caribbean. In 1779 Hannon reportedly boarded a ship bound for the chocolate markets of the West Indies. As the vessel sailed beyond the New England coast, he may have gazed wistfully in the direction of the spot where he had helped found America's first permanent chocolate factory. He was not to set foot in his plant again.

The Irishman simply vanished, never more to be seen. Two rumors about John Hannon's fate arose after he had failed to return to America. The more plausible contended that his ship sank in the Atlantic and took the Irishman to the bottom.

The second conjecture claimed that Hannon boarded his ship and safely reached the West Indies but had no intention of returning to America. Allegedly chafing from a bad marriage to a Boston woman, Elizabeth Doe, and perhaps yearning for his "ould sod," Hannon may have sailed back to Ireland. One fact is certain: The Irish immigrant, who, with Baker, had begun an industry in America, disappeared from history. His name was forgotten, his legacy consumed by another's name—Baker Chocolate.

Baffled no doubt by Hannon's disappearance but with a business to run, Baker could not dwell on his partner's fate. Hannon's wife soon concerned Baker more than the missing Irishman, for she intended to hang on to her husband's share of the chocolate business, although Baker had other ideas.

When Hannon departed Boston, he had left his mill in the capable hands of his apprentice, Nathaniel Blake. But Blake and Elizabeth Hannon spent more time arguing about the operation of the plant than making chocolate. Blake soon quit his post and quickly found a new job—with James Baker.

By 1780 Baker had control of his ex-partner's interest. How Baker finally got his hands on the Hannon plant is open to speculation, with one figuring that the Irishman's "widow," unable to replace Blake, was compelled to sell her share on Baker's terms.

Baker, choosing to consolidate the entire business under one roof, opened a revamped factory at Edward Preston's new mill, on the site of the mill that had burned in 1775. For the next eight years load after load of cocoa beans was roasted in kettles, mashed into steamy liquid between the weighty millstones, and poured into molds, the aroma swirling above the plant. With each brick of chocolate from the spinning stones, Hannon's name faded farther into oblivion. The first name in American chocolate is Baker.

In 1791 Dr. Baker packed up his operation and moved again, to an old paper mill. The reason for the move was probably strained relations between Baker and Preston, who was preparing to open his own chocolate plant and go head to head with his brother-in-law and former tenant for a piece of the chocolate market. Over the years Preston had obviously studied Baker's kettles, stones, molds—and profits. Chances were that the two men were never inclined to chat amicably over a steaming cup of cocoa.

In 1804, nearly four decades after meeting a down-on-his-luck Irishman named John Hannon, James Baker stepped down from his perch as America's chocolate king and bestowed the "title" upon his son Edmund. A new era, one perhaps inconceivable to Dr. Baker and Hannon even in their grandest hopes for their sweet product, was about to dawn for the young nation's chocolate lovers.

Edmund Baker, apparently full of plans to put his stamp upon his father's enterprise, wanted to build a modern mill on the Dorchester side of the Neponset. Meanwhile, as his head swam with his dreams of expansion, he took care of the present by temporarily moving the plant back to the old sawmill in Milton where his father and Hannon had ground their first beans.

The younger Baker forever closed the doors of the venerable old mill in 1806 and started roasting, grinding, cooling, and distributing chocolate in his new plant. For 150 years chocolate was to flow from the site. Edmund Baker also showed general business savvy, opening a gristmill and a cloth mill alongside the chocolate factory and expanding the family's little empire on the Neponset. Small wonder that the Neponset was dubbed "the river of American business," a river where the Bakers ruled.

Baker's chocolate began turning up on store shelves from the East Coast to the western outposts of America's ever-swelling borders. But suddenly disaster encroached upon the Baker chocolate mill: the War of 1812.

America's second conflict against Great Britain cut off the Bakers' supply of cocoa beans and forced Baker to bring his factory to a virtual shutdown. With the plant's huge millstones still and silent, its kettles and its molds empty, Baker probably wondered if his father, who had kept the stones grinding during the Revolution, could have done the same in 1812. But the son could take solace in his foresight in having opened his gristmill, for grain was in demand, and his cloth mill, which he successfully enlarged despite the war. Had he tied up all his family's assets in chocolate—and who could have blamed him if he had?—the saga of Baker chocolate might have ended between 1812 and 1814.

That brown nectar would stream again from his stones was an ironclad reality to Edmund Baker. Despite the lack of beans, he tore down his chocolate mill and built an impressive granite edifice standing three stories, a fitting home, he believed, for the future capital of American chocolate. And with the war's end in 1814, cartloads of Baker's chocolate rumbled in all directions to tickle the taste buds of Americans craving a bit of Baker's best since war had exiled the sweet stuff from storekeepers' shelves.

Edmund Baker, having gotten the chocolate business back on its feet and pointed it toward the future, selected his son Walter as the man to complete his dream of putting the plant's chocolate in every corner of the nation. The son endeavored to do just that.

Walter Baker inherited a business gaining national stature but faced problems his grandfather could scarcely have envisioned at Preston's mill in 1765. Straining to satiate Americans' bottomless appetite for chocolate, Baker increased his work force. In a sign of the changing times in America, he hired not only men but also women. Mary and Christiana Shields, hired in 1834, were the first in petticoats to draw wages from a Baker. The two women worked out well, for by 1846 Baker's payroll was comprised of two workmen, two male apprentices, and *seven women*. As was true of most of the era's bosses, Baker surely paid women less than men.

His employees certainly earned their wages. Conditions inside the plant that smelled like heaven but that must have seemed like hell as the orders piled up were certainly grueling enough to make some workers loathe the very sight and scent of chocolate.

Americans far removed from the heat and noise of the chocolate mill were likely heedless of the labors required to bring the treat to local stores. Chocolate lovers knew only that they could not get enough of their sweet vice.

According to a Milton, Massachusetts, historian, one fellow who learned first hand of his countrymen's passion for cocoa was a tall, craggy-faced man with a shock of unruly black hair. He stocked shelves with Baker's best in New Salem, Illinois, in 1833—and went by the name of Abraham Lincoln.

Americans' readiness to splurge hard-earned cash on chocolate sparked full-fledged competition for the Bakers in the 1830s. By 1835 the Preston mill was churning out 750 pounds of chocolate a day. Walter Baker probably wished that his grandfather had kept old Edward Preston away from the early chocolate plants, for Preston and his family had learned the tricks of the trade well.

Baker's industrial backyard grew more crowded in 1842. A third chocolate mill, Webb & Twombly, rose along the Neponset. Although the new plant owners fathomed little about the business—other than the fact that the Bakers and the Prestons were turning profits—the latest arrivals had lured one of Preston's men to pit its factory against the others. Soon after the opening of Webb & Twombly, the smell of chocolate permeating the banks of the river led locals to name the area Chocolate Village.

"Chocolate Wars" was an apt term for the way the three factories sent out one wagonload after another of their delectable products from Lower Mills, as the knot of factories was known, to the cupboards of American homes. The grinding of each plant's millstones being constant, the chocolate trade was one in which volume meant profit; in the 1840s and 1850s, beans went for ten cents a pound, while Baker charged sixteen cents a pound for his best brand of chocolate and twenty cents for his top cocoa.

Volume and competition were not the only concerns of Baker and the other chocolate makers. Every summer the plants' stones ground to a halt. Effective refrigeration for chocolate was nonexistent; not until 1868 and the advent of "cold" technology could the "generals" of the "Chocolate Wars" wage summer campaigns.

Walter Baker's last campaign in the business came long before refrigeration turned chocolate into a year-round operation. He died in 1852, and with his passing ended the Baker dynasty. For eighty-seven years the family had ruled their chocolate fiefdom on the banks of the Neponset and had persevered in the face of war, embargo, fire, and rivals ruthlessly striving to topple the family that had founded America's first permanent chocolate factory. The leadership of Baker chocolate passed to men with other names.

The company continued to make chocolate along the Neponset until 1965. In that year, two centuries after Dr. Baker and Hannon had filled their first molds, Baker Chocolate shut up along the Neponset, a decision made by the outfit's parent corporation, General Foods, which had purchased the world-renowned chocolate maker in 1927. Baker Chocolate's new home was Dover, Delaware.

More than two hundred years after the first rich brown droplets oozed from the rims of Baker and Hannon's grinding stones, America's love affair with chocolate waxes unabated, testimony to the good taste of Dr. Baker and James Hannon.

10 Minuteman, Minister, and "Mollato": Lemuel Haynes

In a Torrington, Connecticut, church, all eyes stared at a man behind a pulpit. Many faces wore curious looks, lips pursed, eyebrows arched. Other faces glowered, eyes narrowed, jaws clenched.

The man behind the pulpit understood the parishioners' expressions. The people packing the pews and dressed in their Sunday best were whites. He was black.

The year was 1785, and even in New England, where many loathed slavery, the sight of a black minister preparing to preach to an all-white assembly of Congregationalists was unprecedented. If the worshipers inside the church thought for a second, however, that the minister would slink from the pulpit in fear or that his voice would falter, they were wrong. For Lemuel Haynes was made of sterner stuff than they could imagine; at Lexington a decade before, he had stood shoulder to shoulder with fellow minutemen and had faced King George's redcoats and their glinting bayonets.

On that fateful April morning in 1775 Haynes's musket had been his weapon. In the Torrington church his weapon would be oratory. A black minister was about to stand as the first of his race to head a flock of whites.

* * *

If ever an American began life with a heavy burden, that American was Lemuel Haynes. He was born in West Hartford, Connecticut, in 1753, a child of scandal: His mother was a white woman from a family of strong Yankee roots; his father, an unknown black man. The girl and her family, scrambling to rid themselves of her shame as soon as possible, indentured the boy, named Lemuel Haynes by some soul who had realized that bastard or not, the child needed a name, to David Rose, of Granville, Massachusetts. The indenture contract essentially guaranteed that the child was to live in legal bondage to Rose for the first twenty-one years of his life.

As Haynes's early years unfolded, he came to realize that he had been lucky to end up in the care of David Rose. Rose instilled honesty and love of God in his young charge, and in later years Haynes lovingly recalled how Mrs. Rose had reared him with the same love and attention she gave her birth children.

If Haynes ever needed any proof of who his *real* mother, though not his birth one, was, an incident during his youth must have cemented his bond with Mrs. Rose. According to Haynes's biographer, Timothy Mather Cooley, Haynes related that he had accidentally encountered his birth mother in a town near Granville. One can imagine the youth, his knees weak with churning emotions, tremulously approaching the woman who had given him life, then left him. She took one look and ran from him. Hurt but not stunned into silence, he dashed after her and before she could escape unleashed the pent-up fury of a scorned youth.

The trauma of his abandonment notwithstanding, Haynes proved an ideal indentured servant to the Roses, more adoptive parents than master and mistress to the youth, by his treating them with obedience and respect. He chopped and stacked wood for the family's hearth and fireplace, helped plow their fields, and undertook any other chores he was assigned, his strength growing with each arduous and necessary task.

The Roses soon learned that the boy's abilities went far beyond wielding an ax, clearing stumps from fields, and yoking teams of oxen or horses. Like a flame ready to burst into a fire, Haynes's intelligence first flashed in a common school where most, if not all, of the other pupils were white children. His mind eagerly consumed the schoolmasters' lessons, and he read everything he could lay hands on in the schoolhouse and at home. His memory was amazing; long written passages tumbled word for word from his lips whenever he wished.

One Saturday evening, when the Roses huddled in family prayer, Haynes recited a sermon that impressed the group with its piousness and vigor. The youth, asked who had written the words, informed his family that the author was he. Stupefying silence must have hung in the Roses' farmhouse for several moments. Then pride rushed into the family at the glowing erudition of the boy— and perhaps awe that their God had obviously granted such a gift for words to one born with the "tarnish" of his birth parents' sin.

At the urgings of the Roses, the people of Granville soon allowed Haynes to read Sunday sermons at the local meetinghouse. Whether he read standard Scripture or delivered sermons he had written, young Haynes's fervent orations cascading from the pulpit and winning his neighbors' admiration appeared the earmarks of one born to preach; his heart surely racing stride for stride with his lips as he launched into his sermons, he was to the pulpit born.

In 1774 twenty-one-year-old Lemuel Haynes became a free man with the expiration of his term of indenture. He remained in Granville for the time being, pondering his destiny, but his immediate future was soon engulfed by the waves of rebellion surging across Massachusetts. Willing to defend the town and the family that had given a black acceptance he could not have found in many locales of the Thirteen Colonies, Haynes joined the Granville militia. The young minuteman, his wide, deeply set eyes narrowing with concentration, his strong hands wrapped around a musket, drilled once a week with other Granville volunteers on the town green, trying to learn the manual of arms for a blood-chilling prospect: battle with regulars of the Royal Army.

On the night of April 18, 1775, General Thomas Gage, commander of the British troops in Boston, sent some seven hundred redcoats on a march of roughly twenty miles toward Concord to seize powder, shot, and other munitions reportedly stored there by the patriots. The troops also had orders to arrest the rebel firebrands John Hancock and Samuel Adams.

Early on the morning of April 19 the redcoats marched into Lexington. Waiting anxiously on the village green stood about seventy men—farmers, merchants, and tradesmen—with powder horns and various types of muskets. One of those minutemen peering at King George's finest was Lemuel Haynes.

Shots rang out. By the time the smoke cleared, eight minutemen lay dead or dying in the grass. The Revolution had begun.

Haynes and the other surviving minutemen tore from the green, but the battle was just beginning for the colonials and the British. During the rest of that long, momentous April day Haynes and his comrades were joined by other local militiamen and drove the British back to Boston, some 270 redcoats being killed or wounded by Americans firing behind walls and from barns and farmhouses along the route of the redcoats' retreat, sixteen or so miles of hell for Gage's men.

Haynes was never to forget his role on the war's opening day. By the time the first cracks of muskets pealed across Lexington's green, hatred for British tyranny burned hotter than ever in him, and it was to blaze over the years into his revulsion for any form of despotism. "[T]he shot heard round the world," the shot Haynes had actually heard, inspired him to write a poem he grandiloquently entitled "The Battle of Lexington: A POEM on the *inhuman* Tragedy Perpetrated on the 19th of April 1775 by a Number of the British Troops under the Command of Thomas Gage, which Parricides and Ravages Are Shocking Displays of Ministerial & Tyrannic Vengeance. . . ."

He wrote that Americans would rather die than live as slaves under British rule. His choice of the word "slaves" indicates he may have had more than American independence on his mind, for at the poem's end he signed his name as "Lemuel a young *Mollato*." His emphasis upon his race seems testimony to his exhilarating yearning for *all* men's freedom in the heady and frightening days following Concord and Lexington.

Haynes had scarcely a few weeks in which to dwell upon the events of April 19, 1775, for in May he was marching with a force of patriots through northeastern New York on a daring mission that would help make or break the rebellion: the capture of Fort Ticonderoga and its artillery. Among the men on the critical expedition to the British bastion were Benedict Arnold and Ethan Allen, the latter at the head of a rough-and-tumble band soon to win immortality as the Green Mountain Boys.

The Americans took the fort on May 10, 1775. The artillery

Haynes helped seize was later dragged to Boston under the direction of Henry Knox, mounted along Dorchester Heights, and used to drive the British from Boston.

Haynes and at least two other blacks had helped storm formidable Fort Ticonderoga, the future preacher again in the thick of things against the British, the tyrants, to Haynes's way of thinking. He was always to take special pride in his role in Ticonderoga's fall, and the reputed words of Ethan Allen during the fray had paralleled Haynes's feelings during the fall of the fortress: "Surrender in the name of Jehovah and the Continental Congress!" For Haynes, the reverence for God and the blaze of patriotism in those words were the cornerstones of America's struggle for independence.

As the Thirteen Colonies' desperate struggle raged on, the rebels' determination to cast off the chains of monarchy conjured other thoughts in Haynes, thoughts of slavery's evil. The inherent hypocrisy of Americans ranting rightfully against despotism while many of those same rebels dealt in black flesh invaded Haynes's thoughts. He had probably read Thomas Paine's soul-searing tract *African Slavery in America,* a cry for the dissolution of slavery.

With slavery clearly center stage on Haynes's mind as the war neared its end and as freedom—for white Americans—beckoned, he wrote a forty-six-page essay titled "Liberty Further Extended: Or Free Thoughts on the Illegality of Slave-keeping." The work's assault against slavery branded the bondage of fellow blacks a sin against man and God and asserted that blacks were entitled to freedom.

Haynes's eloquent arguments against slavery's evil should have marked a deafening salvo in the antislavery struggle, yet he never published "Liberty Further Extended." Why he poured his soul into the tract but kept it out of the public's sight was, and is, his secret. Modern critics inclined to charge him with cowardice court foolishness; the grim yardstick of war had proved the measure of Lemuel Haynes beyond the words of any would-be detractor.

His thoughts shifted completely to aspirations for the ministry in 1779, two years before the war's end, the ex-minuteman having laid aside his musket at the end of enlistment and having picked up his Bible. He studied Latin and Greek, striving to master the tongues self-respecting Congregationalist ministers comprehended, turning down an opportunity to study at Dartmouth's divinity school in order to study on his own with a pair of ministers in Connecticut.

Haynes's grasp of languages, science, and, most important, the Bible, Old Testament and New, was put to the test in the fall of 1780, when he faced several erudite ministers likely looking as imposing to him as the redcoats. The candidate for a preacher's pedigree endured an inquisition that could dash his hopes for the ministry. Although one of Haynes's mentors, a minister in Wintonbury, Connecticut, believed his charge was ready for the challenge, Haynes, several times throughout the ordeal, must have silently prayed that he would not freeze, would not grope for an answer to find it departed from his memory.

The teacher proved right. After probing the scope of Haynes's knowledge, the examiners pronounced him suitable to preach the Gospel to Congregationalist assemblies.

His triumph hardly surprised the people of Granville, for since the Sundays years before when young Haynes had amazed the locals from the pulpit of the meetinghouse, many had sensed he was to make his mark as a man of God. He delivered his first officially sanctioned sermon at Granville's new church to the approval of neighbors, and as his voice filled the building, few listeners probably spared more than a passing thought to the hue of the preacher's skin. To most souls in Granville, he was simply one of them.

Haynes preached for several years in Granville while awaiting official recognition by a local association of ministers. For Haynes, however, concerns of the soul soon vied with a matter of the heart: He had fallen in love with the Granville schoolteacher, Elizabeth Babbit.

His affections were reciprocated by Babbit, whom he had brought into the Congregationalist fold and who, possessing an education, might have been drawn to her religious instructor by the breadth of his intellect, his growing stature in the town, and, of course, the telltale signals of her heart. There was, however, an obstacle, more a pitfall, to their ardor for each other: the differing colors of their skin.

Haynes was acutely aware that while his neighbors had accepted him as a virtual equal, the idea of an interracial marriage was sure to raise some eyebrows. Probing his heart and mind, he certainly asked himself if his love for the white schoolmistress was powerful enough to withstand the harsh stares, mutters, and outright contempt sure to flare from a local or two. He turned to his faith for strength and presented his case to several ministers; perhaps to Haynes's surprise, his fellow men of the cloth urged him to follow his heart.

Elizabeth Babbit followed hers. The couple defied convention and were married by 1785; their union ultimately produced ten children.

In the summer of 1785 the newlyweds received stunning news that a church in Torrington, Connecticut, wanted Haynes to become their minister. Haynes accepted the post, although the reality of leaving Granville, where he had found so much tolerance, friendship, and love, was surely intimidating for the young preacher and his wife. Still, the time had come to test his sermons beyond an assembly of friendly, familiar faces.

Rehearsing his oratory for future Sundays in Torrington, Haynes took his "show" on the road for part of the summer of 1785, preaching throughout Vermont. The region's sturdy settlers, people not easily impressed, were soon nodding their approval at the intellectual and religious sweep of Haynes's sermons, as the people of Granville had for years.

Approval was surely not on every face when Haynes stepped for the first time behind the pulpit of his church in Torrington. His flock's collective complexion was white, and most of the worshipers knew little of the man in the pulpit except that he was black. Then Haynes's voice rushed at the onlookers and filled most of them with the immediate understanding that no matter his color, the man could *preach*.

With a number of Haynes's fellow ministers valuing his mastery of Congregationalist Gospel and his commanding presence in a pulpit, he received his official ordination from the Association of Ministers in November 1785. His Granville friends, including one from his Revolutionary War years, had pressed the ministers for Haynes's ordination, and the clergymen could scarcely have asked for more telling testimony to his abilities than the words of those who had seen and heard a bright youth develop into a preacher of boundless promise.

News of Haynes's oratory spread rapidly. Every Sunday the

pews of his church in Torrington groaned to their capacity, jammed with people eager to hear his wizardry with words.

The sermons even swayed some bigoted hearts. According to Cooley, a Torrington man had stayed away from Sunday meetings because Haynes was black. Having heard neighbors rave about Haynes's orations, the man attended a service; however, as a sign of contempt, the man refused to remove his hat in the church. Haynes pretended not to notice the insult. Instead he launched into a compelling sermon. A short way into the forceful discourse, he saw that the man had removed his hat.

While Haynes's color ceased to be an issue with most of his flock, he was unable to convince a hard-core cadre of local bigots to shed their prejudice. One can only wonder at the epithets certainly whispered behind the backs of Elizabeth Haynes and her "Mollato" children or muttered loudly enough for anyone to hear. The Haynes family had to find the contempt of the few a ponderous burden. If the Reverend Mr. Haynes had not been married, he might have decided to dig in his heels and drag the circle of bigots kicking and screaming onto the path of tolerance. As it was, he withstood the situation in Torrington for almost three years, winning a victory every time he peered from his pulpit and thundered sermons that few ministers, white or black, could have bettered.

In March 1788, Haynes was offered a church in Rutland, Vermont, a church that may even have had a few blacks in the congregation. His family surely uppermost in his thoughts, he took the job. In the next thirty years the wisdom of his choice was to become ever more evident. However, nobody could deny that Lemuel Haynes had stared the handful of bigots in his former congregation hard in the eye without blinking.

Haynes's way with words gradually swelled far beyond the hills, pastures, and woodlands of Vermont. Refusing to confine his intellect only to religious matters, he penned incisive political polemics, one of them assailing Thomas Jefferson's affinity for France, a nation, in Haynes's view, whose revolution was the bloody excess of atheistic renegades.

On July 4, 1801, the twenty-fifth anniversary of America's independence, the former minuteman began addressing a Rutland gathering about the meaning of liberty. As his oration flowed, the crowd realized that something besides the Revolution was on his

The Reverend Lemuel Haynes, Minuteman and first
black minister of a white congregation

mind, something called slavery. Sentiments seemingly bottled in
his heart during his trying days in Torrington spilled past his lips
in a moving lamentation of the black man's plight. While this only
verifiable instance of his antislavery views was later published, he
apparently avoided airing them in public again.

The first black preacher to lead a congregation of whites
reached, in 1804, another milestone: Middlebury College's award
of an honorary master's degree to Haynes made him the first black
so honored by an American college.

Greater fame serenaded the Vermont minister in 1805, when
he assailed universal salvation, a creed championed by a renowned
preacher named Hosea Ballou. Ballou's assertion that everyone,
regardless of his or her sins, could attain heaven was anathema to
Haynes, schooled in the dogma of repentance, conversion, and
man's innate wickedness, all beliefs at the core of Haynes's soul.

Haynes climbed into his pulpit and, with Ballou in attendance,
branded his doctrine Satan's words. The face-to-face harangue

ignited a two-year war of letters between the two men, and the publication of Haynes's scorching denunciation, *Universal Salvation, a Very Ancient Doctrine (of the Devil)*, won him admirers and foes from Rutland to London.

Haynes's sharp tongue and his scathing pen fueled controversy over the next thirteen years. On such events as the War of 1812, which he staunchly opposed, he made his Federalist views plain. His constant forays into the arena of politics irked his parishioners, who wondered if their best interests were served by such a high-profile minister. A work of unknown authorship later suggested that Haynes himself believed that latent racism was the true source of growing disaffection toward him among some of his church's members.

Whether under a cloud of racism or simply a worn-out welcome, Haynes, sixty-five years old, left Rutland in 1818. The minister, hardly ready for retirement, filled a pulpit in Manchester, Vermont, and wrote a hot-selling examination of the Russell Colvin murder case, a local cause célèbre in which the alleged victim reappeared before his convicted "killers," Stephen and Jesse Boorn, were executed.

In 1822 the seventyish preacher turned over his parish to a younger minister. Haynes and his wife moved to Granville, New York, to spend their remaining days there, except for his guest appearances in regional pulpits. Haynes died in 1833 at the age of eighty, death the only force able to still his zeal for sermonizing.

Haynes, not long before his death, had traveled for a last time to the other Granville, the Massachusetts hamlet where a white woman, Mrs. Rose, had treated the abandoned "Mollato" child as a son, where his remarkable career had begun in the Roses' farmhouse and in the local meetinghouse, where the young black minuteman had drilled so long ago on the town green. If the old preacher's eyes misted with memories of his remarkable life as he glimpsed the town of his youth, he was entitled to his tears of bygone days, memorable days.

In 1836, his beloved Elizabeth, who, like her husband, had defied convention every day of their marriage, joined her husband in the grave. One of their sons was a farmer, one a doctor, and the other a student of law. Like their father, all had surmounted prejudice to grab a piece of what was later termed the American Dream.

The youth who had vainly pleaded for the attention of his birth mother on a rural street earned more renown than ever he could have imagined. On the battlefield, in the pulpit, and in the world of letters, Lemuel Haynes, "Mollato," had proved himself the equal of any American.

11 Thirteen Stars and the Star of David: Francis Salvador

The rebels, three hundred or so, rode beneath the moonless South Carolina sky. If any glanced at a pocket watch, the timepiece read one forty-five in the morning of July 31, 1776. Muskets at the ready, they warily eyed a long rail fence, whose gaps were stuffed with sticks, brush, and leaves from cornstalks, on one side of the route, as well as some scattered houses. In the riders' vanguard was a thirty-year-old man.

Suddenly from behind the fence loud pops pealed and tiny sheets of flame lit the darkness. *Ambush!* the American's minds, as well as several voices, must have screamed. *Tories and Indians!*

Before the man in the saddle could hunch low on his mount and dash for cover, three shots slammed into him and knocked him sprawling from his horse into some brush. He lay there, bleeding, stunned, screams and ragged volleys piercing his ears. Then an Indian, blade in hand, hovered above him. Francis Salvador knew his life was coming to a nightmarish end. What he could not have known was that he was about to become the first Jewish American to die for America's independence and to become the nation's first Jewish war hero. The doomed man, who had also been the first of his faith to hold public office in America, always knew the perilous course he had chosen might lead to the horrible moment he now faced. He had accepted the thought.

*   *   *

The world in which Francis Salvador began his life was as far removed from Carolina's hinterlands as the moon. He was born in London in 1747 to a family of vast wealth, his uncle Joseph Salvador being a renowned financier who was the first member of Britain's Jewish community to serve as a director of the East India Company, a fabled repository of the British Empire's riches.

Francis Salvador had received an excellent education and, as with many young Englishmen whose families possessed bottomless purses, had indulged in the "Continental tour," in which rakish young lords and merchants' sons richer than many lords traveled to Europe's great cities, many of the young tourists drinking, gambling, and womanizing their way through Europe. How, young Salvador may have wondered, could life be better?

His life did get even better. He inherited the fabulous sum of sixty thousand pounds and joined the family business. And what a business the Salvadors enjoyed: Joseph Salvador had gained influence as a liaison between Britain's Jewish community and King George III. Winning further royal favor, Joseph lent the king's ministers money for a number of government projects.

Given his family's affluence, Francis Salvador could certainly afford a wife and family, and by the early 1770s he had a spouse and four children, heirs to the family fortune. And in his fashionable wig, costly silk or velvet waistcoats, silk stockings, and fine shoes or boots, the proud husband and father gave the appearance of not only a man of means but also a man of noble birth.

Being an accomplished man was not the same as being titled in British society, no matter how wealthy and sophisticated he might be. Salvador might have rubbed shoulders with noblemen in London's coffeehouses and theaters, and he knew that the king and his ministers would not turn down loans from the Salvadors and other successful men of Britain's Jewish Community, but in Great Britain's class system, the Salvadors, no matter how prosperous and influential, no matter how genteel their life-style, were not on equal social footing with lesser families bearing titles.

In 1773 the unthinkable happened to the Salvadors' financial footing: Ruinous investments and the collapse of the Dutch East India Company gutted the family fortune; one historian speculates that Francis Salvador lost seventy-three thousand pounds. The stunned clan still had a financial card to play, but that card was a huge land tract in South Carolina, a site too distant for aging Joseph Salvador to inspect for its moneymaking potential. To Francis Salvador fell the task of traveling to the colonies.

Salvador reached the breathtakingly beautiful harbor of Charleston, South Carolina, in December 1773. To his advantage in his new locale, he found a small number of Jews settled in and around Charleston; from their ranks was to come a military unit—"the Jew Company"—to fight with valor in the Revolution. Salvador was perhaps surprised to discover that many Protestant Carolinians were inclined to judge him on individual merit rather than on religion.

From Charleston Salvador made his way to the present-day Greenwood region of South Carolina and got his first look at his family's acreage. He realized that establishing an indigo plantation was the best way to garner profits from the land, and he learned the ins and outs of the business by cultivating friendships with neighboring planters and merchants. Soon Salvador's plantation, near Coronaca Creek, was a reality, covering six to seven thousand acres. The London city boy was on his way to becoming a country squire.

The region's newest plantation owner quickly embraced the talk of independence peppering the conversations of many of his neighbors. Perhaps he recalled snide remarks made by some Londoners about his religion; he must have remembered that no matter how far his family rose in Britain's financial realm, many nobles would never view the family as equals. One thing grew certain: Francis Salvador, finding the ways of his new neighbors more to his liking than the manners and mores of Londoners, was a budding zealot for American independence.

Salvador's bent for independence notwithstanding, he relied upon at least thirty slaves to run his indigo plantation. If he felt pangs of conscience while overseeing the backbreaking labors of his field hands, he knew, as a pragmatic businessman, that few, if any, whites would voluntarily work his crop and that the only way to launch his venture was to buy his workers on the slave block. For most indigo planters, their trade ran on an appalling axiom: blacks or bankruptcy.

Superseding Salvador's business concerns as war with his former homeland loomed was his evolving patriotism for his new country. His neighbors thought so much about his abilities and apparently so little about his religion that they selected him to represent them in December 1774 at the First Provincial Congress of South Carolina, making him the first Jewish American to hold a popularly elected office. All the more remarkable about Salvador's status in locals' eyes was that the worldly Londoner had been in their midst for roughly a year.

Throughout 1775 and 1776 Salvador's intelligence, sophistication, and patriotism blazed in Charleston's turbulent political arena, where Tories and patriots clashed daily. Salvador found a powerful ally in John Rutledge, a rebel heavyweight destined to serve as the second chief justice of the United States.

The Revolution's outbreak in April 1775 made South Carolina a flash point for the rebels to tangle with desperate Tories and their Cherokee Indian allies. One of Salvador's first wartime services, however, was not on the field of battle but in the field of his expertise—finance. He helped keep a lid on spending by the beleaguered new government, stopping a move by some legislators for high salaries. He also helped create South Carolina's constitution. But his financial prowess and legislative abilities aside, he apparently coveted a chance to serve his struggling country on the battlefield.

His chance to fight came in the summer of 1776. With Tories and Cherokees gathering near his plantation, Salvador garnered an appointment as chief aide to Major Andrew Williamson, the commander of twelve hundred men facing the enemy in Salvador's backyard. The roughhewn militiamen, in all manner of dress, lacked military polish, but Salvador, knowing his countrymen were ready for a fight, urged Williamson to hurl an offensive at the foe, already plaguing the region with their guerrilla tactics.

At 6:00 P.M. on July 30, 1776, Williamson led about 330 men on a prospective search-and-destroy mission of an enemy encampment. Two prisoners had agreed to guide them to the camp, the Americans counting on reaching the target by the dawn of July 31. Riding near the head of the strike force was Francis Salvador. His heart must have throbbed with anticipation and trepidation. What a strange course of events, he may have thought on the march into enemy territory, had thrust an erstwhile London dandy to the vanguard of such a rough-and-tumble band of colonials. Homespun Americans and dandy alike, all were brothers in liberty's cause.

The Americans' plan was to dismount two miles from the

enemy camp, the Indian Village of Essenecca, and surround the sleeping foe before guards could raise an alert. With each step of his horse's hooves, perhaps Salvador wondered if he would freeze when the time to shoot and kill came.

Near two in the morning the riders came to a rail fence and several scattered dwellings. Suddenly musket blasts tore into the startled Americans. Three balls tore into Salvador and knocked him from his saddle. He landed in or near some brush.

As his comrades overcame the shock of the ambush, regrouped, and began pushing back their assailants, an American captain glimpsed Salvador, crumpled on the ground, and a man crouching over him. The captain, certain that the man was an aide or a soldier stanching Salvador's wounds, returned to the battle. The captain never saw the blade in the Indian's hand.

After driving off the enemy, the Americans found Salvador near the bush. He had been scalped. Still coherent, he asked Williamson if they had won.

"I told him yes," Williamson wrote. "He said he was glad of it, and shook me by the hand—and bade me farewell—and said, he would die in a few minutes."[1]

At 2:30 A.M. Francis Salvador died, the first Jewish American to die in his country's service, a price he willingly paid although Jewish settlers did not yet have a full stake in America's fortunes. Many of his faith also made the ultimate sacrifice in the Revolution and in wars to come.

Francis Salvador had set foot in America to help replenish his family's fortune, but what he had found in his new country was far more valuable than land and profit. What he found was a place where a Jewish settler could not only live and work in freedom but also *serve* in freedom's cause. And serve he did. By doing so, he opened America's doors a crack to future generations of his coreligionists, the price of admission being his own life. Unfortunately most Americans have forgotten the name of Francis Salvador, the first Jewish American martyr for the nation's independence. The oversight is unpardonable.

Today, in Charleston, a plaque preserves the indomitable character of Francis Salvador, the first of his faith to hold elected office in America and the first of his faith to die for American independence:

Memorial plaque to Revolutionary War hero Francis Salvador, Charleston, South Carolina

Born an aristocrat, he became a democrat,
An Englishman, he cast his lot with America;
True to his ancient faith, he gave his life
For new hopes of human liberty and understanding.

Although apter words have not been written, Francis Salvador deserves more than mere mention on a plaque. He merits a place alongside Crispus Attucks, Nathan Hale, and the other American martyrs of independence.

12 A Connecticut Yankee's Cookery: Amelia Simmons's Little Cookbook

Amelia Simmons was a woman on a mission. As she hurried through the streets of Hartford, Connecticut, on an early spring day in 1796, she clutched forty-seven handwritten pages unlike anything written before by an American. On the pages, written by Simmons for "the improvement of the rising generation of Females in America," was America's first true cookbook, *American Cookery*.

Eighteenth-century New England's answer to Julia Child remains a woman of mystery; glimmers of her personality appear in the pages of her modest book, but her history remains unknown. She lived in or near Hartford, but few would have heard of her had she not strolled into the office of Hartford publisher Hudson & Goodwin in 1796 with her little collection of "receipts," or recipes.

The practice of writing receipts and filing them in a catalog of sorts was not an uncommon practice among colonial housewives able to read and write. Eighteenth-century women whose husbands had a shilling or two to spare reached for such early cookbooks as the popular 1742 edition of *The Compleat Housewife*, by Eliza Smith; *Housekeeper's Companion*, by Hannah Glasse; *The Frugal Housewife*, by Susannah Carter; and *The New Art of Cookery*, by Richard Briggs. The cookbooks, with titles that would have been popular in the America of the 1950s, let alone the 1750s, were collections of standard English recipes prepared with Old World ingredients not always available in colonial kitchens. Printers in Williamsburg, Philadelphia, and Boston happily ran off copies of the English cookbooks despite the works' shortcomings and counted the profits.

With American ingenuity and practicality, colonial readers added to the traditional British fare their own touches, especially Indian corn, or cornmeal. Innovation, however, went only so far for some cooks. Where, many American women wondered, were trusty, *printed* recipes for colonial menus—Indian slapjacks, pumpkin pie, corn bread, roasted wild turkey, and other dishes? Book printers had no need nor much inclination to answer the question.

In the spring of 1796 Amelia Simmons took it upon herself to tackle the problem. No local printer, of course, was eager to finance her project. Hudson & Goodwin agreed to print copies of her forty-seven pages of receipts if, in the era's equivalent of vanity publishing, she dug into her or her husband's purse to cover the printing costs. She agreed to the terms, likely with her condition that she receive all or most of any future profits.

What her printers saw as they set type for her sheafs of recipes was a work similar to familiar English cookbooks. But there was a landmark difference between the Hartford housewife's book and those of her predecessors, a difference trumpeted by her missive's gargantuan title:

AMERICAN COOKERY
OR THE ART OF DRESSING
VIANDS, FISH, POULTRY AND VEGETABLES,
AND THE BEST MODES OF MAKING
PASTES, PUFFS, PIES, TARTS, PUDDINGS,
CUSTARDS AND PRESERVES,
AND ALL KINDS OF
CAKES
FROM THE IMPERIAL PLUMB TO PLAIN CAKE
ADAPTED TO THIS COUNTRY
AND ALL GRADES OF LIFE

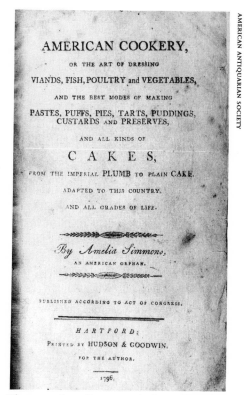

AMERICAN COOKERY,

OR THE ART OF DRESSING

VIANDS, FISH, POULTRY and VEGETABLES,

AND THE BEST MODES OF MAKING

PASTES, PUFFS, PIES, TARTS, PUDDINGS,
CUSTARDS AND PRESERVES,

AND ALL KINDS OF

C A K E S,

FROM THE IMPERIAL PLUMB TO PLAIN CAKE.

ADAPTED TO THIS COUNTRY,

AND ALL GRADES OF LIFE.

By Amelia Simmons,

AN AMERICAN ORPHAN.

PUBLISHED ACCORDING TO ACT OF CONGRESS.

HARTFORD:

PRINTED BY HUDSON & GOODWIN.

FOR THE AUTHOR.

1796.

The start of a culinary revolution—American style: the title page of *American Cookery* by Amelia Simmons

Simmons's major break with past cookbooks lay in the line "adapted to this country." Her message was long-winded but clear: She was an American who had assembled recipes for *American* kitchens. She was the first to assert in print that a genuine American cuisine—gasps from European cooks, then and now, aside—had been simmering in Great Britain's former colonies.

The price of *American Cookery*'s first edition, two shillings, three pence, indicated that Simmons was a sharp businesswoman who wanted her book to be affordable for the wives of prosperous merchants and the thrifty spouses of farmers, frontiersmen, and tradesmen alike. In a young nation still brimming with a newfound flush of democracy (the Constitution was not even a decade old), the Hartford housewife had fittingly penned a cookbook for the masses, a work intended to help women of "all grades of life."

On April 28, 1796, Connecticut's district court granted a

copyright to *American Cookery,* ostensibly to receive protection from imitators through the land's first true copyright law for writers. A month or so later, the office of the U.S. secretary of state, Thomas Jefferson, officially received a copy of the book for the government's first repository of copyrighted works. One assumes that the ever-curious Jefferson pored over the pages and perhaps instructed a cook or two to whip up one of Simmons's tarts or puddings.

Simmons had a smash hit on her hands by the end of summer 1796. Advertisements in the *Connecticut Journal* and the *Middlesex* (Connecticut) *Gazette* sent housewives or their husbands with two shillings, three pence in hand to the papers' offices, where copies of the book were sold. Word of mouth spread the news that a collection of recipes tailored to American palates had finally arrived in New England.

Once Simmons's book was opened on kitchen tables throughout the country, readers found a familiar cookbook format, a combination of recipes, housekeeping hints, home remedies, and advice for food shoppers. Anyone who had read Susannah Carter's 1772 cookbook noticed that Simmons had lifted some of her predecessor's recipes for use in *American Cookery,* hinting that the Hartford housewife shrewd enough to seek to copyright her own work was not above the eighteenth-century practice of running verbatim another's work without permission.

Few readers of 1796 cared that Simmons had "borrowed" some of Carter's recipes, for as American housewives perused the pages of Simmons's book, they delightedly realized that for the first time one of their own was speaking to them in colloquial American terms—and with American ingredients in the recipes. In *American Cookery* appeared words never seen in Old World cookbooks—"emptins," for emptyings; "slapjacks," for griddle cakes; "shortning"; "cookie"; "slaw," for salad; "squash"—and many other Americanisms, Dutch words, and Indian ingredients.

The truly American flavor of Simmons's book was apparent in many recipes dependent upon cornmeal, the longtime staple of colonial diets. In receipts for "Johnny Cakes," "Indian Slapjacks," and "Indian Puddings," Simmons proved that her determination to adapt recipes to Americans' tastes was no idle boast of her book's title page.

Other dishes appearing in *American Cookery* were enough to

set readers' mouths watering and survived the test of time even into the 1990s. Her suggestion to serve roast turkey with cranberry sauce, a widely held practice by her day, remained a tasty Thanksgiving tradition. Her molasses-flavored gingerbread was a fluffier, Americanized version of European gingerbread, more cake than cookie, and is similar to the variety still found in America's bakeshops and supermarkets.

Another instance of Simmons's adaptations of American foods to her recipes was her praise of the Irish potato, first cultivated in America by Scotch-Irish immigrants in Londonderry, New Hampshire, in 1719. As evidenced by the popularity the potato was to gain in America, she obviously knew a good thing when she tasted it.

Some of Simmons's recipes sound as if they required preparation in the barn as well as in the kitchen. To make "Syllabub from the Cow," she told readers to "sweeten a quart of cyder with double refined sugar, grate nutmeg into it, then milk your cow into your liquor."[1]

Simmons knew her way not only in the kitchen and in the barn but also in the market. Dishonest merchants and farmers had to be careful whenever she showed up to buy groceries, for she had sniffed out every dirty trick an unscrupulous vendor could conceive, and she was eager to impart her shopping savvy to her readers. She warned unwitting housewives to beware of fish sellers who wet fins and tails and painted gills with animal blood to hide spoilage. With rotten meat a chronic problem for housewives forced to rely upon cuts shipped from the countryside, Simmons counseled readers that bagged meat carried to market on "sweaty" horseback was likely to be tainted and that meat transported by wagons was a better bet for any American's table.

Among her other peeves were cheese sellers who, like sleazy fishmongers, disguised spoilage with a range of ingredients confusing buyers' sight and smell. Dishonest dairymen also earned her scorn, the sage Simmons urging readers to find a butter seller who shipped his cargo at night or early in the morning to avoid the sun's ruinous effects upon butter, milk, and cream.

According to the historian Mary Tolford Wilson, one of the most remarkable aspects of *American Cookery* was its mention of a colonial cooking ingredient called pearl ash, which was wood ash and was used like modern baking soda. Wilson suggests that Simmons was the first to cite American cooks' use of pearl ash in various receipts.

Along with Simmons's receipts and her warnings about untrustworthy merchants appeared fascinating glimpses of American homelife in the 1790s. She advocated that housewives raise rabbits for food and a few shillings on market days. Her cautioning women to be wary of unruly boys raiding apple trees evokes an image of Simmons's head craned toward her orchard as she tended to her rabbits.

Simmons, so full of homespun advice and kitchen know-how, was left, in one respect, with the proverbial egg on her face: Her book's first printing contained some disturbing errors, which included the omission of flour for her pudding and a wrong amount of "emptins" needed for a cake to rise. Thoughts of readers muttering as their puddings turned into watery messes and their cakes lay flat as rugs sent Simmons scrambling back to Hudson & Goodwin. This time she carried but one page: corrections to run in the second 1796 printing of her book.

The extra page, as much an apology as revisions to her readers, indicated that success had not swayed the Hartford woman's modesty:

> The author of the American Cookery, not having an education sufficient to prepare the work for the press, the person that was employed by her, and entrusted with the receipts, to prepare them for publication (with a design to impose on her, and injure the sale of the book) did omit several articles very essential in some of the receipts, and placed others in their stead, which were highly injurious to them, without her consent—which was unknown to her, till after publication; but she has removed them as far as possible, by the following Errata.[2]

The "Errata," or apology, offers Simmons's testimony that the person she had trusted to clean up her copy had deliberately sabotaged American Cookery. Her words boiling over like a recipe carelessly tended, Simmons showed an understandable, almost endearing rush of temper, not to mention honesty in her frank admission of her lack of formal education.

According to Simmons, the ongoing demand for her book made the second edition necessary—and profitable, no doubt. Not one to rest on her literary laurels, she set to work augmenting her original cookbook with new recipes and revisions of familiar dishes. In 1800 the second edition of *American Cookery,* featuring such culinary concoctions as Election Cake, Independence Cake, Federal Pan Cake, and that old New England tradition "chouder," was printed in Albany, New York. The names of her cakes, so redolent of patriotism and freedom, offered not only tastes of her skill in the kitchen but also insights into the minds of men and women still exhilarated by the creation of their young nation.

The success of Simmons's cookbook bred imitators. Her copyright did little to protect her work from appearing under other writers' names, a development Susannah Carter might have deemed fitting for the Hartford woman who had shown no qualms about "borrowing" some of Carter's recipes for *American Cookery.*

Simmons's compilation of receipts had proved, in her own words, a success. But what of her aim to aid "the improvement of the rising generation of Females in America"? Her ideas of improvement—well-prepared meals, smart shoppers, and efficient households—were hardly suited to win the writer accolades from women yearning to stretch their traditional boundaries beyond the home. However, if her work made life in the kitchen a bit easier for hard-pressed American housewives of the 1790s and early 1800s, she had improved their difficult lot, if only a bit.

Before 1990s' minds dismiss Simmons as some domestic drone who penned a quaint little cookbook, they should note that *American Cookery* not only outsold the printed offerings of many *male* writers of the 1790s but also provided future historians with the sights, smells, and tastes of eighteenth-century America. Would-be critics should also note that in the 1990s every writer whose recipes reach the shelves of America's bookstores shares in the legacy of Amelia Simmons, the Hartford woman who wrote the first truly American cookbook and foreshadowed the modern cookbook industry.

Potential detractors of Simmons's little collection of receipts should also note one other fact: Today the 1796 editions of Simmons's cookbook, sold in her day for two shillings, three pence, command prices of up to nearly nine thousand dollars.

Part IV

A Heavyweight, "A Woman's Place," a Woman's Wit, and a Wood Stove

13 "The Great Black Hope": Tom Molyneux

He had done it! Tom Molyneux, a freed Virginia slave, stood in a downpour and stared at the white man crumpled on the floor of the boxing ring. Molyneux had to know that his fallen foe, Tom Cribb, British heavyweight champion, would not answer the call, or "come to scratch," for the twenty-ninth round. For the first time in history a black man was about to claim the undisputed heavyweight titles of both the United States and Great Britain.

Nothing, Molyneux must have thought, could rob him of his moment in history's sun. He was wrong.

Tom Molyneux was born a slave in 1784, the property of a family of Virginia planters named Molyneux. As the young black matured, his rippling muscles led to his being given to one of the Molyneux sons as a personal servant and bodyguard. The slave was lucky to have earned the task. The position spared him a life of backbreaking labor in his masters' fields, although chances were that at least a dose of fieldwork had helped hone the slave's incredible strength.

Molyneux's master was a young man who loved to wager, and at some point the rake learned that his manservant was not only powerful but quick-fisted. Soon the well-heeled planter's son began pitting his servant in makeshift rings against the slaves of other masters and laying heavy bets on his man. Luckily for the high-rolling dandy, his slave pummeled his opponents, the brawny fighter being an eighteenth-century facsimile of Roman gladiators who had battled fellow slaves for the enjoyment of haughty, blood-thirsty masters. Whatever the boxer's feelings about pounding other slaves, he surely kept his mouth shut.

According to several accounts, when Molyneux was twenty, his master laid a foolhardy bet on his servant: the rake wagered that his man could beat another gambler's slave boxer, a larger, more experienced fighter than Tom Molyneux. The bet was higher than Molyneux's master could cover, and the sporting man realized his mistake only after sobriety slapped him.

Unable to welsh on his wager, seeking a way to improve his chances of winning, the rake hired an English sailor with ring savvy to drill Molyneux in the finer points of the "sweet science" he would need to overcome the bigger slave. The Englishman went to work preparing Molyneux but told the gambler that the slave was still likely to lose the bout—unless there was a way to ignite a fire in the belly of the boxer. When the Virginian asked the trainer what such a stimulus might be, the Englishman suggested that the master offer his slave freedom and a cut of the fight's purse in exchange for victory. Molyneux's master agreed.

Molyneux clobbered his opponent and soon after the bout rushed to New York City with his freedom and five hundred dollars, his share of the bet, before his master could change his mind about setting the young boxer loose. With the freed slave in New York was the sailor, a fact that leads to suspicions that the trainer and Molyneux had tricked the master into thinking that the promise of freedom to the fighter had been the sole way to propel him into fighting beyond himself and rescuing a seemingly unwinnable wager. Thanks to his trainer's stratagem and to his own pugilistic prowess, Tom Molyneux, who chose to keep his former master's last name, was a free man.

Molyneux, now able to reap the profits of his fists, strode into New York's boxing rings and flattened his opponents. In 1809 he proclaimed that he was the boxing champion of America. No one apparently disputed the claim of the brawny young fighter, his self-styled crown coming nearly a century before Jack Johnson (the subject of the movie *The Great White Hope*) punched his way to glory and hardship as the first black to win the modern heavy-weight title.

Molyneux fixed his fighter's gaze on another title, that held by the superb British champion Tom Cribb. In 1809 Molyneux stepped aboard a ship bound for England; he had to work his passage, either his success in America's ring having won him little more than bragging rights to his title or his later affinity for life in the fast lane of "wine, women, and song" having already punched its first gaping hole in his winnings.

He reached London later that year and was directed to the popular pub of Bill Richmond. Richmond and the black fighter forged a kinship from the virtual moment the young boxer stepped into the pub and professed his desire to strip Cribb of his title.

That the boxer and the barkeeper struck up an immediate friendship was not surprising, for Richmond, too, was a black man who had left America behind in search of a better life in England. During the American Revolution a British general had employed Richmond as a servant, and the hireling had accompanied his boss to England. The genteel general had taken a liking to the servant and had seen to a basic education for Richmond, who had also learned carpentry. The young black had put his hands to use in another trade, prizefighting; although never threatening to win a title, he had saved his winnings, opened his pub, and become a popular fixture among Great Britain's rabid boxing crowd, the "fancy."

Richmond could undoubtedly gain Molyneux access to the British ring, and at Richmond's first look, Molyneux's five-foot-eight-and-a-half-inch frame, his chiseled muscles and unusually long arms and legs likely impressed the fighter turned barkeep. But could the hulking American *box*? Richmond had to wonder.

He soon had his answer. He put Molyneux through his pugilistic paces and discovered that behind the newcomer's brawn and his affable manner lurked the flinty resolve of one who could pound another man senseless within the ropes of a ring. He also discovered that Molyneux's desire was matched by thunderous punching power and the critical ability to withstand bareknuckled punishment that smashed bones and sliced the skin of even the hardiest pugilists of the early 1800s. Richmond decided to get the eager Molyneux his shot at the title.

Even with his connections to the fancy, Richmond had to start

Molyneux at the bottom echelon of Britain's boxers; the ex-slave would have to prove he could trounce a journeyman boxer or two before he had any chance of a shot against the champion himself. Despite the obvious talent of his charge, Richmond, too, must have wanted to gauge if Molyneux was truly the "great Black hope," the man who could wrest London's heavyweight crown from its white owner.

On July 14, 1810, Molyneux, looking to prove himself to Richmond and to introduce himself to the fancy, stood poised in a ring to box Jack Burrows, a run-of-the-mill pro from Bristol. The bout, as all of Molyneux's professional titles in Britain were to be, was held under the specifications of the London Prize Ring rules.

The rules were hardly so civilized as their name implies. A bareknuckled fight was one to the finish, the victor and his corner taking the entire purse. Rounds ended only when a fighter was knocked down or hurled to the ground. Since a round could end in little more than a blink or could stretch a seeming eternity for two fighters flailing away at each other but unable to land a knock-down blow, the total of a bout's minutes were more indicative of a fight's fury than the tally of rounds. Fighters had thirty seconds to rest between rounds, and before a round could begin, both boxers had to come to scratch, or set their feet on opposite sides of a square etched in the ring's center. If a battered fighter could not come to scratch, his opponent was the victor.

British rings of the day were square in shape, with each side ranging from sixteen to thirty feet. Championship bouts generally featured a twenty-four-foot ring perched on a pile of turf or a wooden platform with no cushioning to support boxers careening face first to the ground.

As Molyneux surely saw when he gazed past the ropes, in a Prize Ring rules prizefight, spectators of all social classes watched from behind a roped-off area around the ring, a measure intended to dissuade rambunctious fans from storming the ring, a measure that did not always work. At the crowd's edges, aristocrats perched in or on costly carriages peered over the throng at the ring.

The group gathered to watch Molyneux's first British fight must have stared curiously at the stocky black, stripped down to his breeches, his powerful torso tensed for the fray. Then the fighters came to scratch, the ex-slave aware that the Englishman was larger and obviously ready to give his all. Molyneux knew what was at stake: A loss to Burrows, an ordinary fighter, could ruin the American's hopes for a title shot against Cribb.

The two fighters broke from their scratch and began punching. Bare fists thudded against flesh and bone, tearing grunts and yelps of pain from the combatants' lungs; blood sprayed about the ring. Molyneux was clearly the better fighter, but Burrows kept coming back for more of the American's fistic fury. Finally Molyneux floored the valiant but overmatched Burrows for good at the fight's sixty-five-minute mark. Although Molyneux had surely wanted to dispose of his foe sooner, the American had his first overseas victory, not to mention purse, under his belt.

Molyneux's second British bout came on August 21, 1810. He was paired against Tom Blake, who, at forty, was sixteen years older than the American but was a shrewd warrior whose nickname of Tom Tough was more than apt. To any observer of the fancy, Blake posed a greater hurdle to Molyneux than had Burrows.

From the moment that the two fighters unleashed their opening blows, Molyneux's brutal punches showed that all of Tom Tough's ring cunning would not be enough to beat the American. Only if Molyneux dropped his guard for an instant and waded into a lucky knockout shot from the older man could he lose. He was not about to give the veteran such a chance.

Molyneux's crunching blows finished Blake in eight rounds. The former slave now had a name in the fancy.

He soon made sure that every boxing buff in Great Britain heard that name. In Richmond's pub and anywhere else he frequented in London, Molyneux issued challenges to Cribb. The American, wearing fine clothes, indulging himself with women and liquor, his high spirits shouting for all to hear that he could beat the estimable British champ, was straining for a chance to back up his boasts with his fists.

Cribb heard the challenger's boasts. Although the champ had served as second to both of Molyneux's British victims, he believed he could defeat Molyneux despite the American's punching prowess. But the newlywed owner of a profitable coal concern had apparently lost his hunger for the ring. He had not come to scratch in nearly two years; he hated to train and knew he would have to whip himself into prime condition to take on Molyneux. If he never had to strip to his breeches and climb into the ring again, he would likely have been a content man.

Pressure from the fancy mounted upon the recalcitrant champ. How could he let a black—an *American*—taunt him so boldly? When would the champ come to scratch against the boisterous challenger? Cribb surely heard the questions again and again from his friends and his fans alike. In the macho world of prizefighting, Cribb's manhood was on the line; so too, many Englishmen might have asserted, was England's honor in the face of a black American's dare. Cribb agreed to fight the challenger.

Although Molyneux had to be ecstatic that he was to have his shot at the boxing crown, he must have sensed that he had never faced such a threat as Cribb inside the ropes. Molyneux had never seen the champ fight, but such was Cribb's reputation that the American plunged into diligent training for the upcoming bout, the fight of his dreams. If Molyneux flashed any signs of cockiness about his opponent, Richmond probably quashed them with vivid details of Cribb's abilities and warned Molyneux not to assume that the champ's nearly two-year layoff from the ring had softened the starch of his punches.

The date of the bout was set for December 18, 1810, but both the time and the site of the fight were kept secret from the public. Prizefighting was illegal in Great Britain, and even though bouts were generally tolerated, the law might be compelled to act if the day and site became common knowledge. The fancy would know when and where.

On December 18, more than five thousand people gathered in a downpour at Copthall Common, between London and Brighton. Shivering in the rain and frigid gusts from the English Channel, the crowd, which ranged from working-class men to high-rolling lords, surrounded a boxing ring, where popular Tom Cribb was to take on insolent Tom Molyneux.

The sodden weather could dampen neither the crowd's excitement nor gamblers' bets. The odds makers had established Cribb as a four to one favorite, with Molyneux expected to crash to the ground courtesy of the champ's fists fifteen to thirty minutes into the bout.

Cheers for the champ rose in the damp air when the fighters

Tom Molyneux and Tom Cribb brawl with bare knuckles for
Great Britain's heavyweight title, c. 1810–1811

SCHOMBURG CENTER FOR RESEARCH IN BLACK CULTURE, THE NEW YORK
PUBLIC LIBRARY, ASTOR, LENOX AND TILDEN FOUNDATIONS

made their way into the ring. The minute the boxers stripped to
their breeches, fans saw that both men had trained fiercely to buff
their muscular physiques for the ordeal to come. Cribb stood two
inches taller than Molyneux but at 196 pounds was but 1 pound
heavier than the American. Molyneux's compact body seemed to
radiate power, and veteran boxing fans surely noticed that the
shorter man had a longer reach than his British foe.

Perhaps a long look at the American spurred some bettors to
lay a quid or two on him just before the fighters came to scratch.
Most of the gamblers, however, probably waited to see how the
first few rounds developed.

The fighters came to scratch for the first round, broke, and
warily probed each other's styles. Molyneux soon realized that
Cribb was not a smooth fighter; the Englishman's strategy was to
absorb countless blows until his opening came. Molyneux went
face-to-face with the champ in one thrilling exchange after another

for the first seven rounds, cutting Cribb up with some telling punches. But if the blood on the champ's face led the American to think he had him, Cribb taught Molyneux the folly of such a notion with a blow that clobbered Molyneux to the ground.

Despite the knockdown, Molyneux's quickness was unimpaired. The plodding Cribb, striving to slow down the action, crouched, stolidly retreated, and counterpunched against the challenger's savage combinations. Molyneux stalked his foe and rocked Cribb with blow after blow. How much more of the onslaught could Cribb endure?

By the seventeenth round the odds favored Molyneux four to one. Fans, furious that a black American was about to tear the heavyweight title from Cribb, screamed their dismay to the gray sky. Cribb, meanwhile, lurched about the ring for the next few rounds, blows pounding his head, his stomach, and his ribs. He took them with the grit of the champion he was.

The fancy knew that its favorite could take a punch but that not even Cribb could take Molyneux's merciless blows indefinitely. The champ had to find a way to stop the churning arms of the black boxer—or else the London Prize Ring's title would belong to the *American*.

His pride and his fans' entreaties must have sent a rush of adrenaline through the reeling champ. In the twenty-third round he leveled a frightening volley of punches against Molyneux, and the odds dropped to even money on the fighters.

Once he shook off any effects of the champ's counterattack, Molyneux regained control of the bout. Still, at the beginning of the twenty-eighth round, Cribb came to scratch. The bloody, grueling work began again, with Molyneux undoubtedly frustrated that Cribb was yet on his feet. Suddenly one of Molyneux's bloody fists knocked down Cribb. A sense of dread gripped the crowd as the fighters went to their corners for the mandatory thirty-second break between rounds. Everyone saw that the battered champ was in trouble.

As soon as the thirty seconds elapsed, Molyneux came to scratch. He stood on the mark alone. He waited.

Cribb, covered by his handlers from the rain, was slouched in his corner; but the referee did not declare Molyneux the winner. Time must have stood still for the American. He had defeated

Cribb! Why, Molyneux must have thought and Richmond may have yelled, did the referee do nothing?

Suddenly one of Cribb's seconds dashed to Molyneux's handlers and charged that the American had been hiding musket balls in his fists. Molyneux was forced to open his hands. Neither musket balls nor other foreign objects fell from his palms. Nothing but his punching power had rocked the champion.

Several minutes had passed. The referee called again for the fighters to come to scratch. This time Cribb lumbered to his mark. Realizing any complaint would be useless, Molyneux was determined to finish the champ a second time, likely believing that his bruised fists could deliver a climactic blow from which no ploy by Cribb's corner men could save their fighter.

Cribb, having gotten a second wind, had other ideas. He took the action to Molyneux in the twenty-ninth and thirtieth rounds. As the crowd roared its approval of the champ's resurgence, Molyneux kept his wits, refusing to buckle, waiting for his chance to land a decisive shot.

In the thirty-first round Molyneux lunged at Cribb, slipped on the wet ring, and tumbled headfirst against one of the ring's posts. Dazed, wobbling, he somehow climbed to his feet, but the post had accomplished what Cribb's fists had failed to do: It had landed a critical blow against the challenger.

Cribb smelled blood and went in for the kill with the fancy's raucous approval pounding in his ears. Molyneux, his limbs suddenly as heavy as his scrambled thoughts, staggered through the thirty-second round, surviving Cribb's ruthless attack, but as the thirty-third round loomed, not even Richmond probably believed the challenger could shake off the post's effects.

Molyneux, all but finished, tottered to the square at the start of the round. In short order Cribb drove him to the floor. The fight was over.

The champion had kept his crown courtesy of his cheating second and an unyielding ring post, but the bout's fifty-five minutes had probably proved the longest of Cribb's career.

In the days after the tainted fight Molyneux demanded a rematch. One can only imagine his anguish as his thoughts replayed his incredible misfortune on Copthall Common. Cribb surely did not relish the prospect of a second bout against the tough Amer-

ican, but he agreed to it—with the stipulation that both fighters
ante up three hundred pounds for the purse.

The sum was stiff, and Molyneux did not have it in hand. To
raise part of his share, Molyneux fought Joe Rimmer in May 1811
and handily beat him. Molyneux and Richmond raised the rest of
their share through an exhibition tour through Great Britain by
the challenger; the rematch was scheduled for September 28, 1811.

With the fancy's interest in the bout at feverish intensity, some
twenty thousand spectators flooded Thistleton Gap, the crossroads
of Leicester, Lincoln, and Rutland shires, for the rematch. The
fighters stepped into a twenty-five-foot ring atop a wooden platform. The sky was lovely, the weather balmy.

Cribb was in perhaps the finest condition of his career, eleven
hellish weeks of training at the hands of a noted Scottish athlete
having whittled the fighter's usually problematic weight down to
a rock-hard 185 pounds and having tuned his stamina to a peak
level. The defending champ, his memories of Molyneux's heart
and thrashing fists undoubtedly painful, was leaving nothing to
chance in his second meeting with the ex-slave.

Molyneux was not in the same sterling condition he had attained for his first crack at the title. In trying to raise money for
the purse through his exhibition tour, he had been unable to train
as diligently as he had the first time. Still, he was capable of fin-
ishing any fight with a torrent of blows.

The blows came fast and furious from both fighters during
the opening rounds. Molyneux scored heavily to the champ's face,
and Cribb, shaking off the damage, slammed endless blows against
Molyneux's body, a sound strategy designed to impair the challenger's breathing and turn his arms leaden. Body punches were
an even more effective tactic than usual against a fighter who was
not in superb condition.

Cribb was clearly winning the battle at the end of six rounds.
Although Molyneux hurled potent shots against him throughout
the seventh and eighth rounds, the splendidly conditioned champion did not waver and continued hammering at the challenger's
body.

In the ninth round Cribb went "upstairs" and drove a left to
Molyneux's chin. Waves of pain ripped through Molyneux's face;
the blow had fractured his jaw. He came to scratch for two more

rounds, but at the opening of the eleventh he could go on no longer. The fight was stopped at the twenty-minute mark, his hopes for the title as splintered as his jaw. Tom Molyneux was never to have another chance at his dream.

After defeating Molyneux at Thistleton Gap, Cribb never stepped into the ring again. Perhaps the bloody bouts against Molyneux had taken their toll upon the champ; he was likely determined never to undergo the same rugged training he had suffered through prior to the rematch against the American.

Molyneux was able to live off his reputation for a time, perhaps dreaming of yet another crack at the title. He made a great deal of money by putting on sparring exhibitions throughout England, but almost as quickly as he earned his pound notes, he blew them on liquor and women. In part, perhaps, because of his wild life-style, which surely impeded proper training, Molyneux and Richmond ended their partnership.

Between his boxing exhibitions and his carousing, Molyneux stepped amid the ropes to defeat two professionals. Many members of the fancy, however, likely noticed that Molyneux's once-dazzling skills had been all but absent in both victories. Perhaps some spectators attributed his lackluster efforts to the limited caliber of the two foes; maybe Molyneux had been only as sharp as necessary. His next scheduled bout would prove whether the American had been holding back or was finished as a serious contender.

The test came in Scotland in 1815. Molyneux came to scratch against George Cooper, a flashy and dangerous opponent in the ring. For fourteen rollicking rounds of action, the fans got more than their money's worth. Then Cooper floored Molyneux in the fourteenth. The American champion did not come to scratch for the fifteenth.

From that dark moment in the Scottish ring, Molyneux's life spiraled slowly, inexorably into oblivion, the once-dominant athlete became a caricature of himself, winding his way through the British Isles in shoddy boxing shows. On an exhibition tour he fell grievously ill in Galway, Ireland: too much liquor, too many loose women, too many late nights, and probably too much heartbreak having exacted a terrible toll upon the thirty-four-year-old fighter. Death stilled the great heart of Tom Molyneux on August 4, 1818.

Today Americans know the names of Joe Louis, Muhammad Ali, Joe Frazier, George Foreman, and even Jack Johnson, whose fame is recorded on blurry film footage of the early twentieth century. Few Americans know, however, the name of Tom Molyneux, America's first black heavyweight champ. As surely as the fancy robbed him of a title, so history robbed Tom Molyneux of the acclaim his fists deserved.

14 Crusader in the Classroom: Emma Hart Willard

In the spring of 1814 something was happening inside a Middlebury, Vermont, house, something never before seen in America. A small group of girls mostly in their late teens stared at a schoolmistress in her late twenties. Beneath her light, neatly combed hair, her blue eyes surely glinted with the zeal of a crusader bent upon a noble cause. When she called the girls to order, she sounded a call to revolution in the young nation's school system. The teacher, Emma Hart Willard, was opening America's first school for the higher education of women.

The crusader for women's rights in America's classrooms began life on February 23, 1787, on a farm in Berlin, Connecticut, the ninth of ten children born to Samuel Hart and his wife, Lydia. Samuel Hart's "human" crop was as prolific as the products of his fields; he had fathered seven children in a previous marriage.

The traditional role of most eighteenth-century women as appendages to men was known to Emma Hart in her childhood. Her father, however, recognizing the girl's intelligence and that of her younger sister, Almira, encouraged Emma not to shortchange herself in at least one aspect of her male-dominated world: education. When she was not hard at work on some household chore, she buried herself in books, reading the words of such renowned thinkers as John Locke and discussing them animatedly with her father. By her early teens he often told her to forget about whatever task she was working on and to plunge into intellectual discourse with him. Her youthful cheeks probably flushed with excitement, she eagerly laid down a broom or abandoned a churn for any chance to talk of history, philosophy, and religion with Hart, surely amazed at the precocious mind of his daughter, who had taught herself the intricacies of geometry at the age of thirteen.

Why waste your time encouraging the girl to study subjects that could never help her run a proper American household? neighbors of the Harts probably wondered. On the other hand, they may have thought, What else would one expect from a man who espoused the views of Thomas Jefferson and his Democratic Republicans in a community where many "right-thinking" men advocated the aims of the Federalists, spearheaded by such titans as Alexander Hamilton? The differences between the two factions were complex, rooted in regional and national ties, but a perception among many Jeffersonians that the Federalists would try to turn the country into a monarchy clashed with the Federalists' fear that the Democratic Republicans craved rule by mob. During her political discussions with her father Emma Hart came to embrace many so-called Republican views.

Hart's political leanings were not the only thing that made him and his large brood appear a nest of radicals to conservative neighbors. The Harts were Universalists, people whose faith held that *all* souls would find salvation in God's grace. The creed was anathema to Congregationalists and other entrenched sects unable to accept the idea of universal salvation, a doctrine promising God's mercy to even the most grievous sinners.

"Tainted," in neighbors' eyes, by her father's politics and his religion, armed with a passion for books perceived as unnatural in a woman by most Americans, men and women, Emma Hart marched into the Berlin Academy in 1802 and enrolled for classes. Few fifteen-year-old farm girls of the era saw any need to advance their education beyond basic reading, writing, and arithmetic skills, and many girls never even had the chance to gain the basics. Emma Hart, however, wanted every scrap of learning she could glean.

Among teachers dismayed by Universalists, the Hart children did not have an easy time in Berlin classrooms. Still, Emma Hart earned her academy diploma. But to her frustration, the Berlin Academy appeared to be the end of her academic journey: America's colleges accepted only men. No matter how qualified Hart was to continue formal studies, applying to any university was certain to win silence or outrage or guffaws from male educators. Unwilling to give up the classroom, Emma Hart had but one choice: She became a teacher.

For a year or two she taught small children the basics at the Berlin Academy, some neighbors undoubtedly keeping a wary watch to make sure that Samuel Hart's daughter did not slip in a radical notion or two between the children's ABC's and rudimentary arithmetic. She was operating her own school in her father's house by 1805 and ran the academy's winter semester the following year, her ardor for her profession growing as she gazed at boys grappling with the only formal education many would receive before full-time farm work or apprenticeships for some youths to local tradesmen called. For the girls, domestic skills—sewing, cooking, cleaning—taught largely at home were the cornerstones of women's education.

Only girls from families of means could afford private boarding schools, and while such daughters of privilege were taught a smattering of the basics, perhaps French, and a dollop of the arts, they also learned embroidery and other domestic skills befitting the nation's image of a woman's secondary role in society.

Churning within Emma Hart was a growing resentment of the deficient education offered the "fairer sex." To provide her students the best possible lesson plans during their often limited stints in her classroom and to continue expansion of her own voracious intellect, she took a variety of courses at two women's schools in Hartford. But no matter how many courses she enrolled in, she could not earn a college diploma—because men decreed that their "little women" were simply incapable of tackling demanding courses. She chafed for a chance to prove America's men wrong.

Hart, realizing that she would never prove them wrong in Berlin, accepted an offer to teach in Westfield, Massachusetts. Before long, however, a better offer came along from a small Ver-

mont town, Middlebury. Emma Hart was to be preceptress, head
teacher, of the Middlebury Female Academy, taking to her new
post her undeniable talents for educating children and her dreams
of bringing challenging higher education to older girls.

In 1807 twenty-year-old Emma Hart first glimpsed her new
town. Nestled around both sides of Otter Creek and amid graceful,
grassy slopes, featuring a common as picturesque as any landscape
artist could conceive, the little town also featured more than scenic
beauty: In 1800 Middlebury College had been chartered there.
The existence of a college in the rustic setting may have raised the
new schoolmistress's hopes that here, where locals had already
displayed an affinity for higher education, she might find fertile
ground for her dream of bringing college-level courses to promising
women students.

Before hinting of her ambition to any of her new neighbors, Hart first sought to prove her teaching mettle in the job for
which she had been hired. Her classroom was on the town school's
second floor, above the boys' grammar school; the faces of her
students, all girls, ranged in years from very young to teenaged,
compelling her to prepare lesson plans for students of different
ages and abilities. The preceptress was unfazed by the formidable task of juxtaposed grade levels and juggled her curriculum
expertly.

Hart was also ready to handle an even more strenuous task
familiar to all teachers of the region: how to battle bitter New
England winters. Whenever winter roared into the Vermont town,
heaping snow outside the schoolhouse's door and hurling icy
gusts that rattled the building and stifled any warmth from the sput-
tering flames in her classroom's fireplace, she led the girls in a
vigorous dance to get the blood flowing again in their chilled
limbs.

To Hart's students, the sight of her forming them into lines
for a dance did not seem outlandish in any way. The young teacher,
unlike so many educators of the period who ran their classrooms
with the iron discipline of drill sergeants, was an accessible, open-
minded figure to her girls. Her nonconformity, however, tame as
it was, irked some locals, afraid that any newfangled notions might
cause havoc with the girls' sensibilities. In what surely seemed a
case of déjà vu to the schoolmistress, some neighbors also grew

nervous about her liberal religious views. A battle was brewing in Middlebury, and at its center was Emma Hart.

The embattled teacher found a firm ally in a local physician, John Willard. Close to fifty, twice a widower, Willard was a respected man in the community, whose outspoken views on religion, politics, and social issues must have evoked memories of Samuel Hart for the teacher. She had found an intellectual soul mate, for John Willard harbored Democratic Republican leanings and was a proponent of higher education for women. With Willard at her side, Emma Hart weathered any attempt to rein in her teaching methods or to remove her from her post.

Soon Hart's feelings about Willard turned into something more than respect: She fell in love with him. On August 10, 1809, the twenty-two-year-old teacher and the fifty-year-old physician, the father of four children from his prior marriages, were wed, and the new bride's students, while undoubtedly happy that their teacher had found love, learned the dismaying news that she was resigning from her job to devote herself to the duties of a wife.

A new duty quickly followed: In 1810 Emma Hart Willard gave birth to a son, John Hart Willard, who was to be the newlyweds' only child. Even with the demands of motherhood, Emma Willard continued to read and study, refusing to curtail the development of her intellect. Her husband's nephew John Willard, a Middlebury College student, boarding at his uncle's house, proved the perfect vehicle for the former schoolteacher to give herself the college education she desired. During countless conversations with the young man, she picked his mind for every detail of his teachers' classroom methods. She studied his books, his homework assignments, and his examinations and came to a conclusion she had always believed but had been unable to put to a test: She could absorb college courses. If she could, she knew, so could other women given the opportunity.

A sudden onslaught of financial woes struck the family in 1814, and Emma Willard hit upon an idea to help raise money direly needed to pay their bills—and to aim a blow at discrimination against women in the classroom. In her house she opened a school, the Middlebury Female Seminary, a school unlike any that America had ever seen. Her seminary offered young ladies higher education, college-style courses.

If Willard had the slightest misgivings about her pupils' abilities to handle advanced coursework, her little band of students, thriving under her tutelage, soon allayed any doubts. She even went so far as to ask the officials at Middlebury College to let her girls audit its classes. Her bold gambit, probably causing the college's bigwigs to gape in disbelief at the uppity schoolmistress, earned a resounding no from Middlebury administrators. But the zeal flashing in her blue eyes must have again unnerved locals convinced that a woman's place was in the home, not a college classroom. They had to sense that Willard was not about to muffle her radical campaign to bring higher learning to women and that no local could appeal to her husband to hold his "little woman" in check—not when he was actually encouraging his wife's maverick project in his own house.

News of the landmark school seeped beyond the undulating hills and valleys of Vermont. To the astonishment of American men, mathematics, philosophy, classical studies, and other rigorous courses were not prompting Emma Willard's girls to collapse on her floor from mental and physical strain. Her girls were holding their own academically. Many men did not like what was happening in the Middlebury Female Seminary; some wives perhaps hid smirks as their husbands ranted against the schoolmistress and her revolutionary ideas.

For a time it appeared that the stand for equal education begun in Middlebury by the daring schoolmistress was to take root in Vermont. Such was not to be, for Willard soon realized that her plans needed more governmental support than she could woo in the state.

Vermont's loss was New York's—and America's—gain. In 1819, with the sponsorship of New York Governor De Witt Clinton, Willard founded a school in Waterford, New York. Slowly her notions of equal education spread across America.

Over the next five decades Willard achieved success beyond her boldest imaginings; her seminary in Troy, New York, opened in 1821, became a world-famous model of advanced education for young women. John Willard died in 1825, having lived long enough to view the changing landscape of American education, the vision realized in his Middlebury home.

For the rest of her life Emma Willard fought and won victories once thought inconceivable by men and women alike in America.

Portrait of landmark educator Emma Willard

Although she never became immersed in women's political causes, her voice continued to ring above all others in the struggle for the liberation of women's minds, helping establish women's schools across the country, convincing countless girls to join her crusade by becoming teachers, and paving the way not only for high-school-level education of young women but also for America's first women's colleges and eventually coeducational universities. Even though she struck up friendships with Lafayette and other prominent figures from Europe and America and enjoyed dressing in silks and satins as her success grew, she never abandoned the goals she had imbued in her landmark Middlebury school, whose young women had served as the bright, eager shock troops in her crusade to win higher education for all of America's women. Nothing, not even a disastrous second marriage to a scoundrel named Dr. Christopher Yates, a gambler who turned her life nightmarish for nine long months until she was granted a divorce in 1843, could divert her from her devotion to young women seeking a better education.

Emma Hart Willard died at eighty-four in Troy, New York,

on April 15, 1870. Few Americans of her era had had such an impact upon the nation's life. Her legacy to America was a simple and righteous credo: Women have equal rights in the classroom, rights for which women must always be prepared to fight. She was the first American woman to set that momentous creed of equal education into irresistible motion.

15 Frances Whitcher's Poison Pen

Pen poised above paper, a wry smile likely flitting across her lips, the writer chose her target. Her quarry might be a person, a place, or some foible of American life in the 1840s; but no matter who or what her prey, Frances Whitcher's pen would skewer its intended with the satire and accuracy that her legion of fans adored—and that those who saw themselves lampooned loathed.

Before Mark Twain created legends with his folksy cast of characters, long before the wit and whimsy of Erma Bombeck ran in newspaper pages, the barbed humor of a woman from upstate New York regaled readers throughout America. Her name was Frances Miriam Berry Whitcher, and she was our nation's first best-selling woman humorist, a writer whose vivid style remains a unique but unfairly overlooked nugget of nineteenth-century American literature.

Frances Miriam Berry was born in Whitesboro, New York, on November 1, 1814, the eleventh of Lewis and Elizabeth Berry's fifteen children. Her father owned Berry's Tavern, a popular watering hole for local farmers and merchants.

Frances Berry soon proved a child whose startling intelligence belied her years. In addition to her incredible memory, keen enough to make even some of her elders edgy, she displayed a talent for drawing caricatures guaranteed to make anyone they depicted livid. Family members, neighbors, playmates—almost all around her winced from the sting of the girl's "poison pen" or pencil. One of the initial and most furious victims of her wickedly accurate sketches was her first schoolteacher, whom Berry later described as a sharp-tongued shrew.

Because Berry's drawing hand continually fired the wrath of her "models," the dark-haired, dark-eyed girl was constantly in trouble. She had a hard time keeping friends since her classmates were understandably jittery about having their flaws of face or personality captured in her sketches. Making matters worse for the talented and feared girl, many people misinterpreted her quietness as conceit. Her dilemma leaves one to speculate that her sketches, inflammatory as they were, were the voice of a shy, lonely child seeking attention.

As Frances Berry grew, she studied at a local academy, but she never received formal training in art and writing. The erstwhile terror of the neighborhood became an attractive, graceful young woman with a voracious passion for reading and writing poetry and prose. Seeking an outlet for her stories, she joined a local women's literary group, the Maeonian Circle; her humorous tales about a fictional creation she named Widow Spriggins lampooned the social-climbing aspirations of bucolic women and elicited plaudits and laughter from the literary circle. For Berry, whose sketches years ago had earned anger and ostracism from neighbors, the praise of her small group of readers must have soothed any wounds lingering in her psyche.

Encouraged by her friends' reaction, Berry submitted several stories to a Rome, New York, newspaper. To her surprise and delight, a few of her Widow Spriggins pieces soon ran in the paper.

Obviously emboldened by her whiff of success, Berry summoned the nerve to send samples of her work to *Neal's Saturday Gazette,* a popular, nationally circulated magazine based in Philadelphia. Her submissions, chronicling the outrageous doings of another fictional widow, this one named Widow Bedott, were signed with the nom de plume Frank.

Joseph C. Neal, the editor of the *Gazette* and a gifted caricaturist and humorist himself, was enthralled by the stories' colloquial speech, intentionally fractured spelling, rustic malapropisms, and satirical sketches. He bought pieces by "Frank" and printed them; when readers clamored for more, he persuaded Berry to become a regular contributor to *Neal's Saturday Gazette*. America's first female humorist had been discovered.

Berry wasted little time in taking advantage of her opportunity, one for which countless struggling male writers of the era would have begged Neal on their knees. "The Widow Bedott's Table-Talk" rapidly became one of America's best-loved serials. *Gazette* readers simply could not get enough of the ugly, libelous, backstabbing widow, an unbridled busybody stirring up trouble in every corner of her town. Berry's rambling colloquial style, broad comic scenes, and delightful sketches brought to vivid life a vexing gossip whom readers knew, for most of Berry's fans surely had Widow Bedotts in their worlds.

With her marriage to Reverend B. W. Whitcher, an Episcopalian preacher, on January 6, 1847, the satirist's world took a new turn. The couple moved to Elmira, New York, where her husband had been assigned a church.

The bride shared the religious convictions of her groom, but if the Reverend Mr. Whitcher held any expectation that she would curtail her writing to assume the conventional duties of a preacher's wife, he was in for a jolt. Frances Whitcher's writing career was about to soar to heights beyond *Neal's Saturday Gazette*.

Louis Godey was an admirer of the Widow Bedott pieces; he was also the publisher of *Godey's Lady's Book*, the *Ladies' Home Journal* of the day. Certainly figuring that Whitcher's work not only would amuse his readers but might reel in new ones, he offered her a deal requiring her to create a series similar to the Widow Bedott for his publication. She agreed and created for Godey her Aunt Magwire, the Widow Bedott's sister, a much more likable and well-intentioned character than the troublesome widow.

From 1847 to 1849 Aunt Magwire's folksy monologues, rendered in Whitcher's familiar barbed style, satirized small-town American life. This latest character mocked a rural sewing society beset by pettiness, gossip, quarrels, and prejudice and dominated by an arrogant, pretentious, wealthy woman.

Her words depicting an era when many women still looked balefully at anyone questioning the traditional female roles of wife and mother, Whitcher, through her characters, satirized such "strange creatures" as suffragettes. In one of her Aunt Magwire

A daguerrotype portrait of Francis Miriam
Berry Whitcher, who usually hated to be
photographed or sketched

pieces, Whitcher introduced Samanthy Hokum, "a wonderful, tall,
slab-sided, coarse-lookin' critter, who hild that the men hadent no
bizness to monopolize everything and trammil the female sect."

Another Aunt Magwire tale chided the notion of role reversal
between a man and a woman of the nineteenth century. Whitcher's
words lambasted the Professor, "a ridiculous man" who cleaned
house and churned butter while his wife chopped wood and performed other male tasks of the 1840s. Ironically, the writer sati-
rizing women's rights proponents was a woman whose roles of
wife, mother, and career woman were to appear more akin to
1990s "supermoms" than to the "little women" of her era.

Whitcher's facile pen poked fun at not only country folk,
social climbers, and suffragettes but also materialists and city slick-
ers. Beneath the jumbled English and homespun antics of Whitcher's rustics lay a message: The values of "simple" country folk, in

Whitcher's mind, were superior to those of "sophisticated" city dwellers.

In Elmira, many of the country folk of the Reverend Mr. Whitcher's church failed to grasp that the preacher's wife was laughing with them, not at them. They felt themselves maligned in the stories of the Widow Bedott and Aunt Magwire, and while the writer may have rationalized their understandable pique as a bump in her literary turf, her husband, who had to face irate churchgoers each Sunday from his pulpit, probably found their bruised egos more than a mere nuisance, especially when one indignant local threatened a slander suit against Frances Whitcher.

In November 1849, shortly after the birth of her daughter, angry neighbors were the least of Whitcher's worries, for the humorist contracted tuberculosis, a deadly scourge throughout America. She returned to her girlhood home, Whitesboro, to recuperate and started work on a novel entitled *Mary Elmer*. Perhaps because she now faced her own mortality, her book was a religious work bearing scant similarity to the humorous style for which she was noted by her readers.

Whitcher eventually joined her husband at his new parish in Oswego, New York, but her condition worsened. She soon went back to Whitesboro.

On January 4, 1852, tuberculosis claimed the life of Frances Miriam Berry Whitcher. The poison pen of the thirty-seven-year-old humorist would never again flow with the shrill, bellicose words of the Widow Bedott and the less strident opinions of Aunt Magwire. Although over a hundred thousand copies of a Widow Bedott anthology were reportedly sold, time's passage nudged the work of America's first woman humorist from readers' attention.

Today Erma Bombeck, Fran Leibowitz, and many other talented women writers offer keenly satirical glimpses of American life. They are the descendants of Frances Whitcher, the first lady of American humor.

16 The Original Spruce Gum Man: John B. Curtis

In 1848 a sharp aroma rose from a Franklin stove in a Bangor, Maine, kitchen. The smell—spruce resin—was familiar to anyone in Maine, but as John Bacon Curtis and his father cooked up a batch of the sticky stuff in their cast-iron oven, they used the resin in a way that was to set the nation's collective jaws into grinding motion. The American chewing gum industry was about to be born in the form of State of Maine Pure Spruce Gum.

The future founder of the industry that proved the delight of chewers and a windfall for generations of dentists was born in Hampden, Maine, on October 10, 1827, to John Curtis, a farmer and lumberman, and his wife, Mary. The parents instilled the Yankee work ethic in their son, and by the age of twelve, young John B. Curtis toiled in Penobscot's fields and woods to help his family survive. Although the youth's only education was a smattering of the basics, dreams of fortune blazed within him. He was determined to raise his family from the hard life they had always known.

Twenty-one-year-old John Curtis found his angle to fame and fortune as he worked as a swamper in 1848. The gum oozing from the trunks of spruce trees gleamed like gold. He likely knew that

New England Indians and woodsmen had chomped on chewy spruce resin for centuries; however, young Curtis was the first to see the gooey gum as a cash crop. Why not gather the gum, cook it into a more attractive form, and sell it?

When he described his idea to his father, the elder Curtis's pragmatism, rooted in life's hardships and offering scant room for dreams, put little stock in the idea. Who, the father wondered, would pay hard-earned cash for something anyone could scrape off trees? But Mrs. Curtis came to her son's aid, persuading her husband to help the would-be entrepreneur.

Soon the reek of bubbling spruce gum—"the first gum made anywhere or by anybody"[1]—rose from the family's rude Franklin stove, filling the Bangor house. John B. Curtis knew, however, that he needed a bigger market than Bangor for his gum. His eyes were already turned toward the region's commercial heart, Portland.

He took the first batch of State of Maine Pure Spruce Gum on the road to Portland, joining the ranks of America's drummers, or traveling salesmen, with "little besides his gum and his supreme confidence in himself."[2] After many days of fruitless drumming, he convinced a Portland shopkeeper to give the gum a trial run.

The gum sat on the shelves at first, but when a few hardy souls finally tried the pungent, chewy stuff and liked it, word of mouth began to sell the product. Soon State of Maine Pure Spruce Gum was an item that had people's jaws chomping throughout the city. John B. Curtis later said: "It [the chewing gum business] was hard starting, but it rolled up like a big snowball after it was started."[3]

In 1850 the Curtises moved to Portland, set up a small factory, America's first chewing gum plant, and dubbed it Curtis & Son. John B. Curtis drummed New England, the Atlantic seaboard, and the West in search of store owners eager to add the fast-selling chewing gum to their wares. Using teams of speedy horses and stagecoaches, Curtis traveled America's roads in the hours before dawn, embodying the Yankee tradition of getting up earlier than one's competitors. Meanwhile, at the brick factory in Portland his father turned out box after box of spruce gum to fill the seemingly endless orders sold by his son; in the factory's first year, Curtis & Son turned a profit of six thousand dollars, a substantial sum for the era and a figure the family could only have dreamed of before 1850.

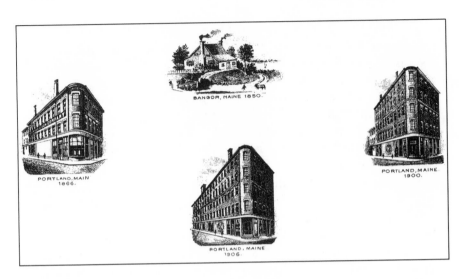

The evolution of an industry, 1848–1923: the incarnations of the Curtis Gum factories from Bangor, Maine, farmhouse to brick plants in Portland, Maine

THE MAINE HISTORIC PRESERVATION COMMISSION

As the demand for the gum jumped, the Curtises hired hordes of workmen to gather raw spruce gum from Maine's forests, the crews often harvesting the resin for two to three weeks at a time. John B. Curtis's tapping of markets throughout America had put countless American mouths to work on pieces of State of Maine Pure Spruce Gum, and from the bustling factory came new "chews": Yankee Spruce, American Flag, and Trunk Spruce. A popular brand whose name probably scared off all but the strongest jaws was 200-Lump Spruce. Wagons creaking with loads of spruce resin became a familiar sight outside the factory, and the Curtises bought up to ten tons of raw gum in single shipments, the elder Curtis once writing a thirty-five-thousand-dollar check for a delivery of the sticky stuff.

The tang of spruce was too strong for many Americans' taste buds. For gentler palates John B. Curtis had an answer: paraffin. His paraffin-based gums, laced with sugar, licorice, and other appealing flavors, were unquestionably tastier than spruce gums; Four-in-Hand, Sugar Cream, Biggest and Best, White Mountain, and especially Licorice Lulu were among the paraffin gums that rolled off the machinery at Curtis & Son and added to the family's escalating wealth. A hard-core legion of gum chewers, however, remained loyal to State of Maine Pure Spruce Gum and the other spruce gums cooked up by John B. Curtis.

By 1866 the Curtises enjoyed a virtual monopoly in America's chewing gum business. Their Portland headquarters, their third factory, was an impressive three-story brick building with a giant sign emblazoned CURTIS & SON COMPANY proclaiming the family's Colossus-like status in the realm of gum making. The company employed about two hundred workers; production, forty hand-packed boxes a day at the firm's beginning, reached a high of eighteen hundred boxes a day, thanks to innovative, relatively inexpensive machinery designed by John B. Curtis.

After his father died in 1869, Curtis continued to reap the spoils of his tooth-spoiling products. He also made an addition to his personal life: In 1878 the man who had spent much of his adult life on the move from Portland to the Mississippi and the Pacific finally put aside business long enough to take a bride, Alice Bacon, an Illinois woman. The newlyweds bought a Portland mansion and were eventually blessed with a son.

The man Alice Bacon had married did not fit the mold of nineteenth-century American robber barons. Curtis was a genial tycoon who downplayed his success, quietly made large charitable contributions, and earned a reputation as a scrupulously honest businessman. A contemporary lauded him: "Mr. Curtis is a man of immense energy and perseverance and great business sagacity . . . [who] has made a high and enduring mark for himself in the industrial world."[4] Throughout his life the gum magnate never wallowed in notoriety of the sort sparked by the excesses of some other American captains of industry.

Although Curtis's private life was low-key, his venture's success inevitably bred competition from aspiring entrepreneurs determined to cut the gum titan down to size. New Yorker Thomas Adams introduced chicle-based gums to America in the early 1870s; by 1890 his six-story factory employed 250 workers.

In 1892 a midwesterner jumped into America's "gum wars." William K. Wrigley, a Chicago soap salesman, introduced Wrigley's Spearmint Gum to Americans in that year; a year later he marketed Juicy Fruit. Although Curtis & Son tried to compete with the new titans, the family's hegemony in the chewing gum business was ebbing. Wrigley was to become a household word; Curtis & Son a forgotten milestone.

The rise of other gum makers did not ruin John B. Curtis, for his business interests were hardly confined to the gum factory in Portland. He had money in shipbuilding, dredging, coal mining, cattle, and real estate, and he had founded a steamship line.

On June 13, 1897, John B. Curtis died of heart failure in Deering, Maine, at the age of sixty-nine. His Portland gum factory, America's first, shut its doors in 1923.

Curtis's recipes for spruce gums were soon lost. Many scientists, however, believe that his gums' ratio of base, both spruce and paraffin, to flavorings was similar to the process of modern gum makers. According to the Maine Department of Labor, the last-known producer of spruce gums was a small Monson factory operating in 1964.

The life of John B. Curtis was the embodiment of the American Dream. A real-life Horatio Alger, he turned spruce into gold and became America's first chewing gum giant—the Original Spruce Gum Man.

Part V

A Rogue, a Real (?) Man, and a Royal

17 Landmark Hero or Landmark Traitor?: Lambdin P. Milligan

On the evening of October 5, 1864, a train backed out of the Union Depot in Indianapolis, chugged along the tracks for the ninety miles to Huntington, Indiana, and hissed to a stop near a sprawling wood and stone house. A Union Army provost marshal and an aide stepped from the train, walked warily to the house, and pounded on the front door. Rousted from sleep, a tall, bleary-eyed man opened the door and was brusquely hauled off by the soldiers to the train.

Moments later the train was hurtling back to Indianapolis. The ordeal of Lambdin P. Milligan, a stormy drama that was to spark a landmark decision by the Supreme Court of the United States, became the first case, in many scholars' estimation, to clarify fully the superiority of civil law over military law in areas where civil courts still functioned. In short, Milligan's case was to define, in landmark legal terms, Americans' right to due process and a fair trial—the Sixth Amendment of the Constitution—even in wartime.

Years before the roar of cannon and the crack of muskets shattered the air above Bull Run and Gettysburg, Lambdin P. Milligan had established himself as a southern sympathizer and an

"A traitor and an apostle of liberty":
Lambdin P. Milligan

unabashed supporter of states' rights. He was to prove steadfast
in his convictions.

In 1856 a group called the Knights of the Golden Circle,
advocating states' rights and the creation of a southern empire
stretching from the Mason-Dixon line to Mexico and Cuba, had
attracted followers from Illinois, Ohio, and Indiana, men who
wholeheartedly believed that the federal government had trampled
the states' individual interests. Lambdin P. Milligan was one of the
Knights.

Milligan, in his early fifties and one of Indiana's foremost
attorneys, was a so-called Peace Democrat; as such, he was opposed
to any act leading to a war between North and South. Usually
clad in a well-tailored frock coat and a tall top hat and standing
six feet four inches with wide shoulders and deeply set, piercing
blue eyes, the Irish Catholic lawyer was a man who looked every
bit the zealot.

When the Civil War erupted in 1861, Milligan railed against
the Union, eastern industrialists, and the newly elected President,

Abraham Lincoln. The Huntington man's fiery rhetoric was to land him in deep trouble.

As the war raged from Virginia to New Mexico, Governor Oliver P. Morton of Indiana came to believe that the region's Peace Democrats were actively aiding the Rebel cause and had supported the abortive but bloody raid into Indiana by the Confederate cavalry commander John Hunt Morgan and his riders. With the staunch support of Union Secretary of War Edwin Stanton, Morton began cracking down on alleged southern sympathizers and stymied the Golden Knights—now known as the Sons of Liberty—in their vigorous campaign to seize statewide power at the ballot box. The Sons' unsuccessful candidate for governor in 1864 was Lambdin P. Milligan.

The Sons' leaders, thwarted by Morton's shrewd, sometimes ruthless political tactics, made a fateful decision: to launch an armed insurrection in Indiana.

The scheme divided the state into four military districts and named Milligan major general of northeastern Indiana. Whether or not Milligan actually knew he had been accorded this rank was to fuel historians' conjecture.

The Sons began to stockpile weapons, some of them pistols hidden in crates marked "Sunday-school books," for a planned uprising in the summer of 1864. Meanwhile, Morton and the Union Army had planted daring, resourceful agents inside the Sons' regional temples, or cadres. One of the agents, Henry L. Zumro, was ordered to befriend Milligan and to infiltrate Milligan's temple, the Men's Bible Class.

Zumro and his fellow spies dispatched alarming intelligence to Morton and General Alvin P. Hovey in Indianapolis. The Sons of Liberty apparently planned to assemble in late August 1864 near Camp Morton, on the outskirts of Indianapolis. They aimed to overthrow the state government and release thousands of captured Confederates. Milligan, who had been delivering scathing speeches condemning "Federal misrule, usurpation, lawlessness and crime" and branding Lincoln "a tyrant and an usurper,"[1] was already under attack from the Republican press and was on a Union Army short list of suspected traitors.

The August coup never came off, but on October 5, 1864, Hovey ordered Milligan's arrest. An unscheduled train rolled out of the gabled expanse of the Union Depot and headed for Huntington with the provost marshal of Indianapolis, Captain Place, on board. The train lumbered backward along the rails, for if trouble exploded from Milligan's supporters in his hometown, the train could retreat full throttle forward to Indianapolis. To his undeniable relief, Place grabbed his man without incident under cover of night.

Milligan was not the only suspect seized. Dr. William A. Bowles, of French Lick (a town now familiar as the home of basketball immortal Larry Bird); Stephen Horsey, of Shoals; and Horace Heffernan, of Salem, were also rounded up by the government.

News of the arrests spread throughout the state, and citizens followed the evolving drama with rabid interest—and rabidly opposite opinions, in many cases. When Milligan's treason trial opened on October 21, 1864, excitement mounted.

The trial blazed with controversy from the onset. In a blatant disregard for the alleged traitor's Sixth Amendment right to due process, General Hovey ignored Indiana's fully functioning civil courts and hauled Milligan before a military commission to try the case *without a jury.* Several officers on the commission had already stated their view of Milligan's case: Anyone criticizing the government or its war effort was a traitor.

Among the witnesses testifying against Milligan would be Zumro and several Sons of Liberty turning state's evidence in exchange for clemency. The charges filed against Milligan included conspiracy, aiding the enemy, inciting insurrection, and, of course, treason.

Into early December 1864 the Indianapolis courtroom rang with damning testimony against Milligan. John R. Coffroth, Milligan's counsel and a longtime friend of the accused's, fired back against prosecutor Judge Advocate Major Henry L. Burnett with a two-pronged defense of Milligan during the rancorous proceedings, refuting all the charges and protesting the fact that Milligan was being subjected to an "illegal" military trial in a city where the civil courts were open. On what grounds, Coffroth asked, could a military court justify such trampling of Sixth Amendment rights?

Burnett countered with witnesses painting a damaging picture of Milligan's treasonous activities (Coffroth labeled one prosecution witness a "mudsill of infamy"), but the judge advocate never conclusively tied Milligan to a concrete plot against the government. Typical of the prosecution's witnesses was a reporter who had heard Milligan deliver a "traitorous" speech at Fort Wayne, Indiana, but had not taken down the speech word for word. Coffroth compellingly argued that the reporter's "omissions might give a different construction to what was said [by Milligan]."[2] The defense attorney also forced the journalist to admit that Milligan had said in his speech that citizens believing that the war was right should not grumble about the Union Army's draft.

Despite Coffroth's skillful defense, the defense attorney's task was futile in the face of a "drumhead court." Milligan's debatable knowledge of the Sons of Liberty's military aims notwithstanding, the accused was linked to the secret society; the trial's verdict was a foregone conclusion. In early December 1864 Indianapolis newspapers trumpeted the fact that the military commission had sentenced Milligan "to hang by the neck until dead." The execution was fixed for May 19, 1865, between noon and three in the afternoon on the parade ground between Camp Morton and Burnside Barracks, just outside the city.

In a strange sequence of events, Governor Morton, so instrumental in Milligan's arrest, now launched a campaign to save him from the noose. Abraham Lincoln studied an account of the trial and seemed willing to commute Milligan's death sentence.

John Wilkes Booth's derringer ended Lincoln's life and brought Milligan closer to the scaffold. Lincoln's successor, Andrew Johnson, harbored no inclination for clemency toward the Confederate sympathizer languishing in an Indianapolis jail. The new President was determined that Milligan would hang, and in the days just before May 19, 1865, the air above Camp Morton rang with the smacks of hammers and the rasps of saws: Milligan's captors were erecting a gallows.

Although Milligan believed that nothing could save him from the hangman and had chosen his pallbearers, Coffroth frantically filed an eleventh-hour appeal of his client's sentence on May 18, 1865. The Indiana circuit court could not reach a decision on the legality of Hovey's commission and passed the appeal to the United States Supreme Court.

Morton had hurriedly sent an aide, John U. Petitt, to Washington, D.C., in a last-minute plea for Milligan's life. President Johnson grumblingly asked: "Does Morton think he's running the whole shebang?"[3] The President agreed to a stay of execution only until June 2, 1865. He was still determined to hang Milligan.

Milligan's wife, Sarah, also arrived in Washington. However, rather than seek an audience with Johnson, she marched into the office of Milligan's former friend and law school classmate Edwin Stanton, the secretary of war. Sarah Milligan left Stanton's office with his assurance that her husband would not be hanged.

Shortly after this meeting Morton received a telegram from Washington, D.C., halting the execution. Rumors abounded that Stanton had boldly issued the order when Johnson, hoping that his absence from Washington would ensure Milligan's death, was on a Potomac cruise. Later the secretary of war convinced the President to order a commutation of Milligan's death sentence. The date of the commutation was June 2, 1865, the day intended to be Milligan's last hours on earth.

His life spared, Milligan, was taken from Indianapolis and thrown into a squalid cell in the penitentiary in Columbus, Ohio. The stench of an adjacent hog slaughterhouse filled the prisoner's cell day and night. His captors sometimes threw his meals on the filthy floor; before long Milligan was seriously ill.

While Milligan suffered in prison, a team of some of America's most brilliant legal minds, including the future President James Garfield, argued Milligan's appeal before the Supreme Court. The Milligan case was the first to have dropped the dilemma of citizens' constitutional rights in wartime so squarely into the justices' legal laps.

In early 1866 Justice David Davis rendered the Supreme Court's landmark decision on the Milligan case, one of the milestones in America's legal annals. Davis, in the Court's majority opinion, declared: "The Constitution of the United States is the law for rulers and people, equally in war and in peace, and covers with the shield of its protection all classes of men, at all times, and under all circumstances. . . . Martial law can never exist where the courts are open, and in the proper and unobstructed exercise of their jurisdiction."[4]

The Court ruled that General Hovey and his military commission had possessed no legal right to traduce the principle of habeas corpus and to impose sentence upon Milligan, a civilian. The court also stated that no *military* court could try civilians in an area where the civil courts were open.

From the beginning of Milligan's ordeal, he and Coffroth, canny lawyers both, had seen their legal trump card, but they had nearly run out of time before they could play it. Milligan, realizing how close he had come to the noose, acknowledged his debt to his old law school classmate. "I owe the commutation of my sentence to Edwin Stanton,"[5] Milligan said.

Milligan was released by an act of Congress on April 2, 1866, his health, but not his anger, almost broken. The civil charges against him were eventually dropped.

Two years after his release Milligan sued Hovey and the military commissioners for damages. An Indiana jury decided in Milligan's favor but awarded him only five dollars in damages. His jurors obviously believed that the Army had trampled on his constitutional rights but that Lambdin P. Milligan was guilty of something, if not outright treason.

Rarely have the proceedings of any American trial surpassed in importance the case of *Ex parte* Milligan (for the side of Milligan). On September 17, 1987, the Huntington (Indiana) *Herald-Press* asserted: "It [the Milligan case] clarified 6th Amendment guarantees and stands today . . . as a key safeguard to the integrity of the civilian judicial system." Another writer declared, "The decision is a rebuke to those who would forego liberty in the name of security."

What of the man "who remains variously a traitor and an apostle of Constitutional liberty," who was the first to force the Supreme Court to examine, so momentously, citizens' rights during wartime? Before his death in Huntington in 1899 Lambdin P. Milligan flatly stated: "I do not want pardon—I have done nothing I would not do again!"[6]

18 "Go West, Young *Man*"?: One-eyed Charley Parkhurst of the High Sierras

During the 1850s and the 1860s a stage-coach driver, or whip, hailing by the name of One-eyed Charley Parkhurst drove six-horse carriages up and down the twisting trails of the Sierra Nevada with a skill and a nerve few, if any, western whips ever matched. Parkhurst, "profane to the extreme, scarred and angular,"[1] chomped on tobacco, shot dice, smoked cheap, rancid cigars, belted down tumblers of whiskey with the best of 'em, and wielded a black snakeskin whip with savage accuracy in barroom brawls. Of all the macho men who swaggered their way across the Old West, Parkhurst was as manly as any.

Parkhurst was also "different" from the other men, his wild and woolly western peers. The whip guarded an incredible secret, a secret America finally learned at Parkhurst's death in January 1880. The secret? One-eyed Charley was a *woman*—the first and only woman to drive that most legendary vehicle of western lore, the Wells, Fargo stagecoach.

Parkhurst may also have garnered another American first: Although in a man's guise, she may have been the first woman to cast a vote in an election.

The bizarre and astonishing saga of Charlotte Parkhurst began in 1812 with her birth in New Hampshire, far from the western mountains and valleys that would be her home. She was raised in an orphanage, and at some point in her difficult youth, she decided that boys had a better chance in life and that she would become a "he." She cut her hair, donned boys' clothing, and ran away to Worcester, Massachusetts, to pass herself off as "Charles" Parkhurst.

Possessing a way with horses, Parkhurst applied for a job at the stable of Ebenezer Balch. Balch, sizing up the desperate "boy" pleading for work, offered Parkhurst a position as a stableboy and vowed "to make a man" out of "him."

The new stableboy proved to be a wise hire, showing Balch a deft hand with teams of two, four, and even six horses. The budding young reinsman moved with Balch to Providence, Rhode Island, in the 1840s. Parkhurst quickly became a favorite coachman of the city's blue bloods, driving swells and their ladies to various glitzy social affairs and pocketing tips.

The driver's "sex change" was working. To allay any suspicions about her "manhood," Parkhurst sewed shirts with box pleats to conceal her bosom and spoke in a raspy voice designed to pass as a whiskey tenor. Whenever fellow drivers teased Parkhurst about "his" shyness with women, Parkhurst replied that "he" preferred the company of horses to people, not an unheard-of notion among horsemen of the day.

In 1849 the excitement of the gold rush lured Parkhurst to fabled California, but the goldfields were not to be the site where she hung her hat. Instead she won a job with California Stage Lines, beating out some fierce competition from skilled drivers. The whip's wiry five-foot-seven-inch frame, tanned face, gray-blue eyes, and tobacco-stained lips soon became familiar and soothing sights to stagecoach passengers braving stage runs along the tortuous trails of the Sierras and the Mother Lode country. Parkhurst's unerring skill in keeping a jostling coach on track and applying the brakes "as light as a feather and without a jar"[2] won her the plaudits of her passengers, peers, and bosses. Had any known the grizzled driver was a woman, mouths would have opened as wide as some of the chasms along which she guided her teams.

A harrowing exploit during one of Parkhurst's regular Sierra runs cemented her reputation as a wonder among western whips. As she guided her coach across a swaying bridge over the Tuolumne River in the midst of a fierce rainstorm, she heard the heart-stop-

ping sound of cracking timbers above the howling wind. Below
the lurching bridge the river's frothing waters promised death.

Parkhurst coolly swung her snakeskin whip and lashed her
team forward. At the instant the stage's rear wheels touched the
opposite bank the bridge collapsed.

None of Parkhurst's passengers was hurt, although one had
fainted. They all were lucky; a lesser driver might have panicked
and caused the stagecoach to plummet into the churning river.

Parkhurst's skill with whip and reins was matched by her
toughness. One of her horses kicked her in her right eye, and when
it could not be saved, she donned a patch, giving her a roguish
appearance and a nickname, One-eyed Charley. The moniker soon
became familiar throughout the High Sierras.

Parkhurst and her fellow whips faced not only nature's perils
but also a human menace: outlaws. The words "Throw down the
[cash]box!" growled by robbers leveling six-shooters and shotguns
at drivers and passengers, were always a grim possibility on stagecoach runs.

Bandits quickly learned that One-eyed Charley was the wrong
driver to stick up. A notable holdup artist called Sugarfoot surprised Parkhurst on a run and had the draw on her before she
could grab her shotgun. She handed the strongbox to the outlaw.
"Next time I'll be ready fer ya,"[3] she vowed. Sugarfoot should
have heeded the whip's warning.

When the bandit struck again, Parkhurst whipped out her
shotgun and loosened a load of buckshot before Sugarfoot could
fire. The outlaw, mortally wounded, rode to a nearby miner's cabin
and with his dying breaths told the miner that One-eyed Charley
had plugged him. So ended the robber's reign of terror—at the
hands of a woman.

Another legendary western outlaw, Black Bart, learned that
tussling with One-eyed Charley was a painful no-win contest. Bart
was not the typical robber of the Wild West. He sported the latest
in men's fashions, carried an old, unloaded shotgun, and wrote
poems about his "derring-do." His verses, run in local newspapers,
infuriated stagecoach officials.

Black Bart, who had the strange modus operandi of robbing
stagecoaches on foot, had another reason to stay out of a saddle
after he tried to hold up Parkhurst. A dose of buckshot from One-
eyed Charley's shotgun had "decorated" Bart's posterior.

Sketch of One-eyed Charley Parkhurst, the enigmatic Boss of the Road during the heyday of Western stagecoaches

Despite Parkhurst's well-deserved reputation as a gruff loner, she was known as a soft touch for people in need. Always, however, she eschewed close friendships, even with the people she helped from time to time. She slept on her runs alone in stables at stage stops.

One look at One-eyed Charley was probably enough to dissuade the curious from posing questions to the tough whip. Clad in a long buffalo-skin duster, a buffalo-skin cap, a muffler, and blue jeans, urging six-horse teams of twenty-passenger stagecoaches forward, One-eyed Charley won another nickname, the Boss of the Road. Her reputation as a rugged customer quelled most suspicions about her sometimes high-pitched voice and her beardless cheeks.

Her formidable reputation aside, a few of Parkhurst's acquaintances still harbored questions about the whip's avoidance of intimacy with women. In the eyes of many who knew "him," Parkhurst, holding a steady job and stashing away "his" earnings, seemed a decent catch for some marriage-minded "little woman." Throughout the Sierras rumors were rife that Parkhurst had been brutally jilted by a woman and did not trust any female.

Chasing women was assuredly not Charley's "vice," but she did enjoy a sip or two of whiskey. However, she rarely got drunk, fearing perhaps that liquor might loosen her tongue and reveal her secret.

One night in the 1860s too much liquor did bring near disaster to Parkhurst. She had uncharacteristically tossed down too many shots, staggered into the house of her boss, Andrew Clark, and passed out in a heap. When the Clarks put the inebriated whip on a bunk and started to undress Parkhurst before placing the driver under the covers, the family discovered that "he" was a "she."

The Clarks guarded Parkhurst's secret. After all, One-eyed Charley was a friend, not to mention one of Clark's best whips.

Thanks to the Clarks, Parkhurst continued to hide her sex from the world. Passengers awed by the driving skills of One-eyed Charley kept on marveling at the Boss of the Road. J. Ross Browne, a famous California writer of the 1860s and 1870s, left a vivid account of the driver near the end of her career. "I was proud and happy," Browne wrote, "to sit by the side of Charlie. . . . The way he handled the reins and peered through the clouds of dust and volumes of darkness and saw trees and stumps and boulders of rock and horses' ears . . . was a miracle of stage driving."

Parkhurst told Browne that she could sense the road's twists and turns by the sound of the stage's wheels and that if she chewed more tobacco than usual, the road was bad.

What would Browne, or virtually any nineteenth-century male, have thought had he known that the weather-beaten crack driver was a *woman*?

Parkhurst, her hands racked by rheumatism, the scourge of teamsters, laid down her reins and retired in the late 1860s. Unlike some of her stagecoach cronies, who had drunk, gambled, and "womanized" away their earnings, One-eyed Charley had saved her money. She tried her hand at running a stage stop and saloon and raised cattle on a ranch near Watsonville, California.

At some point after her retirement Parkhurst met a widow and her daughter who were about to lose their ranch. The ex-whip bought the ranch and handed the deed to the grateful woman. The daughter was more than grateful; she told neighbors that she would like to become Mrs. Charles Parkhurst. The former whip ran nearly as fast from the would-be bride as the team of horses across the collapsing Tuolumne River years before. Parkhurst's acquaintances must have shaken their heads and remarked, "That's old One-eyed Charley—skittish 'round women. . . ."

Parkhurst the "man" ran *from* women, but Parkhurst the "woman" ran *to* a place where no American woman was allowed: the ballot box. When One-eyed Charley registered to vote in Santa Cruz County in 1868, few locals likely gave her action much thought because every man had the right to vote. When the ex-whip, however, listed on the rolls as "Charles D. Parkhurst, age fifty-five, born in New Hampshire and a farmer," marked a ballot, she was likely the first American woman to vote in an election.

In the years following her landmark trip to the ballot box, Parkhurst's rheumatism worsened. She spent more and more time alone in a cabin she had purchased at the Moss Ranch, about six miles from Watsonville. In 1879 she contracted tongue cancer, the probable result of a lifetime of smoking cheap cigars and chewing on endless plugs of tobacco. She threatened to shoot any doctor approaching her cabin, a message local medical men wisely took to heart; however, she allowed a local man to do some necessary chores around the cabin and befriended fourteen-year-old George F. Harmon. As Parkhurst grew weaker, the youth took care of her to whatever extent she allowed.

Charley Parkhurst died on December 28 or 29, 1879. A doctor arrived at the cabin to examine the body and quickly discovered the ex-whip's lifelong secret, known before only to the deceased and to the Clarks.

Soon newspapers throughout the nation informed their readers that One-eyed Charley, the fearless "six-in-hand" whip of the High Sierras, was a woman. A reporter from *The New York Times* wrote of his amazement that a woman had excelled "in an occupation calling for the best physical qualities of nerve, courage, coolness, and endurance."[4] Countless American men shared the reporter's astonishment.

The public clamored for the hows and whys of One-eyed Charley's double life, and a number of newspapers ran a fabri-

One-eyed Charley Parkhurst's gravestone, proclaiming her "the first woman
to vote in the U.S."

cated story claiming that Parkhurst had lived as a woman in Ohio
and had fled west to a life as a man after a lover—a male—had
jilted her.

Americans soon learned even more titillating scraps of information about the "driver in drag," an autopsy revealing that the
whip had been a mother. Local officials searching her cabin found
a trunk containing a pair of baby shoes and a little red dress.
Charley Parkhurst had carried the child's identity and fate to the
grave.

Many of Parkhurst's friends believed she had taken to her
grave another secret: the whereabouts of her reportedly substantial
savings. She left six hundred dollars to young George Harmon,
but her neighbors claimed that the modest bequest was only a
shred of her actual stash.

Frank Woodward, who had been Parkhurst's partner in a
cattle-ranching venture, "waxed profane"[5] upon learning Parkhurst had been a woman.

Although the news of Parkhurst's secret life must have startled her fellow members of the local chapter of the Odd Fellows, a fraternal group of the day, her former cronies allowed the burial of her body in Watsonville's Odd Fellows' Cemetery. Her gravestone's epitaph reads:

Charley D. Parkhurst, noted whip of the Gold Rush days . . .
The first woman to vote in the U.S.

Charlotte Parkhurst was indeed an "odd fellow," but the first American woman to handle a stagecoach and to cast a vote that actually counted had proved the equal or the better of any male who, like her, had followed the advice "Go west, young man!"

19 "As a Queen Should Go": Queen Emma's Landmark Trip

Excitement wafted through the White House's reception rooms. Washington's high and mighty, men in elegant jackets and stiff collars, women in costly gowns and sparkling gems, craned their necks toward President Andrew Johnson and his wife; to the surprise of the guests, Eliza Johnson, an invalid who served as hostess at only one other reception during her husband's term, was actually on her feet. One look at the Johnsons confirmed that a major event was about to unfold amid the reception room's freshly burnished paneling and plush carpets.

Guests' excited chatter fell to a hush as a lovely woman in her thirties, swathed "in a train dress of rich satin and lace,"[1] glided through the doorway and approached the smiling President and his wife. For the first time in American history a queen stood in the White House. The woman, whose every graceful movement and keen, flashing brown eyes were the very embodiment of her rank, was named Emma, dowager queen of Hawaii, and she was the first queen to set foot in the United States.

Although Emma was not an American, her island home was to be annexed by the United States before the century was out. Her visit was a precursor of future royals' sojourns to the country that had shed itself of monarchy, to the country where

Queen Emma of Hawaii as a young woman

many otherwise democratic sorts were to fawn over royal guests. And long before Prince Charles's and Lady Diana's appearances on our shores attracted gaping hordes, Emma's visit afforded a glimpse of what "royal watching"—American style—was to become.

In April 1865 the *Hawaiian Gazette* broke the news that Queen Emma was about to embark upon a historic voyage to Great Britain. The impending trip elated London but deeply disturbed Washington, for the colonial grasp of both Western powers was spreading rapidly in Hawaii's direction. American politicians and businessmen hoping to set up shop in Honolulu were disturbed that Emma—one fourth English since she was the granddaughter of John Young, the shipwrecked Englishman who had risen to serve as councillor to King Kamehameha I in the early nineteenth century—might help forge an unshakable union between Britain and Hawaii. Although Emma had been educated by American Congregationalists at Honolulu's Royal School, her wedding to King

Kamehameha IV in June 1856 had been an Anglican—Church of England—service.

The colonial agendas of Britain and America, however, were likely the farthest thought from Emma's mind as she and her retinue boarded a British warship, H.B.M. Corvette *Clio,* on May 6, 1865. While the corvette slid from its mooring into the shimmering waters of Honolulu Harbor and she gazed at the vanishing shoreline of her beloved homeland, her mind probably spun with painful images of two who had been unable to wish her bon voyage: her son, who had died in August 1862, and her husband, who had died in November 1863. Her husband's brother and successor, Kamehameha V, had suggested the trip to Britain in part to ease Emma's aching grief.

The image that Americans in Hawaii quickly passed on to Washington was that of Hawaii's widowed queen traveling on a British warship and accompanied by Commissioner William W. F. Synge, Queen Victoria's representative to the islands. Soon an American warship, the USS *Lancaster,* was speeding to Honolulu; aboard the vessel was Admiral George Pearson, commander of the Pacific Squadron, with orders to forge friendly relations with King Kamehameha V. Emma's voyage, barely begun, had already set off a diplomatic scramble between Honolulu, Washington, and London.

As the political waters roiled around Hawaii, Emma and her retinue landed in Panama, crossed the isthmus, and set sail for England aboard the royal mail steamship *Tasmania.* The dowager queen arrived in London two months after leaving Honolulu.

The British simply went wild over Emma, the papers clamoring for every scrap of news about her comings and goings in the British Isles. Queen Victoria received Emma at Windsor Castle, and the two women began a friendship they continued by letter until Emma's death in 1885. As if in pleasant surprise that anyone bred beyond the pale of European royalty could ooze refinement, Victoria wrote: "Nothing could be nicer or more dignified than her [Emma's] manner."[2] The rest of British society concurred, marveling at the loveliness, intelligence, and, in the words of the archbishop of Canterbury, "saintly piety,"[3] of Hawaii's queen.

Emma spent the winter of 1865–66 in France and returned to England in the spring. Her trip had somewhat eased her grief, for many of her new friends commented on her good humor and infectious laugh. She was ready, however, to head back to the warm, lush beauty of her native islands after her dose of Britain's dampness. But King Kamehameha V had other ideas for his sister-in-law.

A letter from the king arrived in London for Emma. He urged Emma to visit the United States, noting that his request would allow her "to see more of the world."[4] But as Emma's wide brown eyes pored over the rest of the letter, the king's true motives materialized: ". . . show that your visits to Europe were not of any political purpose, but for private purposes. They [Americans] are a very sensitive people; your visiting them will disarm all the lies and insinuations directed against our family."[5]

Emma agreed with the king, and on July 28 she set sail aboard the elegant Cunard steamer *Java* for New York City.

Shortly after dawn on August 8, 1866, the *Java* cruised past Sandy Hook, New Jersey, where a telegraph operator had been instructed to relay word to New York at his first sighting of the steamer. For some reason, he did not. His gaffe, according to *The New York Times,* proved fortunate, for if the harbor forts' planned cannonade to greet the queen had taken place, the guns' roar would have rousted the queen and New Yorkers alike from sleep.

America's reception for Emma began when a revenue ship, the *Jasmine,* laden with local dignitaries, slipped alongside the *Java* near 10:30 A.M. Emma and her retinue boarded the American vessel and were ferried dockside, and when Emma's feet touched the wharf, she made history: She became the first queen to visit America.

From the waterfront, sleek carriages carried the queen and her retinue across the city's teeming streets to the Brevoort House, where a luxurious suite had been readied for the city's special guest. Emma barely had time to acquaint herself with her surroundings before R. S. Chilton, sent from Washington, D.C., by Secretary of State William Seward, presented her with an official letter of welcome.

Amid the costly carpets and fine furniture of the Brevoort House, Emma held court, wearing a black dress in memory of her son and her husband. New York's blue bloods and politicians streamed into the hotel for a chance to chat with the dowager queen of the island kingdom as exotic and remote as the moon to most Americans.

Emma quickly cast her spell upon the city, captivating the locals with her refinement and "eyes dark, large and lustrous."[6] In stark contrast with the gaudily gowned matrons who ruled New York society with fists on bejeweled wrists, Queen Emma comported herself with an inbred dignity, leading a reporter to marvel at the genteel widow from the fabled Hawaiian Isles. So impressed were New Yorkers that the *Times* stated that "from . . . the character of this truly gentle Queen, tributes of the kind have been rarely paid to monarchs or their consorts so deserving of it."[7]

From New York Emma traveled to Washington for a historic meeting with President Johnson in the White House. Although Johnson was besieged by the problems of a nation ravaged by the Civil War and by representatives and senators seeking his ouster, he was apparently eager to meet Hawaii's dowager queen. His wife, Eliza, a middle-aged invalid who normally let her daughters, Martha and Mary, serve as hostesses of White House functions while the First Lady remained out of sight in her quarters, decided that the impending reception for the Hawaiian visitor was important and intriguing enough for it to be hosted by her.

The honor of acting as Emma's escort for the gala sparked emotions underscoring the tensions in the President's Cabinet, as well as Congress. Protocol dictated that Secretary of State William Seward accompany Emma, but Seward was not in Washington. Attorney General Henry Stanbery, more than twice Emma's age, was selected to stand in for Seward over the protests of Secretary of War Edwin Stanton, who seethed at what he deemed a slight by Johnson.

When Emma, on the arm of the attorney general, walked into the White House reception rooms on August 14, 1866, she was officially welcomed by Johnson, his craggy face uncharacteristically pleasant beneath his bushy eyebrows. The First Lady, daughter Martha alongside, beamed at Emma. With approval likely gleaming in Emma's eyes, the queen saw that Eliza Johnson's dress was a model of tasteful elegance. After greeting Emma, Mrs. Johnson sat down for the rest of the affair. She stood only for Emma the whole evening.

Emma, regal and lovely in a satin and lace gown, chatting animatedly and humorously with the cream of Washington society, quickly won the admiration of all at the reception, especially Secretary of the Navy Gideon Welles, who later wrote admiringly of

Emma's "well-developed" figure and lively eyes. The dowager queen was the toast of the lively reception, her charm and intelligence bringing the President momentary respite from the snake pit of post-Civil War politics. Thomas Lately, an eminent biographer of Johnson, writes that at the reception for Emma the President appeared happier than he had been in many months— almost jovial.[8]

After her triumphant appearance in the White House, Emma and her retinue visited Niagara Falls and stopped briefly in Canada. Her next scheduled stop was Boston, but before Emma headed for Massachusetts, she received terrible news: Grace Rooke, the aunt who had reared her, had died. Saddened again by the loss of a loved one, Emma canceled the rest of her trip, rushed to New York, and sailed to San Francisco.

In San Francisco the USS *Vanderbilt* stood ready to carry the heavy-hearted Emma back to her homeland. When she boarded the warship, her historic trip to America was over.

The *Vanderbilt,* banners flapping in the breeze, sailors arrayed neatly along the ship's sides as the bow knifed through the Pacific, steamed into Honolulu Harbor on October 22, 1866. A lump undoubtedly formed in Emma's throat as the ship slipped dockside, for a throng of Hawaiians clotted the waterfront, cheering the return of their dowager queen. To exuberant pomp and fanfare, her feet touched her native soil for the first time in nearly a year and a half; then the boisterous procession wound its way to Iolani Palace. Emma knew she was truly home.

Emma, dowager queen of Hawaii, had crossed two oceans and had conquered the collective hearts of two mighty powers with her wit, charm, and grace. In New York and Washington those who had met the first queen to visit America would never forget her. Emma, the American Admiral H. K. Thatcher wrote, had triumphantly traveled "as a queen should go. . . ."[9]

Ironically, the nation where Emma had made such a splash was to absorb the dowager queen's realm.

Part VI

Firsts of Festivity, Flivvers, and Film

20 The King of Christmas Cards: Louis Prang

In a Roxbury, Massachusetts, office in 1874 a young woman waited. Across from her, a bearded fiftyish-year-old man stared at her card-size watercolor, his craggy face furrowed with thought. Her drawing, of a red rosebud with a few leaves and a graceful stem, was simply rendered, but something in the man stirred at the play of the rosebud against a black background. The image had possibilities for a product he had been hatching in his mind.

A short while later, as the young artist, Mrs. O. E. Whitney, left his office, she was probably sporting a wide smile. Louis Prang, an internationally acclaimed printer of lithographs and business cards, had bought *her* watercolor. Although she could not have known at the time that her little painting was to become a hot property, Prang intended to turn her work into a landmark creation. For in 1874 the lithographer was to feature Whitney's design and other artists' work on America's first Christmas cards.

The future king of Christmas cards was born in 1824 in the town of Breslau in Prussian Silesia, and grew into an unhealthy youth whose education suffered because of his frequent absences from school. His father owned a calico-printing business and took in his frail son as an apprentice when the boy was thirteen. Young

Prang, taking to the trade, was introduced to the intricacies of print design, wood and metal engraving, dyes, and color schemes, all lessons he was to carry for the rest of his life. As a bonus his health apparently improved; his schoolmates, not to mention his own family, could scarcely imagine that the once-ailing boy was to live a long life.

When Prang turned eighteen in 1842, he left Breslau, seeking to enhance his knowledge of his craft with other mentors and likely straining to throw himself into the world beyond his hometown with the independence of eighteen-year-olds of all eras. He worked for a time at his brother-in-law's paper mill in Westphalia; he also avoided a stint in the army; his family, perhaps concerned at how the formerly frail young man might hold up under the strains of military drill and barracks life, apparently knew someone able to pull official strings to keep him out of the service.

No strings could keep Prang in Westphalia, as he had a desire to hit the road again. After leaving his brother-in-law's employ, Prang worked for printers and dye shops in Austria-Hungary, Switzerland, France, and Great Britain. He was not merely accumulating knowledge in his trade but also, if his later life was any indication, commencing a lifelong love affair with art, a passion inspired no doubt by European masters' paintings and prints he viewed in public galleries and museums.

In 1848 the meandering trail of the twenty-four-year-old Prang led him back to Prussia, where the flames of revolution against Prussia's nobles, the Junkers, nearly engulfed Prang. His affinity for some of the radicals' democratic ideals was mainly confined to thought rather than deed, but by the end of the turbulent year, when King Frederick William IV and his Prussian Army had reinstituted the Junkers' order, Prang had fled to Switzerland with his eyes on a new land, a land whose revolution had succeeded.

On April 5, 1850, Louis Prang, twenty-six years old, set foot in New York City, bracing for the biggest adventure or nightmare of his young life. He was better off than countless other immigrants to America's shores, for he could read and write, and most important, he had a trade.

He did not stay long in New York. Perhaps he was unnerved by a glimpse or two of the city's squalid tenements, where hordes of immigrants were bitterly learning that for most of them, America was not the land of opportunity but the land of despair.

Prang soon headed to Boston. The former bastion of Puritanism was hardly an oasis of tolerance for immigrants, but Prang found that his knowledge of printing was a strong selling card to local businesses. He worked for an architect and designed engravings for book illustrations. He made an excellent contact through his illustrations for Frank Leslie, art director of *Gleason's Pictorial* and future publisher of a widely popular periodical, *Frank Leslie's Illustrated Magazine*. Except for a brief foray into the leather goods trade, Prang came to realize that engraving, a craft he enjoyed and one at which his proficiency was rising, was his likeliest path to the American Dream. In a new land where a foreign accent garnered cold stares or worse, where most immigrants were limited to backbreaking manual labor for miserable wages, Prang had to recognize that he was one foreigner lucky enough to practice his chosen field.

In 1851 he became lucky in another realm, love. Prang married Rosa Gerber, a Swiss woman who remained his wife and companion for nearly fifty years. Soon the printer had another Prang to work for, a daughter.

The Silesian immigrant, seeking to provide a steady income and a stable life for his new family, wanted far more than to hire out his talents to local printers and engravers. He craved to run his own business, to be his own boss, not an easy prospect for any immigrant.

He dug into his savings in 1856 and started a lithography business, a highly competitive field in which players scrambled to turn a dollar selling business cards, invitations, and the like and to place their artwork in magazines free to pick and choose from talented engravers throughout America. Initially in partnership with a man named Mayer, thirty-two-year-old Prang poured into Prang & Mayer all that he had learned of printing, colors, and engraving.

At his Boston plant Prang placed designs coated with greasy material on flat stones or metal plates, then carefully added water and ink to the design. The greased images soaked up the ink and repelled the water. The results were lithographic prints, which in the hands of a shoddy craftsman could emerge as a blotted mess.

Inferior workmanship did not slip past the sharp eye of the meticulous Silesian.

By 1860 his plant, which had become Prang & Company, was successfully running off business cards, formal announcements, and other moneymaking staples of the printer's trade in and around Boston. However, Prang was not content to remain just another printer straining to keep his ledgers in the black. Always scouting for avenues to put his lithographs on the national "map," which usually meant magazines and books, he found his way to acclaim beyond Boston—with a *map*. Shortly after Confederate batteries had bombarded Fort Sumter into submission on April 12, 1861, and had unleashed the Civil War, Prang printed a map of the surrendered fort and Charleston Harbor; with northerners clamoring for every possible scrap of information about the portentous event, Prang's lithographic map sold well. He was on to a vein of commercial gold, which he mined for the rest of the war, printing battlefield maps and small cards bearing the images of Union Army leaders (an idea we have recently seen again in the form of Desert Storm trading cards). Prang's business sense was shrewd enough to set the head of any captain of commerce nodding in admiration.

As the war raged into 1864, Prang took his wife and child on a trip to Europe. The lithographer, his eyes gazing once again at the glorious artwork all around him, was developing a business scheme he was to bring back to America. His concept, one certain to win snickers from well-heeled sorts in costly brownstones from Boston to Philadelphia, was to bring prints of masters' oil paintings into the homes of average Americans.

Shortly after his return to Boston, Prang began experimenting with ways to put his concept into inked reality at his busy plant. By 1866 he had developed a technique he called chromo, lithographic copies of great paintings. Many businessmen believed Prang's venture was doomed to fail: too steeply priced at six dollars a copy, they warned.

The naysayers were wrong. Buyers intrigued by the notion of owning a reproduction of a masterpiece snapped up Prang's chromos from the shelves of stationery stores. Largely because of the chromos' success, he relocated in 1867 from Boston to a new state-of-the-art factory in nearby Roxbury, where he and his staff strove to meet the rising demand for Prang's skillfully rendered chromos, including the masterful seascapes of Winslow Homer.

Prang not only had begun bringing great art to average Americans but also had brought a splash of color to the usual black-and-white world of the nation's printers. The same use of color upon business cards was to help steer Prang toward a Christmas novelty that captured the fancy of millions.

Business cards were on Prang's mind and in his hand as he passed them to potential clients at the Vienna Exposition of 1873. The eye-catching cards featured colorful floral designs adorning backgrounds of various hues, the moniker of Prang's company etched in the card's center. The cards won not only new customers for Prang but also the scrutiny of Mrs. Arthur Ackermann, the wife of Prang's British agent, in London. She envisioned Prang's products as something more than business cards: She saw Christmas cards.

Christmas cards had turned up during the 1840s in British stationery shops but had not fared well initially. The seasonal trifles, derived from religious cards exchanged on or near Catholic holy days, had begun tugging at some English hearts and purse strings in the 1860s. Mrs. Ackermann, who had perhaps signed with a flourish London-style Christmas cards destined for friends, perhaps including Prang himself, helped convince the Boston lithographer to design Christmas cards for sale in Great Britain.

Enamored with the idea, Prang wasted little time. His first line of Christmas cards, bearing his trademark of vivid colors, was on British shelves for the holiday season of 1874. The small novelties from the Roxbury plant proved a hot seller among the English, who gladly dropped a shilling or two for the delightful cards of the master lithographer, a fact that must have ruined holiday cheer for a few London card makers.

In Prang's office, on the other side of the Atlantic, the sales figures from London must have raised the printer's bushy eyebrows and brought a smile peeking through his dense beard. The time was right, he sensed, to introduce Christmas cards to America. One of those cards was to be Mrs. Whitney's rosebud.

If Prang knew America's history, he grasped the irony of introducing Christmas cards to a region whose first white settlers, the Puritans, had abhorred any celebration of the yuletide, a holiday they associated with "Papist" rituals. Now, on turf where the Puritans had trodden, Prang & Company was fashioning a celebration of Christmas inside the firm's printshop.

Prang's impending sale of America's first Christmas cards was not his first attempt to package Christmas novelties to New Englanders, for in 1868 he had offered illuminated chromos with Christmas themes intended to grace customers' walls. He had also offered small yuletide greeting cards for placement in albums. But the concept of mass-producing holiday cards that people could offer each other as heartfelt tokens of holiday cheer was an idea whose prospects of success—no matter what Prang's instincts— were as murky as some of the inks splashed across his flat lithographic stones. Success in Great Britain did not guarantee a similar triumph in America.

Not even Prang's most optimistic hopes for America's first Christmas cards could have exceeded buyers' reactions during the preholiday weeks of 1875. One glance at the cheery cards, crafted with the same chromolithography techniques that had won popularity for Prang & Company's reproductions of oil paintings, was sufficient to make many Americans joyfully open their purses with a desire to purchase Prang's cards and hand their loved ones the novel holiday notions.

Knowing he had a hit on his hands as he counted the receipts of Christmas past, Prang swung into production for Christmas future. From his factory over the next few years poured a delightful array of Christmas cards. Buyers' faces grinned at the choices of yuletide cards, brimming with vibrant floral images such as Whitney's; pictures of birds or butterflies; Nativity scenes; angels of all shapes and sizes; picturesque winterscapes; elves; and, of course, Santa Claus. Prang himself, with his whiskers and bushy eyebrows, could have served as his artists' model of "Old St. Nick," whose rosy face was helping turn Christmas into a merry holiday indeed for Prang & Company.

The holiday wishes inscribed on some of the cards were words from such poetic titans as Longfellow, Whittier, and Bryant. Many cards featured the written musings of Celia Thaxter and Emily Shaw Forman, both poetesses part of Prang's yuletide team.

Production of Christmas cards soon soared to upward of five million a year. Small versions, roughly the size of playing cards and printed on only one side, sold for a dime apiece; people un-

A Yuletide treasure: a Louis Prang Christmas
card of the 1880s

concerned about pennies parted with a dollar for larger cards
embossed with elaborate designs and festive ribbons, the steep
price tag the result of lithographic costs in which the use of many
inks and stones produced a beautiful card but pushed along
chromo costs to customers. Few apparently complained about the
prices, for as the ever-rising production of the cards proved, Americans of the 1870s and 1880s were willing to pay their dimes and
their dollars for Prang & Company's quaint product. Thanks to
his cards' booming sales, Prang was indeed finding his Christmases
merry and his new years happy.

America's budding market for Christmas cards kept Prang on
the prowl for new themes for his holiday money-makers. He ran
contests in which artists of the early 1880s designed potential
Christmas cards for Prang & Company. The competition was stiff,

and for anyone—in 1880 or now—viewing Prang's cards as crass commercialization of a religious holiday, one look at the talent bursting from many of the contestants' entries should have been proof that America's early Christmas cards were a union of profit and art. Such prizewinning entries as Lizbeth Humphrey's 1882 drawing of a benevolent Santa gazing down at a child pensively awaiting the jolly old elf were more than money in the bank for Prang; the entries were the work of skilled artists, and Prang, a lover of fine drawing and clever brushwork, proved his affinity for contestants' work by paying generous awards for prizewinning submissions, testimony to his own Christmas spirit.

Prang showed little affinity for card themes smacking of the avant-garde to his way of thinking, but he allowed his production people latitude in cards'configurations, those cut in the shapes of diamonds and stars making their way into his holiday stock. A bit of glitz from his designers sometimes passed his muster, as evidenced by a Christmas card cut into the shape of a star and gleaming with tinsel.

As his card sales continued to soar, so did Prang's unflagging zeal to bring appreciation of art into the mainstream of American life. From 1882 to 1908 under the imprint of the Prang Educational Company, Prang's instructional books on drawing, painting, and art appreciation enriched classrooms throughout the nation. *Teacher's Manual for Prang's Shorter Course in Form Study and Drawing, A Course in Water Color, Art Education for High Schools*—those works and other projects weaned some future American artists. Perhaps more important, Prang's primers infused a lifelong love of art in many students who were never to draw and paint with the skills of more artistically apt pupils but who were to gain an understanding of art previously reserved for the offspring of America's well-to-do. "Art for the masses" could have been Prang's motto, proving that at least one successful American capitalist understood that art should belong to blue bloods and poor alike.

In the early 1880s the man who had brought a new Christmas custom to Americans and was in the midst of getting the Prang Educational Company off the ground floor hired a Syracuse, New York, woman to help with his campaign to bring art appreciation to America's students. His hiring Mary Amelia Dana Hicks was to prove a pivotal event in both the business and the personal life of Louis Prang.

Hicks, a widow in her mid-forties, was the sort of woman who sent hard-boiled male chauvinists of the nineteenth century into fits of rage and teeth gnashing. After the death of her husband in 1858, she had taught art to support herself and her daughter and had risen to become art director of Syracuse's public school system. A mix of art lover, educator, and administrator, she soon showed that her business acumen and her knowledge of art were second to none of the boys at the Prang Educational Company.

Hicks was named director of Prang's art classes in 1884, and as the 1880s and 1890s unfolded, she was a strong force in production of virtually every Prang art manual, her editorial eye sharp as that of any male peer. There was little doubt that Mary Hicks was one of the company's most valuable players, a woman whose abilities certainly captured the notice of her bewhiskered boss.

By 1890 the efforts of Hicks and others involved with Prang's art manuals had taken center stage at the company, which had opened offices in New York and Chicago. Prang's Christmas cards had been shoved to the background not only by the firm's art books but also, according to Prang, by cheap cards produced in France, Great Britain, and his birthplace, Germany. Waning American interest in Christmas cards prompted Prang to shut down his yuletide operation in 1890. He was wise to do so. The sale of Christmas cards in America virtually died for the next decade or so. A wistful twinge or two must have pulled at the heart of the sixty-six-year-old printer whenever he recalled his first Christmas cards, painstakingly crafted with stones and ink, and the delight those yuletide scenes had brought to countless Americans of all ages.

Eight years after the demise of Prang's cards, he suffered a far more grievous loss: His wife, Rosa, died on June 2, 1898. The following year Louis Prang retired.

Retirement was not to be a slow slide into utter inactivity for Prang. In what might have seemed a miracle to the seventy-six-year-old widower, he and sixty-three-year-old Mary Amelia Hicks found themselves spending more and more time in each other's company. They exchanged vows on April 15, 1900, and over the next ten years the former lithographer and the ex-art teacher traveled far and wide, bound by their companionship and by their passion for art. Prang must have wondered if fate had brought Hicks into his factory years ago not only to share his crusade to bring art's wonders to average Americans but also to bring joy to the remaining years of his remarkable life.

Louis Prang died in Los Angeles on June 14, 1909. His widow, Mary, went on to earn an arts degree from Radcliffe in 1916, and in 1921, at the age of eighty-five, she earned a master's degree from Harvard. She had become a great philanthropist of the American art scene, her role one that the man who had awarded generous stipends to Christmas card artists would have approved. Mary Hicks Prang died in Melrose, Massachusetts, on November 7, 1927, having kept the name of Prang a proud and cherished one in the arts.

Few remember Louis B. Prang today, but every time Americans walk into a store during the holiday season, select boxes of Christmas cards from a shelf, and smile, the shoppers experience the same yuletide warmth that Americans of 1875 felt.

To modern Scrooges, Christmas cards are overpriced, commercialized, saccharine sentiment. To holiday revelers, the cards are—and will always be, no doubt—a heartwarming tradition. Both opinions aside, Americans *buy* Christmas cards. Today's greeting card giants know that fact well, for in 1875 the ink-blotted stones of Louis Prang told the nation so.

21 The Father of the Automobile: George B. Selden

In a Rochester, New York, machine shop in early 1878, George B. Selden's heart pounded. His breath quickening, he lit the ignition of a one-cylinder engine and spun its flywheel as his assistant frantically turned the contraption's crank. Suddenly a small explosion jarred the engine. A second bang followed, then another and another in staccato bursts.

The din was no reason for the thirty-two-year-old Selden to flee the foundry. Far from it. To Selden's ears, the engine's sputters were sweeter than a symphony's strains; his noisy invention was the heart and soul of America's first gas-powered automobile.

After some eight years of tortuous trial and error in his workshop and in the foundry, Selden's dream to replace the horse with his self-styled "road locomotive" was within reach. But even in his wildest hopes, little could the attorney turned inventor grasp to what heights and depths his creation would push him. Little could he envision what would happen when twenty-five years later his crude car thrust him into the path of a titanic roadblock named Henry Ford.

That George B. Selden was someday to achieve success, even fame, was expected in the Selden household. Born in Clarkson, New York, in 1846, one of the twelve children of Judge Henry R.

Selden, the future inventor was son to a man who was one of New York's most eminent legal lions and a potent force in the state's Republican party. According to family tradition, Judge Selden came within an eyelash of serving as Abraham Lincoln's Vice President, the incident fueling family speculation that had he taken the nomination, he would have succeeded the assassinated President to the White House in April 1865. As it was, the judge served a stint as New York's lieutenant governor and acted as famed suffragette Susan B. Anthony's attorney during a controversial voting rights trial.

A man such as Judge Selden, in whose veins law and politics flowed, naturally expected his sons to inherit the same passions. But George Selden inherited a different interest, one his father shared but viewed as a foolhardy notion on which to base one's life. That interest was invention.

George Selden later asserted that his love of invention had been kindled when he was a fourteen-year-old boy eavesdropping on a conversation between his father and a client. The two men were animatedly discussing an idea they deemed intriguing but impractical: a horseless carriage. Young Selden, hanging on every word from the men's lips, felt his imagination flare with visions of such a wondrous vehicle; somewhere in the hinterlands of his thoughts rose a voice that grew loud, insistent that he was just the one to create a horseless carriage. Another voice quickly shoved its way alongside the first: The judge, it warned, would not tolerate his son's frittering his life away tinkering with foolish gadgets and crackpot ideas. For years to come the two thoughts were to vie for Selden's soul.

By 1859 the family had moved from Clarkson to Rochester. Acutely aware of his father's fervent hope that the young man would eventually study law and join the judge's practice, Selden enrolled two years later at the University of Rochester.

To the judge's horror, his son, having meandered through his courses for a time, studies of little interest to his scientific bent of mind, abruptly left school and enlisted in the Union Army. Ironically, the young man who dreamed of replacing horses with motorized carriages joined the Sixth U.S. Cavalry; during his stint in the saddle he was bedeviled by a war-horse notorious for its ill temper and its habit of throwing its rider—equine sins, one of his

sons later wrote, that hardened the bruised and battered caval-
ryman's resolve to shed saddles for car seats.

Judge Selden had no intention of letting his boy become a
victim of the Civil War's carnage and used political clout to yank
the runaway from the ranks of Federal blue. No doubt after haranguing his son in a few heart-to-heart conversations, the judge
sent him packing off to Yale, where relatives living in New Haven
could keep a wary eye on the young man.

One look at an 1864 photograph of George B. Selden depicts
what a formidable task the judge and his relatives faced in trying
to make the boy put his nose to the proverbial grindstone. The
twenty-two-year-old Yalie, perched on a seat, was garbed in silk
top hat, a jaunty frock coat, well-tailored pants, and shiny boots.
His mustachioed lip was clamped around a cigar, and his eyes,
brimming with a devil-may-care gleam, pored over a small book,
in which, given the rakish visage of the handsome undergraduate,
he was searching for just the right bit of poetry to recite to some
pretty young woman.

If Selden majored in any course of study at Yale, it was rest-
lessness. A letter from the judge, dated January 24, 1864, testified
to the generation gap, 1860s style, between a father annoyed by
his son's academic drift but loving the boy enough to encourage
him to study science—as long as his studies led him on the career
path to be a college professor rather than a harebrained inventor.

The letter contained two amusing asides. The first, capturing
the ageless clash between lawyers and doctors, found the judge
writing: "I am wholly opposed to your studying medicine. . . .
Anything else rather, from a Greek professorship to a woodsawyer
[woodcutter]."[1]

The second aside was one with which any parent of a college
student, then and now, could commiserate: "I sent you a draft for
$50 on Saturday," the judge wrote, "and when you need more, let
me know."[2] Doubtlessly George Selden let his father know.

To Judge Selden's continuing anguish, if not his surprise, his
son was a washout in New Haven except in courses of the Sheffield
Scientific Institute. Henry Selden, fed up with what he perceived
as the young man's aimlessness, likely employing the stony courtroom eyes of the jurist, laid down the law to his floundering son:
time to get serious and to join the judge's practice.

Selden acquiesced to his father's stern advice; the prodigal son went to work in the judge's office, studying briefs, writs, and massive legal tomes. In 1871 young Selden, who had failed in most of his studies, passed the New York bar.

In what seemed another telling indication that he was finally taking his life seriously, Selden married a young Rochester woman, Clara Drake Woodruff, who, as she gazed into the eyes of her handsome husband, must have figured she was wed to a man destined for success in his law practice. Perhaps, as the newlyweds started a family that resulted in two sons and two daughters, Clara Selden even dared hope her husband might garner the legal and political laurels his father had. Indeed, George Selden was to garner notoriety, but hardly the sort won by the judge.

Selden's passing the bar was an event for which his father had longed, but the new attorney quickly showed where his true aspirations still lay: He chose to practice patent law in order to work for local inventors. He also intended to patent the future gadgets of a would-be inventor named George B. Selden, a man whose imagination blazed with a dream from his boyhood, a vision of a horseless carriage.

Selden had gained enough maturity to realize that with a wife and children to support, he could hardly give up his law office for a workshop. But he was determined to launch a second career, as an inventor.

At the onset of the 1870s he fashioned a workshop in the basement of his father's house. Armed with data from French and British patents he had researched in 1870 while filing a patent application in Washington, D.C., for a client, Selden plunged into his self-appointed mission of creating America's first car. He soon abandoned the idea of steam-powered cars and began experimenting with volatile fuels—including nitrous oxide, or laughing gas—in his attempts to design an internal-combustion engine. If Clara Selden was fully aware of the dangerous scope of his experiments with explosive fuels, she must have been worried sick about her husband.

Night after night for nearly eight years Selden, ignoring fatigue from his daily legal labors, holed up in his Rochester workshop, drawing and redrawing sketches of engines and carriages, tinkering endlessly with his models until his eyelids drooped and his mind grew numb. Then he trudged home and caught a few hours' sleep before heading to his law office.

Selden was not merely excited by his labors in his lab; he was obsessed, so much so that one of his brothers warned the inventor that his experiments were like "throwing money into the water." Setting aside all admonitions from colleagues or family, Selden refused to abandon his quest. As he strove relentlessly to make that quest for a horseless carriage a reality, he also found time to invent a typewriter and a machine that made hoops for barrels, both contrivances actually fetching him a few dollars, money he probably spent on his road wagon experiments.

In 1876 Selden's passion for science drove him to the world-famous Centennial Exhibition, in Philadelphia, where the newest technological wonders of the civilized world were on display for scientist and layperson alike to ponder. As the thirty-year-old patent attorney shoved his way through the jostling crowds of sight-seers gaping at the technological displays, his eyes must have widened at the sight of a mechanical behemoth, the internal-combustion engine of a British inventor, George Brayton. Selden, staring at the metal monster, studying its parts with the eager scrutiny of a potential rival to the British inventor, had a revelation, one that perhaps struck him with the force of a mental thunderclap or one that dawned in an instant of cold scientific logic. Whatever the form of the epiphany, Selden decided that somewhere within the more than half a ton configurations of the Brayton engine lay the basis, in much reduced form, for the car engine he was seeking.

Once he was back in his workshop, his pencil scratching countless notes and numbers on sheets of paper, his hands shaping new models, he slowly began to sense that he was on the right track to his dream; even when nagging doubts about his labors flashed, as they must have in the aftermath of failed experiments and mechanical blind alleys, he manifested the timeless persistence of thick-skinned inventors from Archimedes to Edison and refused to cave in to despair.

By the end of 1877 Selden had reshaped Brayton's principles into a form that would have arched the Englishman's eyebrows. Selden's most obvious innovation was to reduce the British engine's ponderous weight by designing an enclosed crankshaft that eliminated the massive heft of Brayton's bedplate. Selden's version weighed about four hundred pounds, a reasonably manageable weight to attach to a sturdy carriage. Besides shedding the cumbersome bedplate, Selden discarded or revamped other pieces of the Brayton.

By no stretch of today's science was Selden's evolving design streamlined, a later scientist branding the machine a "fearful" concept. But compared with the Brayton engine, the patent attorney's concept was infinitely more practical.

If developing a design for his automobile engine was difficult, Selden's ongoing experiments to find the right hydrocarbon fuel to power the contraption continued to be downright dangerous. He ran tests with benzene, kerosene, nitrous oxide, and gasoline. The fact that he experimented with various fuel-air mixtures that he ignited with an *open flame* leads one to believe that his hands and nerves were steady and his luck steadier. When he came home at night with his hands reeking of fuel, his wife perhaps wondered if she was married to a lawyer or a mechanic.

With the specifications for his internal-combustion engine on paper, Selden knew it was time to lay aside his makeshift models and construct the real thing. The inventor, his excitement palpable (if his letters are any indication), strode into the shop of Rochester machinist Frank H. Clement. After convincing Clement and an assistant machinist named William Gomm that the engine could work, the three men set to work to prove Selden's assertion. People passing by the shop figured that the banging and grinding echoing from the foundry were part of Clement's usual jobs, repairing a farm implement or the like. Few except Selden and his helpers realized that the first gas engine intended to power a horseless carriage was materializing in metal inside the shop.

The Selden engine's trial by fire, a literal one, given the machine's open-flame ignition, occurred in early 1878. Selden's design called for a three-cylinder engine, but the prototype he, Clement, and Gomm crafted had only one cylinder, Selden suspecting that the reduced version would be ample to prove his idea's feasibility—or, a dread thought maybe chided him, to disprove his theory.

On that fateful day in 1878 Selden spun the flywheel, Gomm frantically turned the crank, and a mixture of gasoline and air was forced from an outside chamber into the engine's working cylinder and ignited by a tiny, open flame. For three to five minutes the engine sputtered—but worked.

Like the brevity of the Wright brothers' first flight, the short maiden run of the Selden engine signified far more than the mere tick of seconds could tell. Jubilation coupled with a warm sense of vindication coursed through Selden. If he had shouted, "It works!" or broken into a victory jig, who could have faulted him? Each rasping vibration of his engine was balm for any doubts in the inventor's heart. As he stared at his prototype, Selden was viewing the future of transportation: the gasoline-powered car. And he had seen it first.

Selden, with the aid of a draftsman, honed his design and its specifications and filed for a patent on May 8, 1879. One of the required witnesses who signed Selden's application was one of his friends, a young bank clerk named George Eastman, whose future innovations in photography far eclipsed Selden's measure of fame in the world of automobiles.

The application described far more than an internal-combustion engine: Selden's plans called for a fuel-driven car with a clutch and a compressed-air self-starting ignition system. His design also featured something that, thankfully, never really caught on: two steering wheels.

Selden informed the Patent Office that his invention was "a road locomotive including a liquid hydrocarbon gas engine of the compression type, comprising one or more power cylinders." His use of the word "compression" was to spark controversy in a courtroom, but that day was still more than two decades away.

Selden captured his vision of transportation's future in a small-scale model required along with his application by the Patent Office. The diminutive archetype was a four-wheeled buggy with its engine attached beneath the driver's seat—a horseless carriage.

With his filing of his patent application, Selden embarked on a course of action that was to lead critics to deem him at worst a fraud and at best a greedy opportunist. Selden, as a patent lawyer, realized that government regulations offered inventors two years to respond to any communication from the Patent Office; he also knew that each time an inventor sent an amendment of a design to the office, patent officials would contact the inventor and set the two-year response time into motion. Through a chain of amendments Selden delayed issue of the patent by *sixteen and a half years.*

Selden's critics and even many of his supporters were to ask why such a lengthy delay. His legion of detractors was to charge that realizing that the automotive age was years away and that the life-span of an issued patent was seventeen years, Selden deliberately delayed his patent until industry caught up with his invention. His tactics, according to foes, were sneaky and greedy, for he opted to let others pay the price of financing the necessary technology to build cars and held his patent in ambush until he could unleash his design upon unwitting car manufacturers and siphon their profits.

Another alleged sign of Selden's underhanded tactics was his failure to construct a full-size automobile or even a prototype three-cylinder engine before he sprang his patent upon the automobile industry.

In his defense Selden later claimed that he had tried to woo financial backers as he amended his patent application again and again but that he was unsuccessful in his efforts to find moneymen. There is some evidence to support his claim, but even so, he seemingly did not wear out a path to the doors of prospective partners from 1879 to 1895.

The charge that Selden's delaying of his patent's issue was wholly unscrupulous was specious. In his era many inventors took advantage of the government's regulations to hold back an idea until an opportune moment. To excoriate an inventor for using the best lawful means, even if they were stall tactics designed around a legal loophole, to reap a profit from an idea was to be more than a bit self-serving on the part of Selden's foes.

On November 5, 1895, the Patent Office issued Patent 549,160, to become known from coast to coast as the Selden Patent. Virtually hidden from the world for sixteen and a half years, the patent was to send shock waves through the fledgling American car industry.

Even with the patent's issue, Selden reaped nothing for a few years. Then, in 1899, William C. Whitney, a multimillionaire and the founder of the Electric Vehicle Company, an enterprise turning out battery-powered taxicabs, launched a search for any patents that could make a blanket claim to the very concept of the automobile. The investigation led him and his aides to the Selden Patent, and despite the patent's description of a fuel-powered engine, Whitney suspected the document's wording could be applied to any gas or electric automobile. If it could, Whitney wanted to be the one wielding the patent in any legal action claiming infringement of Selden's "road locomotive."

In 1899 Selden exchanged his exclusive patent rights to Whitney and the EVC for fifteen dollars per car sold and a minimum of five thousand dollars per year for the Rochester inventor. The partnership was to win Selden far more than the original terms.

Selden must have wondered at first if he had erred grievously in the deal, for as sales of gas-powered cars left electric cars in the dust because recharging electric batteries was a chore, Whitney's company soon slid into rough financial straits. Desperate to rescue his outfit from ruin, Whitney turned to the Selden Patent.

In June 1900 two major players in the young American automobile industry—the Winton Motor Carriage Company and the Buffalo Gasoline Company, the latter a builder of internal-combustion engines—received a shocking notice from the Electric Vehicle Company. "You," the EVC letter warned, "are manufacturing and advertising for sale vehicles which embody the invention of the Selden Patent. . . . We notify you of this infringement and request that you desist from the same and make suitable compensation to the owner of the patent therefore."[3] EVC and Selden had fired the first salvo of America's "car wars."

Astonished executives of Winton and Buffalo Gasoline asked, "*Who* is George Selden?" They were about to learn more than they ever wanted to know about the Rochester inventor.

Selden and the EVC also sent infringement notices to three minor car companies. All three of the "little guys" immediately caved in to the notices and cut back—royalties deals with the EVC, which trumpeted in America's newspapers the first victory of the Selden Patent for all the automotive world to hear.

Winton, whose first reaction to the Selden suit had been to fight the interlopers, opened settlement negotiations with EVC, whose president, George Day, served as the point man in the heated talks. Seven other car manufacturers, alarmed by the powerful Winton company's turnabout, quickly sought settlements with EVC and Selden.

Spearheaded by two Detroit car outfits, the Packard Motor Car Company and Olds Motor Works, ten car companies, wary of the Selden Patent but unwilling to sign the store away to EVC, informed Day that the automakers were ready to pay half of 1 percent royalties to EVC. If the offer was rejected, the ten companies, soon to be united as the Association of Licensed Automobile Manufacturers (ALAM), vowed not only to fight EVC and Selden but also to finance Winton's legal struggle against the patent, even though Winton had lost an opening infringement case in which Federal Judge Alfred C. Coxe proclaimed, "He [Selden] must be regarded as the *first* to construct a road-locomotive provided with . . . a gas-engine."[4]

After hard-nosed negotiations, the EVC and the allied automobile companies cut a deal guaranteeing Selden one quarter of 1 percent of *all* car sales of the future ALAM. With the automobile industry already close to a billion-dollar industry, the Rochester inventor was apparently on the verge of Croesus-like riches.

The man whose brother had scoffed at the inventor's gadgets was reaping enough royalties by the end of 1903 to open the Selden Motor Car Company, based in Rochester. With his controversial patent seemingly clutching the car world in a chokehold and not slated to expire until late 1912, Selden, the EVC, and the ALAM were, so to speak, in the driver's seat of the industry.

Not all of America's car makers kowtowed to Selden's patent, some stubbornly resisting settlements and claiming that the inventor's design was some sort of archaic fraud. From the ranks of Selden's foes emerged a newcomer to the car wars, a midwesterner determined to unravel the patent and to bring the ALAM, which he derided as a monopolistic trust, crashing back to earth. His name was Henry Ford.

The Ford Motor Company, founded in Detroit in 1903, was not yet a major force in the industry; however, Ford, a teenager when Selden's crude engine had hissed and sputtered in Clement's machine shop, had shrewdly set his sights on the low end of the car market, his company turning out Model A's (not the same Model A's to gain later renown) at an affordable price of $850. Though full of mechanical glitches, the Model A's sold as fast as Ford's workers could make the cheap buggies. The midwesterner's stock was rising fast.

At first, understandably nervous about the Selden Patent, Ford had reportedly sought entry into the mighty ALAM. Accounts about his approach to the organization were to vary, but its mes-

SMITHSONIAN INSTITUTION PHOTO NO. 41,767F

George B. Selden in the driver's seat of his controversial car, (*right*) his son Henry R. Selden

sage to him had been insultingly simple: to come back when he was "somebody" in the automotive world. Ford later asserted that he had been offered admission into the heavyweights' club if he had agreed to raise the price of his Model A to one thousand dollars but that he had refused. With ALAM cars selling mainly in the three- to six-thousand-dollar range, the sleek Pierce-Arrow touring car fetching a princely seventy-two hundred dollars, Ford claimed that America's little guy was getting squeezed by an ALAM dictatorship. Cleverly he portrayed himself as a Don Quixote-style figure jousting against the evil ALAM. Of Selden, he said that the Rochester man was a tool of the monopolists.

In Ford's eyes, Selden's patent was undeniably the ALAM's key weapon, the target that had to be demolished. War was erupting between Ford and the rulers of the industry; if the ALAM initially scoffed at the upstart from Detroit, the group truly misjudged its foe.

Determined to slap the troublemaker into place, the EVC and Selden, acting on behalf of the ALAM, filed patent infringement suits against Ford and four recalcitrant car makers at the end of 1903. Ford threw all he had into the legal fray, which was to stretch over eight years in one of the longest and most important civil suits in America's annals. Eventually the court records of the rancorous struggle encompassed fourteen thousand pages and five million words. Among the evidence in the case were to be the road tests of a Selden vehicle built loosely to its 1870s specifications by an engineering team including Selden's sons, Henry and George, Jr., and a vehicle built by Ford to allege the "fraud" of Selden's patent. Neither replica performed particularly well, adding little more than hype to the bruising legal battle.

With America's newspapers giving heavy coverage to the raging car wars, Americans clamored to know more about the man whose patent had shaken the very core of the automobile world. And Selden was obviously willing to oblige the press, numerous photos of the era capturing the sixtyish inventor, always dressed in dapper style with his silvery mustache neatly trimmed, posing with his cars or in his workshop. With his paternal visage, he truly looked like the Father of the Automobile.

Selden not only looked the part but also acted it during a memorable courtroom clash with one of Ford's lawyers. On the witness stand, Selden, wearing a jeweled tiepin shaped like his original road locomotive and emblazoned with the glittering numerals 1877, parried, with aplomb, the determined attorney's attempts to discredit the patent. Not long after Selden stepped down from the witness box, he sent Ford an identical 1877 tiepin, the bejewled number signifying Selden's assertion that 1877 had been the year in which the Rochester inventor had developed the design prior to its actual test in Clement's machine shop.

Both sides employed the most formidable patent lawyers of the day, and to Ford's fury, in September 1909 Judge Charles M. Hough, of the United States Circuit Court of New York, upheld Selden's suit against Ford, ordered Ford and his allies to pay one million dollars in back royalties to ALAM and the inventor, and proclaimed Selden "the pioneer inventor of the automobile." A year later *The New York Times,* which helped make Selden famous throughout the protracted proceedings, crowned him the Father of the Automobile, adding insult to injury to Henry Ford.

Henry Ford wasted little time licking his legal wounds; immediately after Judge Hough's resounding blow against Ford's case, the Detroit car maker and his lawyers filed an appeal designed to shatter what he portrayed as the ongoing tyranny of Selden and the ALAM. The irate midwesterner fumed: "The Selden Patent is a freak among alleged inventions and is worthless as a patent and device."[5] He branded as reprehensible ALAM newspaper advertisements warning potential car buyers that purchase of nonapproved ALAM automobiles made buyers liable to legal action by the organization. Ford countered the ALAM scare tactics by running full-page newspaper notices guaranteeing that he would protect customers financially from any ALAM actions and would fight the Selden Patent all the way to the Supreme Court. At stake were not only the validity of Selden's patent but also the future course of the American automobile industry.

With the court battle escalating, Ford was forced to post a $350,000 bond to continue his fight in the wake of Hough's verdict. The midwesterner pledged $12 million in company assets to fight the patent, and he and his lawyers stepped up their public and personal war of words upon the mechanical validity of Selden's work. Throughout the long proceedings Ford and his team based much of their defense upon their belief that an internal-combustion engine known as the Otto was the cornerstone of the industry and that Selden's improved design of the Brayton engine was worthless to modern car makers. Since all car manufacturers—including the members of the ALAM—used versions of the Otto by 1911, how, Ford argued, could Selden's engine be the standard against which all cars were judged? And how, Ford asked, could Selden call his invention a true compression engine when its gas-air mixture was forced from an outside chamber into a working cylinder?

Like some character in a Greek tragedy, Selden's fall from glory came with swift and crushing suddenness. Judge W. C. Noyes, of the court of appeals, decided on January 10, 1911, that if Selden had based his design on the Otto model, the patent would likely apply to all modern cars; however, the judge intoned, Selden's heart sinking with every word the jurist uttered, because Selden had bettered the Brayton, "the claim of the plaintiffs [Selden and his partners] must fall.[6]

"It would have been better that the patent had never been granted," Noyes continued. "We cannot . . . make another choice [the Otto instead of the Brayton] for him at the expense of these defendants, who neither morally nor legally owe him anything."[7]

That the judge had virtually gutted Selden's future earnings was galling enough for the inventor, but Noyes's contention that Selden's invention should not have been granted a patent stunned Selden, who had labored so many years on his engine and *knew* that all arguments about the Brayton and the Otto aside, he, George B. Selden, had invented the first gas engine specifically designed for an automobile.

In public Selden stoically accepted the judge's ruling and decided that because the patent had roughly a year before expiration, appealing the verdict was a waste of money. He remarked to a reporter: "I have succeeded much better than I expected, and as my patent has but a year or two to run, the decision has no severe significance."[8] But his family later stated that his public poker face masked the bitter disappointment the verdict wreaked upon the inventor. Ironically, years before the Otto had destroyed him in court, Selden had called the engine a "God-damned Dutch conception."[9] Perhaps the patent lawyer had sensed the threat it posed to him.

Following the inevitable cessation of his royalties and the eventual dissolution of the ALAM, Selden strained to keep his car company afloat by focusing production on trucks; the company was to survive until 1930, when the Bethlehem Truck Company bought the Selden Truck Sales Corporation, renamed from the Selden Motor Car Company in 1913, and did away with the founder's name.

Ford's landmark victory and the lackluster sales of Selden cars could not completely crush Selden's spirit. The zeal to invent still burned within him, and he returned to the lab to experiment on rotary gas engines, crafting more than three hundred models.

In late 1921 a stroke quelled the inventor's fire. Selden lingered for nearly a month, his mind wandering back to his college days, when he had merely dreamed of inventing a horseless carriage, his son George, Jr., later wrote. But in a fleeting moment of clarity shortly before he died on January 17, 1922, the seventy-seven-year-old automobile pioneer reportedly murmured: "Morally, the victory is mine. . . ."[10]

George B. Selden was buried in Mount Hope Cemetery, Rochester. In the final bitter irony of his saga, an Otto engine powered the hearse bearing his coffin.

Despite detractors' assaults on Selden's patent, the Rochester inventor was the *first* American to apply the concept of an internal-combustion engine to a car and the *first* to file for a patent for a gas-powered car. If Judge Noyes had upheld the lower courts' verdicts, Seldens, not Fords, might have crammed America's highways, and Henry Ford might never have scaled to the pinnacle of the American automobile industry.

Estimates of how much money Selden had made from his patent ranted from two to four hundred thousand dollars, a considerable sum in the early 1900s. Measured against the future earnings of the brilliant Henry Ford, even four hundred thousand dollars was a pittance.

"Although he failed to receive the reward of his achievement, Selden should be remembered as the father of the automobile industry."[11] Selden might have stated his achievement more bluntly: "I—George B. Selden—invented the automobile!"

22 "The Brady Bunch": A Saga of Film, Fisticuffs, and Firsts

On the evening of November 3, 1899, a white blaze of light suddenly bathed the boxing ring of the Coney Island Athletic Club. Two men began slugging away at each other in the ring. All the while a camera followed the action, the cumbersome contraption's every whir sounding momentous firsts in the history of movies and of sports.

A maelstrom of chaos and treachery was to drown memories of the evening's milestones. The debacle was to pit famous promotor William A. Brady and his gang, the "Brady Bunch," against a cast of "villains" featuring a man named Thomas Alva Edison.

The controversy shrouding the heavyweight title bout between Tom Sharkey and the defending champ, Jim Jeffries, was spawned months before the two boxers climbed into the ring of the Coney Island Athletic Club on November 3, 1899. At the onset of 1899 flamboyant William A. Brady was the reigning king of boxing promoters, the Don King or Bob Arum of his day. Brady, a dapper street-smart young actor and producer who was to climb to the top of American show business with a string of smash Broadway shows, numbered such ring immortals as Gentleman Jim Corbett in his promotional stable and was married to the lovely actress Grace George.

Seeking a payoff that could help him direct more of his energies to the floorboards of theaters and less to the bloodstained canvas of the Coney Island AC, Brady planned a risky financial venture, thrusting him into headlong competition against the world's greatest inventor, Thomas Edison. The promoter's scheme, its potential profits of $750,000 dwarfing any prizefighting purse in history, was to alter forever American sports and the movie industry. Brady intended to film a live, completely unstaged fight.

Shooting a prizefight was not a novel concept. Edison had filmed several six-round bouts in 1894 at Black Maria, his Orange, New Jersey, studio. Edison's boxing pictures, however, contained one-minute rounds instead of the regulation three. No moviemaker had ever filmed a twenty-five-round title bout, and more significantly, all attempts to shoot an artificially lighted film of any sort had failed disastrously.

Most moviemakers believed that someone in their ranks would successfully shoot a film with artificial light but were unable to say when. In filmmakers' past efforts to produce moving pictures without sunlight, the vast array of electric bulbs required to light even small stage sets had overtaxed fuses and threatened to turn studios into embers before the cameras began rolling. Edison himself acknowledged the sun's current hegemony over the film industry, having equipped Black Maria with a raised ceiling admitting every precious ray of sunlight into the studio and having built stage sets mounted on rails that followed the sun's path. Yet the audacious Brady proposed to illuminate the Coney Island AC and film history's first artificially lit moving picture—and twenty-five rounds to boot!

Brady's quest for a cameraman up to the unprecedented moviemaking challenge led the promoter to the tiny Vitagraph Studio, in Brooklyn, the workplace of a camera wizard named Albert Smith. Only in his mid-twenties, Smith, an introspective and ambitious man, had cofounded Vitagraph in 1897 and had constructed a portable version of Edison's weighty Kinetoscope, the standard lens of the industry.

Vitagraph's specialty was news events, and the company's most profitable project had been a popular series of short films depicting the Spanish-American War, in 1898. Smith and his associates had conveniently neglected to inform the public, still naïve when it came to screen images, that Vitagraph's battle scenes were

studio re-creations, but American moviegoers, craving almost anything appearing on film, were more than forgiving when the truth
surfaced.

Despite the success of Vitagraph's war films, the company
suffered from a grievous lack of cash. An advance of five thousand
dollars from Brady to Smith cemented a deal with Vitagraph. The
two men prepared to make history—and, they believed, profits.

The deal was not originally struck to film the Sharkey-Jeffries
bout. Brady's sights were set on the heavyweight clash that would
pit Jeffries against Bob Fitzsimmons on June 9, 1899.

On that night a bizarre display greeted the throng of fight
fans clotting the ramshackle Coney Island AC. One hundred huge
arc lamps, designed by Smith and powered by an expensive gen-
erator Brady had purchased, dangled above the boxing ring.

Smith's creations blazed into white-hot life just before Jeffries
and Fitzsimmons landed their opening shots. Vitagraph's camera
cranked into motion, Brady surely counting the profits his film
would cull in America's theaters.

Suddenly the glowing lamps flickered, and with a hiss almost
half the lamps shorted out; Brady reputedly flew into a rage and
tongue-lashed the blanching Smith. The young cameraman fled
from Brady's wrath. When Smith returned later to the arena, his
lamps were gone. Smith had little doubt about who had taken
them.

Brady, still determined to film a live fight, hammered out a
deal with the American Mutoscope and Biograph Film Company,
the agreement's particulars granting the studio "exclusive" film
rights to the November 3, 1899, title bout between Jeffries and
Tom Sharkey. Vitagraph was out of the picture, or so Brady must
have thought.

At the helm of Brady's new partner, Biograph, was an ex-
Edison man named W.K.L. Dickson. A stolid, mustachioed Englishman and an inventor of cameras and camera improvements,
Dickson had chafed beneath Edison's ego; after ongoing scientific
scraps with his illustrious boss, Dickson had resigned his post at
Black Maria in the mid-1890s. Shortly afterward he and several
partners had founded Biograph. The opportunity to beat Edison
to a film first—an artificially lit film—delighted Dickson.

Into the capable young hands of Biograph cameraman Billy
Bitzer, who later rose to fame at the side of the immortal director

D. W. Griffith, fell the immense task of lighting the Coney Island AC for a film. Bitzer, whose motorist's cap, thin mustache, and artistry behind the lens were personal trademarks, went to work immediately on Brady and Dickson's project at Biograph's New York studio, atop the Hackett-Carhart Building, in Union Square.

News of the Brady-Biograph pact angered the chief of Edison's moving picture department, James White. Edison's lieutenant, a lanky man who thrived in the "dog-eat-dog" arena of America's early movie industry, was already miffed that Brady had solicited Vitagraph for the June 9, 1899, bout. The partnership between the promoter and Biograph goaded White into devising a plan that mirrored the fierce competition between 1890s film outfits and Thomas Edison's relentless efforts to monopolize the movie industry.

White's scheme was to ignore Biograph's exclusive rights to film the Sharkey-Jeffries fight and clandestinely use Biograph's lights to shoot Edison's own movie of the bout. A technical barrier, however, could hamstring his stratagem: White needed a camera small enough to conceal inside a man's topcoat. The only such camera in New York was the property of Albert Smith and Vitagraph.

White arranged a meeting with Smith and outlined Edison's intent. Naturally suspicious of White, Smith asked if White was acting independently or as a representative of Edison. The question troubled Smith, for under the terms of a complex 1898 licensee agreement that granted Vitagraph limited access to Edison equipment, Edison automatically acquired legal rights to the first print of any joint moviemaking venture with Vitagraph. In other words, Smith was concerned that Edison would reap most of the profits from an Edison-Vitagraph film of the fight.

White glibly explained that a shadowy financier had approached Edison and had volunteered to pay for a film of the Sharkey-Jeffries clash. The pragmatic fifty-two-year-old Edison had allegedly declined the deal, according to White, who then assured Smith that Edison would have no claim on the proposed film and its profits; the picture would belong to White and Smith.

Weighing his mistrust of White and Edison against the cash bonanza a fight film offered, Smith uneasily accepted White's overtures. Surely driving Smith's acceptance of the deal was another reason: his desire for revenge against Brady, the man who still "owned" Smith's arc lamps from the disastrous June 1899 attempt to shoot history's first artificially lighted film.

As White and Smith worked on the particulars of their secret scheme in the days preceding the Sharkey-Jeffries bout, New York's newspapers teemed with accounts of the fighters' merits, the shifting betting odds, and the news that the fight was to be filmed: "Both fighters are brawny giants ... larger men than were the gladiators that fought for the Roman populace.

"They will battle for a percentage of the gate receipts, which promise now to be about $75,000, and also a percentage of the profits of a moving picture machine," reported the November 2, 1899, edition of *The New York Times*.

Fight news dominated men's conversations in the city's saloons, offices, stores, and residences ranging from ramshackle tenements to elegant brownstones. As New Yorkers' interest in the impending bout surged, the event's promoter was ecstatic. Brady, serving as Jeffries's manager, chief stockholder of the Coney Island AC, and producer of the upcoming Biograph fight film, must have envisioned the bout would prove a once-in-a-lifetime payoff.

On "Fight Night," November 3, 1899, a driving rain and icy Atlantic gusts pounded Coney Island. The elements mattered little to the crowds pressing into Ocean Parkway's hotels and bars, where ticker-tape machines would relay summations of each round to hard-betting, hard-drinking "sports."

Albert Smith and Vitagraph technician Jimmy French met James White and his friend Joe Howard in Room 33 of the Albemarle Hotel around 9:00 P.M. Howard was a songwriter who was to compose such popular ditties as "I Wonder Who's Kissing Her Now"; a show biz man who disliked the bombastic Brady, Howard, as a favor to White, had agreed to procure tickets to the fight for the film pirates and to serve as their lookout inside the arena.

Neither the tickets nor the twenty bodyguards White had guaranteed Smith and French materialized in the hotel room, and since the Edison man and the songwriter were conveniently short of cash, Smith and French angrily scraped together money for four ten-dollar tickets.

A short time later, having gotten their hands on the tickets, the four men headed for the arena. The Vitagraph camera was tied between White's legs, and the film canisters and the camera mountings were inside the other men's overcoats. When they emerged from the sodden night and entered the Coney Island AC, the sweat of eleven thousand fight fans and the acrid smoke of innumerable pipes and stogies filled the foursome's nostrils.

The four men pressed through the mob, the sharp-edged camera gouging White's legs. Suddenly Howard halted; the others followed suit. Manny Friend, Brady's attorney and an acquaintance of Howard's, was standing near the group. Howard recovered his composure, began chatting with Friend to distract his attention from the three moviemakers' bulging overcoats, and brazenly borrowed one hundred dollars from Friend as the three men lumbered past Brady's man. Then Howard excused himself from Friend and rejoined White, Smith, and French.

The four men shoved their way to their seats, in the arena's twentieth row, and assembled the camera. Smith gaped at Billy Bitzer's preparations for the historic filming of the fight: Above the boxing ring hung four hundred giant arc lamps—including, to Smith's fury, the one hundred bulbs he had used in his ill-fated attempt to film the Fitzsimmons-Jeffries fight. Four ponderous cameras rested atop a wooden scaffold some twenty yards from the ring, whose dimensions Bitzer had shortened for better illumination. When one camera exhausted its load of film, the next in line would clatter into action.

Sitting next to Howard was a jockey whose intense eyes and well-trimmed mustache were instantly recognizable in New York sporting circles. He was Snapper Garrison, renowned for stretch-run dashes dubbed Garrison finishes, a term that endured in the horse racing world.

Tom Sharkey emerged from his dressing room beneath the stands at about 10:15 P.M. and strode with his handlers to the ring. A deafening roar from fans whose bloodlines were Irish accompanied the fighter, who had been born and reared in a thatched cottage outside Dundalk, Ireland. When he reached the canvas, he shed a brown robe to reveal a 185-pound physique that he described as "a freak build: stocky, barrel-chested, and hands reaching almost to the knees."[1] His emerald green trunks sent immigrants from the "ould sod" into a frenzy.

A second torrent of cheers signaled the appearance of the

defending heavyweight champ, Jim Jeffries. A dour, heavily mus-
cled 210-pound Californian, Jeffries was nicknamed the Beast; the
nickname belied his excellent agility and quick hands.

The referee for the historic bout was George Siler, a seasoned
arbiter of the ring. His words and decisions would be law during
the bout, for in the boxing world of the 1890s there were no doctors
or bout judges ringside. The referee's choice of a victor was the
sole verdict of a fight.

As the rotund Siler, sporting a jaunty derby, clarified the mar-
ques of Queensberry rules to the fighters and checked their five-
ounce gloves for illegal objects, megaphone-wielding Biograph
crewmen vainly urged the crowd to refrain from smoking.

Moments later the arc lamps' intense white glare flooded the
ring. The lights created immediate problems. "They had lighted
the ring for taking motion pictures—the first time they had ever
tried it indoors, and little they knew of how it should be done,"
Sharkey was to say. "They had a bank of 400 arc-lights hung just
above our heads and so close to us that Jeffries could reach up
and touch them with his gloves. The great lamps poured the light
and heat down on us. It was like standing in front of an open
furnace. Before we got started, we were both wringing wet, our
trunks were soaked, and the sweat burned like acid when it
dropped hot in our eyes."[2]

The first-round bell clanged, and Sharkey charged and unleashed a flurry of blows. Jeffries abandoned his customary stand-
up style for a defensive crouch, counterpunched furiously, and
bloodied the Irishman's ear and nose.

The second round proved more savage. From the twentieth
row the film pirates heard Sharkey's corner men bellowing for the
Irishman to "straighten him [Jeffries] up."[3] A murderous right
uppercut by Sharkey rewarded his handlers' exhortations. As the
champ staggered, Sharkey whistled his fearsome left hook toward
Jeffries's exposed jaw, but the knockout blow never landed. Somehow the reeling Jeffries slammed a left into Sharkey's face, toppling
the Irishman to the canvas. To the relief of fans hungering for
twenty-five rounds and of Brady, who might be hard pressed to
recoup even his costs for the lights if his film ran a mere two
rounds, Sharkey lurched to his feet.

As the slugfest thudded on and the cameras whirred, the sear-
ing arc lamps became an extra foe for the two boxers. Angry burns

Tom Sharkey lands a right to the face of Jim Jeffries in the ring of the Coney Island Athletic Club on November 3, 1899, as the cameras roll.

materialized on the fighters' arms, shoulders, and scalps; then, several rounds into the bout, the lamps crackled and sparks cascaded upon the startled boxers. Biograph crewmen scurried from the arena to a nearby saloon. They reappeared hauling huge blocks of ice, which they heaped onto sizzling switches and plugging boxes before the sparks could ignite a fire.

Sharkey and Jeffries battled on gamely. Between rounds the corner men poured buckets of icy water on the fighters' heads, fanned the pair with towels, and held umbrellas above the combatants to deflect scalding water dripping from the lamps. Nothing, however, protected Sharkey and Jeffries from the blistering heat when they flailed away beneath the remorseless bulbs.

In the tenth round the scorching water streaming from the lights nearly decided the fight. Jeffries slipped in a puddle, and his forehead crashed against Sharkey's face and ripped a gash from the Irishman's left eye to his cheekbone. Although the butt had been unintentional, fans—especially those with money on Sharkey—shrieked: "Foul!"

Sharkey's cut man patched the wound with collodion and tape, but the damage had been done. Jeffries reopened the gash in each succeeding round.

Sharkey's misfortune was a bonus in Brady's eyes: The controversial butt would heighten interest in the film for those who had actually seen it in the arena and for those who had merely heard of it through ticker-tape machines in saloons and hotels.

At the start of the twelfth round the film pirates, whose camera had been filming away from the twentieth row since the bout's onset, were discovered by Brady, who had been peering throughout the arena in fear of just such a stunt by one or more of Biograph's rivals. With the wild-eyed promoter leading a charge, a phalanx of Pinkerton detectives, hired for the night by Brady, began shoving and elbowing their way up the aisles.

As the detectives' prey—Smith, White, Howard, and French—stared in horror at the oncoming group, a boisterous band of New York toughs, men who loathed policemen, Pinkertons, and any other symbols of law and order, gleefully chose to defend the four film pirates. The unruly fans erected a human wall several rows below the Vitagraph camera and repulsed Brady and his hirelings. The Pinkertons mounted two more charges, in the eighteenth and the twentieth rounds, but failed to penetrate the toughs' line and reach the camera.

The Vitagraph camera, scant rows above the tangle of fists nearly upstaging the punishing action in the ring, recorded one of the greatest heavyweight brawls of all time, a fight so dramatic that no filmmaker might have dared script such dramatics on his own for fear of too much melodrama. The underdog Sharkey pounded a left-right combination to Jeffries's chin in the seventeenth round, and the champion's legs wobbled. Sharkey, his cut spewing blood, his battered eyes blue slits, waited for the Beast to fall.

No one could have guessed what happened in the seconds after Sharkey's thunderous combination landed. "The big legs of Jeffries quivered a bit, a funny look flashed across his face, and then he shook his head like a St. Bernard coming out of water and drove his fist into my side," Sharkey later commented. "You want to know why he was champion? There is the answer. That was the blow that broke three of my ribs."[4]

His every breath kindling flames of pain throughout his

bruised body, the Irishman refused to quit. He believed he could still muster a knockout punch. He answered the bells for rounds eighteen through twenty-four, and at the start of the twenty-fifth and final round, he staggered to his feet to the din of eleven thousand fans roaring their admiration for the Irishman's incredible tenacity.

The cheers must have buttressed the battered Sharkey, for he waded into the ring and engaged in a vicious exchange of punches with Jeffries. Then, halfway through the round, the laces of one of the champ's gloves loosened and the glove tore away during a flurry of blows. Before Siler could separate the two fighters, Jeffries drove his suddenly bare knuckles into Sharkey's face—and straight into controversy.

The dazed Irishman struggled to say conscious. Jeers and catcalls poured upon Jeffries from all corners of the arena, for even the champ's most vociferous supporters had to wonder if their man had deliberately fouled the plucky challenger.

Sharkey was not the only man that night who could claim he had been fouled. As the fight ended, the smoldering Brady was facing a disaster. The fourth Biograph camera had broken down, and Bitzer's frantic attempts to reload the machine proved futile. For the second time in less than six months a mechanical mishap bedeviled the promoter. He knew that if Smith and White's movie reached theaters first, the film pirates would snag the lion's share of the profits that a movie of the stunning bout promised. Brady and Biograph had to find a way to stop their rivals.

By the time Siler declared Jeffries the winner of the fight, the four film raiders, well aware that Brady and his boys would come after them, were seeking an escape route from the arena. Smith, surmising that he and White were Brady's chief targets, handed Vitagraph's precious film to Garrison with entreaties that the jockey carry it to the Albemarle. A man thriving on danger, Garrison cradled the film and dashed through the crowd in a different type of Garrison finish.

The pop of champagne corks proclaimed the film's safe arrival in Room 33 an hour or so later, and after several toasts slid down the film pirates' throats, Garrison was reeling. The other men paid little heed when the tipsy jockey slipped out the door. Although he was reluctant to break up the party, Smith began to pack his camera.

A commotion rising from the saloon downstairs caught Smith's attention. He strode out the door and to the landing, then peered down toward the bar.

Inside the saloon Garrison was blustering about how he had spirited the illegal Vitagraph film from the arena and about how his accomplices were still celebrating upstairs, in Room 33. Among the jockey's audience were Jeffries's trainers, Brady, and, Smith claimed, the heavyweight champ himself, whose share in the profits of Brady's film had been undermined by the very man now standing near the bar. That same man suddenly realized the group in the bar had spotted him. Smith scampered into Room 33 and hollered a warning to his cronies as Jeffries and Brady and their entourage dashed up the stairs toward the room.

Smith and his comrades climbed out a window, shimmied down a rope fire escape to the street, and fled with Smith clutching the film. Smith recalled that moments later Jeffries, Brady, and the rest were out the window and in pursuit.

Slowed by the film casing, Smith slipped and stumbled through the dark, wet streets of Coney Island. According to Smith, Jeffries, who had just fought twenty-five rounds under the blazing lamps, and his friends closed in on Smith, but just as they were about to grab him, the cameraman ducked around a corner. Hindered by his swollen eyes, the boxer led the posse past their quarry. Smith could breathe a sigh of relief. He had lost the Beast and the others.

The panting filmmaker hooked up again with White a few minutes later. Their adrenaline pumping, they caught a horse-drawn hack to the sanctuary of the Vitagraph Studio, on Nassau Street.

Smith's work was not yet done. As White settled in a chair and fell asleep, Smith developed the film and laid the gleaming strips across a drying drum. He finished his labors near dawn, collapsed into a chair, and sank into a deep slumber.

A few hours later he was roused from sleep by Pop Rock, a cofounder of Vitagraph. Rock, normally a genial man, was agitated: He could not find the film. The strips were gone from the drying drum.

Smith rushed to Orange, New Jersey, and confronted White at Edison's offices with a demand for the return of Vitagraph's fight film. White coyly replied that he had already run off one copy of the film and that Vitagraph would receive its "licensee" copy as soon as Edison deemed it possible.

Then Smith noticed a box of film on White's desk. The Vitagraph man grabbed it and darted from the office. By nightfall the first copy of the Sharkey-Jeffries film was in the Nassau Street studio. Edison, however, still had the negative.

To recover the negative, Vitagraph's sole recourse was the courts, but the studio possessed neither the funds nor the clout to wage a protracted legal battle against Edison. The 1898 licensee agreement muddled matters further. Another legal aspect of the film fiasco worked against both studios: In a court's eyes, the truly aggrieved parties were likely to be Brady and Biograph.

White's movie department churned out several more copies of the film, and while Thomas Edison's personal involvement in the chaotic project was, and is, murky, it seems unlikely that White would have launched such a venture without at least some sort of go-ahead, tacit or not, from his famous boss. One fact of the drama is undeniable: Edison's fight film was the first to reach theaters.

White's accomplice, Joe Howard, introduced the Edison fight film to a sellout crowd at the Theatre Comique, on Twenty-ninth Street, four days after the bout. As the boxers' images flickered across the screen, few members of the audience likely cared that they were witnessing America's first artificially lit film. All the crowd probably cared about was the punishing action between Sharkey and Jeffries. The film did not show the entire fight because Smith's single camera had not captured all the action inside the ring.

During the film's footage of the fourth round, with the action augmented by an energetic pianist's notes, a man in the crowd rose and began shouting that the film was a fraud and that the "real" film—Biograph's version—would open at the New York Theater the next week. The voice belonged to William A. Brady. Before further trouble broke out, policemen cleared the theater.

Brady's counteroffensive against Edison continued immediately after the incident at the Theatre Comique. His lawyer, Manny Friend, won court injunctions against Edison's and Vitagraph's films of the fight. But the task of preventing all screenings of the films was beyond Brady's—and the court's—capacities. Smith sent his film on the road to Boston and Philadelphia, where the movie drew well. Edison also managed to get its film shown, one location being Professor Huber's Museum of Freaks, on Fourteenth Street.

Brady's prospects of profits from his film ebbed with each day his movie remained unfinished, courtesy of the camera that had broken down before the fight's final round. He wanted to reshoot the last round exactly as it had happened but ran into two huge problems. The first was Sharkey. "Tom said sure he'd fight Jeffries again," Brady wrote, ". . . but once they were in the ring again he'd [Sharkey'd] fight all he knew, regardless of what the movie men wanted him to do. It took all the diplomacy I could muster to get him to see reason, and I still don't think he'd have consulted to play up to Jeffries if it hadn't been for those busted ribs."[5]

Brady's second problem posed as great a challenge as Sharkey's pride. George Siler, the fight's referee, had traveled to Chicago and was unavailable to re-create his role in Brady's missing round.

The Biograph film, its mind-boggling 5,575 feet the only complete version of the bout—including the restaged final round—opened at the New York Theater on November 20, 1899. A reporter for *The New York Times* wrote: "Hundreds of people stood through . . . the twenty-five rounds of fighting. . . . The pictures were clear enough to give one an excellent idea of the fight, though often marred in a slight degree by the flashes which characterize the biograph [a generic term of the era for cameras]. . . . The pictures, however, give Jeffries a little the better of it, especially in the last three rounds."[6]

At the beginning of the Biograph film's final round, the referee's "transformation" into a slimmer man with a weirdly shaped potbelly and wilting mustache surprised the onlookers; then it amused them. Having failed to lure Siler back to New York, Brady, in the grand tradition of the theater, had improvised. A New York *Telegraph* reporter described Brady's improvisation: "Mr. Brady, as referee, is as full of jumps and jerks as a bunch of snakes."[7] Brady's portrayal of Siler was perhaps the most abysmal in the career of the actor and promoter later tagged "Showman."

Biograph's fight film arrived on screen too late to recoup Brady's losses in the deal with the studio. The public's interest in the Sharkey-Jeffries brawl was eroding, a situation abetted by the glut of films depicting the fight.

Even beyond the debacle of his film, November 1899 proved a cruel month for Brady. On the same day that the Biograph movie finally opened, *The New York Times* ran the following headline: DECISION AGAINST W. A. BRADY AFFIRMED.[8] The United States Supreme Court had found the promoter guilty of copyright infringement stemming from the Court's opinion that Brady had stolen a scene from a play called *Under the Gaslight* and had used it in his production of a play entitled *After Dark*. The Court ordered Brady to pay the aggrieved playwright sixty-three hundred dollars in damages.

The legal imbroglio surrounding the first artificially lighted film reflected woes tormenting America's early film industry. Since moviemakers used Edison cameras or modified versions of the inventor's cameras, Vitagraph, Biograph, and several other film outfits hammered out a deal with the Wizard of Menlo Park and formed the Motion Picture Patents Company on December 18, 1908. The corporation shared equipment patents, tried to ban newcomers to the industry, and imposed rigid fees upon theater owners.

Outcries from the theater owners and neophyte film companies drove the federal government to file suite against Edison and his partners for restriction of free trade. On April 9, 1917, the Motion Picture Patents Company was dissolved. The movie field opened up a bit for new players.

The battle between Edison, Vitagraph, and the Biograph-Brady team eclipsed the cinematic milestone of Billy Bitzer and the Biograph band.[9] Forgotten during the fight film furor was the fact that on November 3, 1899, the white-hot glare of Bitzer's arc lamps had begun moviemakers' emancipation from sunlight. As long as the cry "Lights, camera, action!" echoes across movie sets and television sound stages, the legacy of the Brady Bunch lives.

Part VII

A Pilot, a Pundit, and a Pol

23 Avant-garde Aviatrix: Blanche Stuart Scott

Fifteen thousand hearts stood still. All eyes stared at the eastern edge of Fort Wayne's Driving Park.

As an Ely aircraft, its engine droning, clattered down the field, the throng's prayers accompanied the pilot clutching the throttle of the shuddering machine, for the pilot was not some rakish man risking life and limb for the crowd's entertainment. The small figure in a leather helmet and shiny goggles was a woman: Blanche Stuart Scott.

No American woman had ever made a successful solo flight in public. For Blanche Scott, Fort Wayne's skies held immortality or death.

Blanche Scott was born in Rochester, New York, in 1886, the daughter of a patent medicine businessman. In an era when women had yet to win the vote and were expected to remain in their men's shadows, Blanche Scott's father shunned tradition and refused to rear his daughter as a shrinking violet. He imparted a simple rule to her: "Are you right? If you're sure, give 'em hell!"[1] She would give it and raise it for over eight decades.

Scott went to Fort Edward College, in New York, in an era when most young women stayed home and readied themselves for marriage and children. She later recalled: "[I was] a screwball . . . a cocky kid of eighteen."[2] Her petite, attractive appearance belied the need for adventure simmering in her heart.

In 1910 she proved that she would never take a backseat to any man. She drove an Overland automobile sixty-two hundred miles from New York City to Mexico City in an effort to prove that women could handle a car as well as men. The twenty-four-year-old adventuress not only drove the car but also handled mechanical problems from flat tires to engine woes during the sixty-nine-day journey. Her foray into the male bastion of long-distance auto travel completed, she pronounced the experience "too tame"[3] and turned her eyes from the road to the sky. Blanche Scott intended to become a pilot.

The hazards of flying the world's fledgling airplanes injured or killed countless pilots. To the rugged men "flying by the seats of their pants," the notion of a woman at the throttle of a fragile, bucking aircraft was ludicrous.

Blanche Scott, determined to soar into the clouds, refused to take no for an answer. When she approached Glenn H. Curtiss, the aeronautical genius battling the Wright brothers for a piece of America's skies, he wanted no part of her dream. But the manager of Curtiss's traveling air show envisioned a box-office bonanza in the petite young woman begging for a chance to fly; he realized that countless Americans would pay cold cash to watch "a woman freak pilot"[4] risk her life. Grudgingly Curtiss agreed to train Scott.

In the late summer of 1910 Scott began her training at Curtiss's airfield in Hammondsport, New York. She endured three days of intense lectures; the closest she came to flying at first was "grass cutting," short, grueling runs along the airstrip. To make sure she never left the ground, Curtiss always blocked the throttle of the training plane.

Chafing to rise among the clouds, Scott settled into the plane's seat on September 2, 1910, and began another grass-cutting drill. Suddenly the plane surged into the air, climbed, and leveled off at forty feet. A handful of onlookers gaped as she descended deftly and landed with the ease of a veteran pilot. Curtiss was enraged but could not deny that the small woman was a born flier.

Because Scott's first flight was an alleged accident, some historians have refused to recognize her brief jaunt as the first flight

Pioneer pilot Blanche Stuart Scott learning to fly, circa 1910

by an American woman. Years later Scott recalled the flight with a cryptic smile: "Something happened to the throttleblock."[5] Something indeed: An American woman had flown.

Scott soon earned a slot in Curtiss's barnstorming band of aviators. The thrilling air show, featuring a daredevil pilot named Bud Mars, arrived in Fort Wayne, Indiana, in late October 1910; word quickly spread throughout the city that a reckless female pilot was one of the show's headliners.

Fort Wayne had been host to several air shows in 1910, but none of the exhibitions had featured the unique sight of a woman pilot. To the delight of Curtiss's promoter, the people of Fort Wayne eagerly bought ten to fifteen thousand tickets.

If catastrophe were to strike Scott at Driving Park, the crowd would likely witness the last public flight by an American woman for many years; the public outcry to keep women on the ground would prove enormous in the wake of a bungled flight by Scott. Upon her tiny shoulders rested the aspirations of future women pilots.

Thousands of people gathered at Driving Park on October 23, 1910, excitement and tension gripping the throng. Everyone stared at an Ely flying machine resting on the eastern edge of the field. Spectators murmured as Blanche Scott, who had somehow jammed her frame into three petticoats and a pair of thick bloomers, sat in the "undertaker's seat," located in front of the plane's engine, and fingered the throttle. Seconds later the motor churned "like a whirling bolt in a dishpan" and spun the propeller furiously. Scott, handling the controls deftly, nosed the shaking Ely down the field.

Gaping at the brave woman at the plane's throttle, the crowd held its collective breath as the fragile craft gathered speed. Even the staunchest male chauvinists probably urged the female flier to get off the ground.

The Ely quivered and rose into the air. "She's up!" people undoubtedly cried. But could she stay up?

Scott leveled the plane off at twelve feet and soared gracefully above Driving Park, the motor's drone drowning out the crowd's din. Scott summoned her full power of concentration, for her most difficult task—landing the plane without veering into the crowd— loomed.

Scott neared the end of Driving Park, descended from the Fort Wayne sky, and landed safely to deafening applause. The crowd had witnessed a landmark moment in the history of aviation and of American women.

Mobbed by spectators and reporters, Scott climbed from the undertaker's seat. Her face flushed with triumph, she remarked that her boss, Curtiss, had stopped her from performing an even more impressive flight for the people of Fort Wayne. "I believe I could have turned and circled the track [Driving Park's auto track]," she lamented, "but Mr. Curtiss has absolutely forbidden me attempting the turns until I have mastered the straightaway flights."[6]

The delighted crowd had seen ample evidence of Scott's mastery of straightaway flights. Scott's fellow pilot Bud Mars praised: "She [Scott] landed as cleanly and evenly as the most experienced aviator could have done. Miss Scott is certainly a daring little woman and she will make most of the masculine flyers go some to maintain their prestige."[7]

In the skies above Fort Wayne the "daring little woman" not only had made history but had also dented some male egos.

Blanche Scott's feat was front-page news in the October 24, 1910, edition of the Fort Wayne *Journal-Gazette*. Witnesses to the milestone flight relived the spectacle as they spotted the headline MISS SCOTT MAKES BOW TO PUBLIC and read the paper's assertion that when Scott had flown across Driving Park, she had become "the first American woman to make a public flight in an aeroplane." Decades later another writer for the *Journal-Gazette* summed up the local significance of Scott's solo flight: "Fort Wayne's own contribution to the conquest of the air."[8]

Scott's career in the clouds flourished after her flight above Driving Park. Although Glenn Curtiss, unable to overcome his aversion to the idea of female fliers, cut Scott from his air troupe and the Wrights refused to sign any agreement with her, Scott found other air shows eager to reap the profits she could amass from curious spectators. In the years following her Fort Wayne flight, she developed into a flier capable of performing "death dives" from four thousand to two hundred feet. The amazing woman pilot, billed as the "Tomboy of the Air," commanded as much as five thousand dollars a week from her salary and her percentage of gate receipts. She survived two crashes and blithely remarked that one of the crashes had happened because she had been in love.

To Scott's dismay, her flight at Fort Wayne did not herald an era of equality in the clouds. Her triumph paled, the bitter reality of male dominance on and above America's early airfields frustrating her. In 1916 she retired from barnstorming. "In aviation, there seems to be no place for the woman engineer, mechanic, or flier," she said. "Too often people paid money to see me risk my neck, more as a freak—a woman freak pilot—than as a skilled flier. No more!"[9]

Scott went on to work in radio, write for the movies, and serve as the curator of an aviation museum. She was married three times but never had children. "If I had a son, he'd probably be a delinquent,"[10] she said.

In 1948 Scott was offered a ride in a Shooting Star jet. The trailblazing female flier who had fought for the chance to fly the fragile, tricky aircraft of aviation's early days eagerly accepted the chance to soar at speeds the Wright brothers had only imagined. Once again the Tomboy of the Air donned a helmet and goggles. Some historians claim that sixty-two-year-old Blanche Stuart Scott was the first American woman to ride in a jet. As the Shooting Star soared at heights and speeds almost beyond comprehension to Scott and her generation of pilots, she probably recalled her pioneering flights at Fort Wayne and countless other stops across America and momentarily yearned to grab the controls of the jet.

Blanche Scott died in Rochester, New York, in January 1970 at the age of eighty-four. In her flying days Scott herself and the crowds marveling at her hair-raising airborne antics had likely given her two chances—slim and none—of reaching thirty. But throughout her incredible life, the Tomboy of the Air had beaten the odds.

Historians still dispute whether Blanche Scott was the nation's first female flier, but much evidence is available to make a valid claim on her behalf. However, her daring feat above Driving Park— the first *public* flight by an American woman—won her a first in the pantheon of aviation pioneers. Her milestone flight also allowed fifteen thousand Indiana men, women, and children to brag that Blanche Scott had earned her wings over Fort Wayne.

24 First Lady of Fitness: Dr. Lulu Hunt Peters

"My idea of heaven is a place with me and mine on a cloud of whipped cream. . . ."

Somebody unconcerned about his or her weight wrote those words, right? Wrong! The writer was Dr. Lulu Hunt Peters, the "Siren of Slenderizing," a woman who battled her waistline throughout her life and launched a nationwide campaign to improve the collective diet of Americans from all walks of life.

In 1918 Peters's *Diet and Health* became America's first best-selling food and fitness book, shattering traditional American views of diet and altering the eating and exercise habits of millions of readers. Her crusade to reveal to the public the mysteries of calories, vitamins, and nutrients was to revolutionize the realms of nutrition and diet.

Lulu Hunt was born in Milford, Maine, in 1873. She was reared in a comfortable, stable family, but the vivacious, brown-haired girl had a worry: excess weight. Her parents assuaged her concern with assurances that she would shed the extra pounds as she grew, her mother and father's supportive words traditional axioms of nineteenth-century views of diet, in which terms such as "calories" were unknown outside the scientific community.

In the classroom the girl troubled by her weight was able to

The high-school yearbook photograph of a weight-preoccupied teen who would write America's first best-selling diet book—Dr. Lulu Hunt Peters

transcend her concerns. She was determined by her late teens to carve out a career in medicine despite the prejudices of men who believed no normal woman wanted more than a husband and children.

Hunt knew that few professions of her day surpassed medicine for blatant male chauvinism, but no amount of prejudice could deter her from her dream. She was forced to head west to chase her dream because most prestigious eastern medical schools had no place for women in their programs. After all, one can picture college administrators—men, of course—huffing that she would probably start her medical education only to leave it when she met the "right man." The bright, earnest young woman from Down East, however, had other ideas.

In 1909 she won her M.D. from the University of California and became the first woman intern in the history of Los Angeles County General Hospital. The year was one not only of professional triumph for the new doctor but also of personal victory, for she was married to Los Angeles businessman Louis Peters.

Despite her successes, Lulu Hunt Peters was not completely happy. The twenty-eight-year-old physician weighed 165 pounds on her wedding day and was approaching 200 by the beginning of 1912. Summoning the willpower that had allowed her to defy convention and to attain her medical degree, she underwent a regimen of diet and exercise and shed 50 pounds. More significantly, she discovered her true vocation: to aid the millions of Americans battling physical and emotional problems caused by improper diet.

Dr. Peters researched scientific views of nutrition and obesity from 1912 to 1917 and found most of the era's conventional wisdom on food appalling. According to one expert's study she read, "to be acceptable . . . , foods must be tasty." Fruits should be banned from one's diet. Fatty foods, red meats, well-buttered bread, sauces and dressings were preferable.[1]

Peters cringed at the words of other so-called diet authorities, including one who stated, "When we do not like our food, our stomachs will not produce the secretions necessary to the most wholesome digestion." According to this view, everything that you liked was good for you![2] Future hawkers of fast food might consider such nutritionally dangerous views a dream ad campaign.

Eventually Peters began formulating her own theories about nutrition and exercise and revealed her evolving approaches in a newspaper column she titled "Diet and Health." Her witty, well-balanced, well-researched suggestions helping Americans to eat better were quickly in syndication, capturing popularity among an ever-widening readership.

The reason Peters was winning over so many readers was largely the whimsical, often self-deprecating humor that accompanied her advice. Often her written words mimicked the style of religious evangelists: "How you hate it [being fat]. But cheer up! I will save you! Yea, even as I have saved myself and many, many others!"[3] But whenever she preached her gospel of sensible diet, she wanted readers to laugh at her exaggerated "fire and brimstone" as they whittled away unwanted pounds.

The United States' entry into World War I brought Peters's dream of enlightening Americans about proper diet to an abrupt but temporary halt. Upholding the noblest precepts of the medical profession, she closed her medical practice and joined the Red Cross. She was assigned to the war-ravaged Balkans, spending most of her overseas stint in Albania, a land of mind-boggling poverty. In her journal, Peters wrote: "Life [in Albania] is very strenuous. Medical calls on foot in the scorching sun over unkind cobblestones, long-distance calls on unkinder mules, long hours in nerve-wracking clinics, ferocious, man-eating mosquitoes, scorpions, centipedes, sandflies and fleas, and other unspeakable animals kept us hopping and slapping and scratching."[4]

The horrors of war and her draining around-the-clock duties distracted Peters from watching her weight. Then a casual glance into a full-length mirror left behind by French officers shocked her. She asked a close friend if the mirror was "telling the truth."

"Yes," the friend replied. "We have all noticed how stout you have been getting. Aren't you supposed to be some shark on the subject of ideal weight?"[5]

Peters jokingly blamed the loss of her "girlish middle-aged slenderness" on "Albanian food swimming in fat" and on the cover of "big and comfortable uniforms" and began to reduce. But when her tour of duty in the Balkans ended, she visited Paris. Soon she offered another bit of self-deprecating humor: "Paris with its famous dishes! Again I said calories be dashed! I can reduce when I get home!"[6] Her comment was an indication of why her readers loved her. She was not some string bean admonishing those concerned with their weight but was one of them, fighting the same battle of the waistline.

Peters returned to America, shed fifty pounds, and resumed her campaign to make Americans healthier. She had also come back from the war with a second mission: to help postwar Europe's hordes of starving children. The children's gaunt frames and sunken eyes were sights she could not leave behind her. Throwing herself into the postwar relief effort with the same zeal with which she urged her readers to watch their weights, she also pleaded with her fans to donate money to food drives for the hungry children of war. Even in so somber a task, Peters could not resist penning a humorous aside: "If there is a food shortage in Europe, it is not because I was there!"

In late 1918 Peters finished her soon-to-be-landmark book, *Diet and Health with Key to the Calories*. It was an instant success, becoming the first best-selling diet and health volume in America's annals. For the first time many Americans learned about the arcanum of calories, and the public's reaction to Peters's book must have tasted as sweet to the diet doctor as the desserts she so loved but, along with her readers, had to watch rather than eat.

Diet and Health was far more than a winning blend of medical advice and common sense. Every page brimmed with Peters's genial personality and her sense of whimsy. Her book's "characters," all striving to shed pounds, bore such names as Sheesasite, Weyaton, Knott Little, and Ima Gobbler. Allaying the concerns of people who might have thought that Peters was ridiculing overweight people, the author poked more fun at herself than at any of her characters. "All of the characters in my book are friends of mine," she wrote. "Perhaps you had better substitute 'were' for 'are.' "[7]

Throughout her book Peters conducted imaginary conversations with her characters, who served as mouthpieces for her views and her humor. "If there is anything to the joy of taking in your clothes," she wrote, "I have not experienced it." She even included a chapter for readers seeking to gain weight, the title being "The Deluded Ones—My Thin Friends."[8]

Readers were also delighted by *Diet and Health*'s stick-figure illustrations, drawn by "a noted artist." The "noted artist" was Peters's young nephew, and she revealed to delighted readers the artist's stiff fee of an ice-cream cone and twenty-three cents. Some of the boy's funniest drawings depicted exercises and their after-effects.

For all its humor, Peters's milestone book was a serious, practical weight reduction guide providing charts and tables listing caloric and nutritional values of a broad range of foods healthy or unhealthy. She shredded myths about the benefits of fatty foods; devised a formula for ideal weight; discussed proteins, fats, minerals, and vitamins in lay terms; and warned that eating foods beyond what the body's system required for energy, growth, and repair was fattening. Sensibly, she cautioned overweight newcomers to eat right, to shun fad diets, and to build their exercise routines gradually and carefully.

The Siren of Slenderizing, with her own weight problem generally under control and her penchant for fashionable clothes and trendy hairstyles, loved the limelight but never lost her values and her empathy for her readers. Her self-avowed crusade to improve Americans' health was equally unshakable, and to devote herself full-time to her cause, she closed her private practice in 1922 and founded nationwide the Watch Your Weight Club, in which members failing to lose at least one pound a week were to donate a small "fine" to the Red Cross.

Peters's second book, *Diet for Children and Adults,* published in 1924, was also a smash hit. She continued to churn out a torrent of health and diet articles, her work prompting *Collier's Magazine* to dub her "the best-known American authority on diet and health."

Peters received bags of mail from readers thanking her for revamping their health, both physical and mental. "Dearest Doctor," one fan wrote, "I cannot be too grateful to you for your book." Another satisfied customer wrote, "Dear Doctor, for your book . . . words are inadequate to express my thanks."

Throughout the 1920s Peters was obsessed not only by reshaping America's waistline but also by addressing malnutrition among the nation's poor. Much of her work stressed the countless ills of society traceable to meager diets and offered suggestions to bring proper nutrition to all Americans regardless of their financial means.

Another focus of Peters's work in the Roaring Twenties was the "perfect diet." She studied the foods of isolated cultures of the world, especially those of Himalayan tribes whose good health was, Peters believed, the result of their diet of whole grains, fruits, and vegetables rather than the red meat and other fatty staples of Western society.

Before Peters could find her perfect diet for the nation, tragedy overtook her. She suffered a crippling attack of neuralgia while traveling aboard the luxury liner *Adriatic* to London. Weakened from the malady and from her prodigious labors of the past two decades, she quickly worsened. On June 27, 1930, fifty-seven-year-old Dr. Lulu Hunt Peters died of advanced pneumonia in a London rest home.

The legacy of the genial but strong-willed physician endures in the 1990s although few Americans today are aware of the Siren of Slenderizing's contributions to diet and health. While many of her views are outdated, Peters was the first diet expert to make millions of Americans pay heed to that irrefutable maxim of good health "You are what you eat." Long before today's fitness gurus, celebrity doctors, and Hollywood starlets began peddling their diet and exercise "revelations," Peters's premises, conceived through diligent study in an era when the food and fitness field was still in its Dark Ages, opened wide the portals to improved nutrition and sensible exercise for hordes of Americans.

The most fitting epitaph for the doctor who penned America's first best-selling diet and health book is perhaps one of her own sentences: "It is not in vain that all my life I have had to fight the too, too solid."[9]

25 Madame Chairman: Senator Hattie Wyatt Caraway

Every ear was turned toward a truck. There, on a makeshift podium, stood a plump, matronly woman in a black dress and a prim hat. Her voice carried with the aid of the truck's four blaring loudspeakers through the summer air. She peered at the craggy, earnest faces of Arkansas farmers, farmwives, and others who earned their keep with their hands, struggling to subsist in the throes of the Great Depression that summer of 1932.

The speaker knew these people, for she was their United States senator, the first woman ever elected to the office. And now, as she preached her political gospel to faces etched with the tribulations of hard times, she was seeking the crowd's votes in her quest to become the first woman to win a senatorial race against a male opponent—six male opponents.

Few political insiders gave the "little widow woman" from Arkansas the chance of the proverbial snowball in hell. But Hattie Wyatt Caraway, who had already made history, now intended to make a miracle in the summer of 1932.

Once Hattie Wyatt Caraway was the last person anyone would have slated to gather one first after another in the history of the United States. She was born on February 1, 1878, on a farm near Bakerville, Tennessee. Along with the other three children of William and Lucy Wyatt, Hattie was brought up as a traditional southerner of the post–Civil War era, learning that a woman's highest aspirations were home and family and that a man was expected to provide the means to a woman's domestic duties. For many years to come, Hattie Wyatt gave little thought to any other way of life.

When she was four, the Wyatts moved to Hustburg, Tennessee, where her father became proprietor of a general store. Such stores were traditional gathering places of rural American towns, places where farmers, merchants, local lawyers, and all manner of men hashed out politics, regional and national. Young Hattie, a bright child, loved to listen to her father and his customers jawing around the store's cracker barrel about politics and current events; she was too young to realize that somewhere within her was stirring a love of politics that would not bloom until she reached her fifties.

Although Hattie Wyatt was expected to fulfill someday her womanly duties of wife and mother, she was allowed to enroll at the age of fourteen at the Dickson, Tennessee, Normal School, called a college but in reality more of an academy. By the time she earned her B.A. in 1896, she had captured the eye of a fellow student, Thaddeus Horatius Caraway, who hailed from Clay County, Arkansas. Caraway, seven years older than the young woman he fancied, was a young man on the rise, a man aspiring to make his mark in law and in politics.

To a traditional southern woman, the Arkansas attorney had a lot to offer. Hattie Wyatt agreed to his proposal to make her Mrs. Thaddeus Horatius Caraway. They exchanged their vows on February 5, 1902, and soon the twenty-three-year-old bride was on her way to Jonesboro, Arkansas, where her husband launched his career and she settled in to raise a family.

For the first ten years of the marriage, Hattie Caraway was the perfect southern homemaker of the day, changing her three sons' diapers, running the family's cotton farm, and making certain that her upwardly mobile husband had few concerns to distract him from getting his law practice and his political ambitions off the ground. She rarely ventured beyond her household domain except to attend Methodist services and take part in various church-sponsored groups. That life had anything else to offer her was apparently hidden deeply in her mind, if anywhere at all. And if her later comments are indicative of her state of mind during her years in Jonesboro, she was happy to be a wife and mother and to dwell in the shadow of Thaddeus Horatius Caraway.

Caraway's political shadow was spreading, and in 1912 he uprooted his wife and three sons from Jonesboro to Washington, D.C., with his election to the House of Representatives. For his spouse, used to her orderly, busy life in small-town Arkansas, the move to the nation's capital must have posed culture shock. But once she was settled in her new house, the historic Calvert Mansion, in Riverdale, Maryland, she plunged back into her role as her husband's "little lady," holding down his home front as he searched for a foothold in the morass of national politics.

So caught up in her comfortable, customary household tasks was Caraway that in 1920 she paid little heed to a momentous event in the history of American women: the Nineteenth Amendment, granting the "fairer sex" the vote. She had played no role in the long struggle of the nation's suffragettes. She later said that she "just added voting to cooking and sewing and other household activities. Of course," she was to add, "living in Arkansas helped a lot, for down there we don't have to bother about making a choice between two parties."[1] As the wife of a conservative southern Democrat she lived the truth of that statement.

The year 1920 brought another change to the "little woman" of Arkansas that seemed at the time more important to her than her newfound right to vote: Following three terms as a representative, her husband won election to the United States Senate. She now enjoyed status for which many political wives of the 1920s would have sold their souls; true to form, however, Hattie Wyatt Caraway spent most of her time at the family's houses in Maryland and Arkansas, socializing little with more ambitious wives of her husband's colleagues. For the wife of Senator Caraway, her husband did most of the talking outside the couple's home.

Talk her husband did, to the ire of Republicans and the northern press. Senator Caraway, often clad in a brimmed felt black hat and a frock coat, was the visage of fire-and-brimstone preachers and politicians so loathsome to many above the Mason-Dixon line and so revered below it. The *Nation* chided that he "had much of the demagogue and poseur in him." He was known for inflammatory rhetoric often rendered in long-winded orations proving his grasp of the problems and concerns of poor white southerners. "He was true to type," said the *Nation*, "intensely anti-Negro, and he knew well how to hate."[2] But even some of his detractors lauded his stands for America's farmers and his stands against "big-government" corruption, especially his attacks against the Teapot Dome Scandal and against other improprieties in President Warren G. Harding's Cabinet.

In the comfortable trappings of her home, Hattie Caraway was likely the first to hear her husband's diatribes against his political foes; she assimilated many of his views into her own scheme of the outside world, but how much was not to surface until circumstances thrust her outside her home's environs and into the vipers' nest of Washington politicos.

Those circumstances burst into her life on November 6, 1931, the day her husband died. Scarcely had the bereaved widow time to bury her husband in Jonesboro and sort out her emotions than Harvey Parnell, governor of Arkansas, appointed her interim senator to serve out her husband's remaining term, roughly a year. "She was rightfully entitled to the office held by her distinguished husband,"[3] Parnell stated.

There was precedent for that decision, for in 1929 two Arkansas wives had finished out House of Representative terms for their husbands, and a Georgia woman, Rebecca Latimer Felton, had served, by gubernatorial appointment, the final hours of the senatorial term of the deceased Thomas E. Watson. Parnell's move came as a gesture of respect for the deceased Senator Caraway and as a way of allowing Arkansas politicians to scramble for the suddenly vacant senatorial seat in the upcoming election of 1932. Had anyone in Arkansas warned would-be claimants to Thaddeus Caraway's seat that his "little widow" would likewise be infected with "Potomac fever," that soothsayer would have earned guffaws and ridicule.

Hattie Wyatt Caraway was sworn in on December 9, 1931, to serve as her husband's temporary replacement in the Senate. Meanwhile, Arkansas's Democratic heavyweights prepared a special election for January 12, 1932, to rubber-stamp Hattie Caraway's serving out her husband's term, which was to end in March 1933. She faced no opponent in her home state, and the news of her "victory" sent America's reporters scrambling for information about the first woman to win an election—even an unopposed election—for the U.S. Senate.

Many Americans were amused to learn that rather than some

Young Hattie Wyatt Caraway

iron-willed, brilliant feminist, the nation's first female senator was a "widow woman," short, overweight, dressed in black. What a strange sight she seemed as she took her seat amid the country's power brokers, ranging from Brahmin patricians in their muted but elegant suits to a roguish pol from Louisiana known as the Kingfish, Huey Long. To the senators, what a contrast her down-home wit and plain speech, muted at first in her new surroundings, must have seemed in comparison to the fiery bombast of her deceased husband.

The new Senator Caraway trooped up the Senate stairs and into chambers dutifully each day, and while she eschewed taking the floor to deliver speeches from behind the podium, she immersed herself in her husband's former committees, Agriculture and Forestry and later Commerce. She studied each day's *Congressional Record* with the same diligence with which she had studied her Bible. When asked why she preferred airing her views in committee rather than on the Senate floor, she replied: "I haven't the heart to take a minute away from the men. The poor dears love it [speech making] so."[4] Quietly, effectively the black-swathed widow from the South began to show that despite prevailing stereotypes, she was not overwhelmed by the manly concerns of the Senate.

In time, as she pored over Senate bills and listened to the worries of struggling residents of her state, a wondrous thing happened. "The demure little woman who looks as though she ought to be sitting on a porch in a rocking-chair, mending someone's socks,"[5] found that a love of politics, submerged unknowingly so many years in her soul, was suddenly unleashed to the amazement of her and her friends. Suddenly she did not want to give up her seat, the *Caraways'* perch alongside the Potomac. Perhaps the heady wine of politics intoxicated her permanently on May 9, 1932, when Vice President Charles Curtis requested that she preside over the Senate's session. With the nation's press trumpeting the scene inside the Senate that historic day, Hattie Wyatt Caraway ambled into the venerable chamber where only men had held sway, and became the first woman ever to preside over the body's proceedings. Amusement flickered on many of the faces in America's most exclusive men's club. Others likely flashed disapproval. Those holding that no woman had a place in the Senate for any reason probably consoled themselves with the thought that after March 1933 the "little widow woman" would be forever departed from the big boys' turf. The woman, however, had other thoughts.

With the acumen of a born public relations "man," Caraway seized the hype surrounding the unprecedented sight of a woman presiding over the Senate to drop a verbal bombshell spreading political tremors from Washington to Little Rock. "I am going to fight for my place in the sun," she informed stunned reporters and politicians. "The time has passed when a woman should be placed in a position and kept there only while someone else is being groomed for the job."[6] What had Washington done, many of her friends and neighbors back in Jonesboro must have wondered, to the little housewife who had thought voting was little more than cooking and sewing, who was the first woman ever to run against a man—six of them—in a Senate election?

Once the shock of her announcement ebbed, the nation's political pundits smugly declared that the ponderous might of Arkansas's Democratic machine would grind the lightweight challenge of the "little widow woman" into political pulp. "Six mighty champions before the Lord of Democratic Hosts cheerfully conceded that out of a total of possibly 250,000 votes, Mrs. Caraway would poll some 3,000 at the outside."[7]

In July 1932 Caraway's flagging campaign won a sudden and formidable ally: Senator Huey Long of Louisiana. The flamboyant Kingfish was aching to embarrass Arkansas's other senator, Joe Robinson, who had gutted Long's controversial resolution calling for Americans' individual incomes to be limited to one million dollars, with anything over that amount going to the public treasury. Caraway had supported Long's resolution, and what better way, he thought, to swing back at Robinson than to endorse the widow's campaign. To Caraway, Long said: "We can make that campaign in one week. That's all we need. That won't give 'em a chance to get over their surprise."[8] And what a surprise he was about to unleash upon the six unwitting foes of Hattie Caraway.

In August 1932 Long's personal car and seven trucks, two of them each sporting loudspeakers, chairs, a folding table, a pitcher, and glasses, carried the Kingfish and the "little widow woman" on a whirlwind campaign across Arkansas in a political blitzkrieg the likes of which the state's voters had never seen. The caravan wound its way from cities to rural hamlets for nine memorable days, the two senators delivering stump speeches the length and breadth of Arkansas and drawing throngs of up to thirty-five thousand. The frenetic pace of the tour was set by the first day's political rallies in five towns over a distance of nearly 150 miles.

Everywhere the barnstorming caravan stopped, Long delivered riveting, vitriolic speeches portraying the stands of the "little widow woman" against Wall Street's greed and fat cat politicians and her relentless crusades on behalf of America's common folk, all his bombast part of his Share the Wealth campaign. Caraway, reluctant in the past to make public speeches, rapidly discovered that she could effectively expound her ideas from the makeshift podiums of the tour. "I know I can't talk like a statesman," she told a gathering, "but I've always tried to vote like one for you." By the tour's end she had become a winning stump speech maker, even assailing President Herbert Hoover and his "manicured Farm Board." Lauded Hermann Deutsch of the *Saturday Evening Post*: "She . . . spiced it [her rhetoric] with just enough Cayenne to give a fillip to palates that had been jaded by a surfeit of fiery oratory." She also displayed her knack for delivering punchy, pithy replies to reporters' questions. In Jonesboro she was asked where her tour would end. She answered, "In the United States Senate, of course."[9]

Her answer proved correct. She won the Democratic primary in the heaviest voter turnout Arkansas had ever witnessed. She not only won the primary but won it big, amassing more votes than the combined totals of her shocked male opponents and re-proving the brilliance of the "caravan" strategy that had served Long so well in Louisiana. Her victory in the primary in hand, she won election to the Senate for a full six-year term.

Senator Hattie Wyatt Caraway was now a nationally renowned figure, newspaper reporters and magazine writers flocking to her for interviews. And to no surprise of those who had heard her develop as a speaker on her tour with Long, the first woman to have won a successful Senate campaign against male opponents continued to prove good copy.

She also proved to be a politician of sterner backbone than her erstwhile mentor, Huey Long, had ever envisioned. To his dismay, she did not feel she owed him a rubber-stamp vote on any resolution he foisted upon the Senate. He grumbled that she was something of an ingrate. To his complaints she huffily responded, "I am Senator Caraway." During the lightning campaign in Arkansas, Long had praised her as "an unbossed candidate."[10] How true, he angrily discovered, his words had been.

The "unbossed" Caraway, usually clad in her familiar black, often working crossword puzzles during lulls in Senate sessions, continued racking up firsts in the nation's history. She became the first woman to conduct a Senate committee hearing; the first woman to sit as a committee chairman, presiding over Enrolled Bills; and eventually the first woman to serve as her state's senior senator. As her political credits mounted, she stated that her achievements were proof that America had "no need to set women apart from serious consideration as qualified legislators."

In 1938 her qualifications for reelection were assaulted on traditional grounds of chauvinism by her opponent, Congressman John L. McClellan. His campaign slogan said it all: "Arkansas Needs Another Man in the Senate." She faced a bruising run to hold on to her seat; this time, however, she did not have Huey Long, felled by an assassin's bullet, to cull male votes for the "little widow woman." In the words of one reporter, she was to run her race "unchaperoned."

The campaign was as tough as she anticipated, her support

from women's groups, veterans' organizations, the American Federation of Labor, and even a bit of help from President Franklin D. Roosevelt, whom she had supported on many of his New Deal programs, pitted against the parochial backers of McClellan. When the rancorous struggle finally ended, the people of Arkansas spoke their peace: Caraway won by eight thousand votes. The "little people" she had helped through the years had helped her over the political hump to her third term in the Senate.

Caraway's third term unfolded amid the turbulence of World War II, and even before America's entry into the conflict, the little woman from Arkansas grasped better than many in the Senate that America would eventually be dragged into the horror of the fray. She supported such prewar programs of Roosevelt as lend-lease, which helped Great Britain and the USSR in their life-and-death struggles against the Axis Powers.

Once America was in the war, the nation's women manned the factories, embarking upon the greatest display of industrial muscle the world had ever seen. Women's leaders did not intend to let the suddenly crucial role of Rosie the Riveter go unacknowledged by the government; they raised a cry for equal rights. And the cry was heard by an ex-housewife who had once been the epitome of the woman who knew her place in a man's world: Senator Hattie Caraway became the first woman of Congress to support the proposed Equal Rights Amendment. Today the struggle for equality of the sexes still rages, a conflict Caraway likely thought would be resolved long before the 1990s.

In 1944 she attained another first, one she did not relish. She became the first woman defeated in her reelection bid for the Senate, unseated by Representative J. William Fulbright. The sixty-six-year-old Caraway took her loss with typical self-effacing honesty. "The people are speaking,"[11] she said.

Caraway entered the Senate for the final day of the seventy-eighth Congress on December 19, 1944. In a scene described by a reporter as "almost without precedent," the entire Senate, even those who believed that a woman's place was still in the home and nowhere else, rose to its collective feet in tribute to the widow woman, the first of her gender elected to trod those chambers. Her every step in the Senate had made history.

Despite the end of her thirteen years in the Senate, Caraway was not ready to leave the political arena. Roosevelt, certainly remembering the support she had thrown his way on many occasions, appointed her to the Federal Employees' Compensation Commission in early 1945, and in the following year she took a post with the Employees' Compensation Appeals. Politics was still in her blood.

Few foes had been able to best the ex-senator from Arkansas, but in January 1950 a stroke finally yanked Caraway from America's political scene. She remained close to Washington, however, choosing to convalesce at a rest home in Falls Church, Virginia. But her failing health posed a hurdle she was unable to overcome. In December 1950 the first woman elected to the Senate died at the age of seventy-two. She was buried alongside her husband in West Lawn Cemetery, in Jonesboro, Arkansas. There two senators, husband and wife, lay in the soil where their political saga had begun.

Even on her best days in the Senate Hattie Caraway had not been the visage of many feminists' dreams. To blacks yearning for civil rights, she had been a symbol of old-time southern pols unable or unwilling to shed old prejudices, as evidenced by her opposition to an antilynching bill presented in the Senate in 1938. Her dismay that Prohibition had been struck down at about the same time she had taken office surely galled or amused many Americans; after all, many of the Arkansas farmers and laborers who voted for her saw no harm in a nip or two of "pot liquor."

The "little widow woman" from Arkansas was indeed a product of her upbringing and her region, but critics' jibes aside, she had shown she not only could compete with politics' big boys but also had been the first of her sex to best them in the place where senators dwell: the ballot box. Hattie Wyatt Caraway had found her "place in the sun."

Notes

Full bibliographic data for works cited below may for the most part be found in the Sources section.

CHAPTER I: BIG, BAD JOHN BILLINGTON

1. George F. Willison, *The Pilgrim Reader: The Story of the Pilgrims as Told by Themselves & Their Contemporaries Friendly and Unfriendly,* p. 126.

2. Willison, *Pilgrim Reader,* "Mayflower Compact" (appendix), p. 554; Willison, *Pilgrim Reader,* p. 284.

3. Willison, *Pilgrim Reader,* p. 125.

4. Ibid., p. 355.

5. Ibid.

6. Ibid.

CHAPTER 2: THE PENOBSCOT PIRATE

1. Jim McClain, *A Brief Account of the Wicked Doings of Dixie Bull*, p. 13; Massachusetts Historical Society Collections, ser. 4, vol. 33 (Boston: Little, Brown, 1856), pp. 336–337.

2. Sydney Strong, ed., *Roger Clap's Memoirs*, p. 33; also, McClain, *A Brief Account*, p. 24; George Francis Dow, *The Pirates of the New England Coast, 1630–1730*, p. 21.

CHAPTER 3: IN NO MAN'S SHADOW

1. Louis Green Carr, *Notable American Women*, p. 236.

2. *Archives of Maryland*, vol. 1, p. 215.

3. Ibid.

4. Ibid., pp. 238–239.

CHAPTER 4: "THOU SHALT NOT SUFFER A WITCH TO LIVE"

1. George Lincoln Burr, *Narratives of the Witchcraft Cases, 1648–1706*, p. 408.

2. Ibid., p. 408.

3. James K. Hosmer, ed., *Winthrop's Journal*, vol. 2, pp. 344–345.

4. Ibid., p. 344.

5. Ibid.

6. Ibid., p. 345.

7. Burr, *Witchcraft Cases*, p. 408.

8. Ibid.

CHAPTER 5: FOUR FOR FREEDOM

1. Henry Steele Commager, *Documents of American History,* p. 37.

2. Ibid.

3. Albert Cook Myers, ed., *Narratives of Early Pennsylvania, West New Jersey, and Delaware, 1630–1707,* p. 412.

4. Harry Emerson Wildes, *William Penn,* p. 195.

5. Myers, *Narratives,* p. 376 (from a Pastorius letter).

6. Commager, *Documents,* p. 37.

7. Samuel Whitaker Pennypacker, *The Settlement of Germantown, Pennsylvania,* p. 147.

8. Ibid.

9. Ibid., pp. 147–148.

CHAPTER 6: MRS. BUTTERWORTH'S KITCHEN

1. Richard LeBaron Bowen, *Early Rehoboth,* vol. 2, p. 59.

2. *American Dictionary of Crime,* p. 113.

CHAPTER 7: THE PIONEER POETESS

1. Robert Hutchinson, ed., *Poems of Anne Bradstreet,* p. 41.

2. Ibid., p. 47.

3. Ibid., p. 78.

CHAPTER 8: A BARD IN BONDAGE

1. Phillis Wheatley, *Poems on Various Subjects, Religious and Moral,* introduction, "To the Publick."

CHAPTER 11: THIRTEEN STARS AND THE STAR OF DAVID

1. John Drayton, ed., "Letter from Major Andrew Williamson to the President of South Carolina, John Rutledge, August 4, 1776," in *Memoirs of the American Revolution As Relating to the State of South Carolina* (New York: The New York Times and Arno Press, 1969).

CHAPTER 12: A CONNECTICUT YANKEE'S COOKERY

1. Amelia Simmons, *American Cookery,* 1st ed.

2. Ibid., 2nd ed., Errata.

CHAPTER 16: THE ORIGINAL SPRUCE GUM MAN

1. "John B. Curtis Obituary" *Daily Eastern Argus,* June 14, 1897.

2. Ibid.

3. Ibid.

4. C. Bancroft Gillespie, *Men of Progress.* From the collections of the Portland (Maine) Public Library.

CHAPTER 17: LANDMARK HERO OR LANDMARK TRAITOR

1. Darwin Kelley, ed., "Lambdin P. Milligan's Appeal for States' Rights and Constitutional Liberty During the Civil War," pp. 264–265.

2. Ibid., p. 264.

3. John Ross, "Was This a Conspirator's House?" p. 14.

4. Henry Steele Commager, *Documents of American History,* pp. 472–474.

5. Florence Grayston, "A Knight of the Golden Circle," p. 389.

6. Ibid., p. 391.

CHAPTER 18: "GO WEST, YOUNG MAN"?

1. John V. Young, " 'Silent' Charley Weird Figure in Mountain Annals," p. 17.

2. Ibid., p. 17.

3. Cena Golder Richeson, "The Woman in Charles Parkhurst," p. 40.

4. *The New York Times,* "Thirty Years in Disguise," January 9, 1880, p. 2.

5. Young, " 'Silent' Charley," p. 17.

CHAPTER 19: "AS A QUEEN SHOULD GO"

1. Kathleen Dickinson Mellen, *The Gods Depart,* p. 231.

2. Edward T. James, ed., *Notable American Women,* p. 583.

3. Mellen, *The Gods Depart,* p. 230.

4. Ralph S. Kuykendall, *The Hawaiian Kingdom,* p. 202.

5. Kuykendall, *Kingdom,* p. 202; Mellen, *The Gods Depart,* p. 230.

6. "Our First Royal Lady Visitor," *The New York Times,* August 9, 1966, p. 5.

7. Ibid.

8. Thomas Lately, *The First President Johnson: The Three Lives of the Seventeenth President of the United States of America,* p. 478.

9. Mellen, *The Gods Depart,* p. 231.

CHAPTER 21: THE FATHER OF THE AUTOMOBILE

1. Dana Roberts, "Two Letters in Old Desk Sketch Inventor's Trials," *Rochester Times,* May 8, 1929.

2. Ibid.

3. Robert F. Scott, "I Invented the Automobile," *Automobile Quarterly* (Winter 1966), p. 318.

4. Joseph W. Barnes, "Rochester and the Automobile Industry," *Rochester History* 43 (April and July 1981), p. 7.

5. Advertisement by Ford Motor Company. *The New York Times,* February 13, 1910, p. C4.

6. "Did Not Infringe on Selden Patent," *The New York Times,* January 10, 1911, p. 5.

7. Ibid.

8. Scott, "I Invented," p. 325.

9. George D. Selden, "Horses Hated Rochester Alumnus, Pioneer, Inventor of Automobile," p. 17.

10. Scott, "I Invented," p. 325.

11. *The National Encyclopedia of American Biography,* p. 223.

CHAPTER 22: "THE BRADY BUNCH"

1. Tom Sharkey with Morrow Mayo, "Fighting the Champions," p. 35.

2. Ibid., p. 120.

3. Ibid, p. 121.

4. Ibid.

5. William A. Brady, "Showman," *The Saturday Evening Post*, March 21, 1936, p. 80.

6. *The New York Times*, "Biograph Fight Pictures," November 21, 1899, p. 4.

7. Edo McCullough, *Good Old Coney Island: A Sentimental Journey into the Past*, pp. 180–181.

8. *The New York Times*, "Decision Against W. A. Brady Affirmed," November 21, 1899, p. 4.

9. Some particulars of the fight-film controversy—among others, Edison's complicity or noncomplicity and some of Albert Smith's memories (see Albert E. Smith and Phil A. Koury, *Two Reels and a Crank* [1952; reprint, New York: Garland, 1985] can still spark debate among film historians.

CHAPTER 23: AVANT-GARDE AVIATRIX

1. Blanche Scott obituary, *The New York Times*, January 13, 1970, p. 40.

2. Ibid.

3. "Miss Scott Makes Bow to Public," *Fort Wayne Journal-Gazette*, October 24, 1910, p. 6.

4. Valerie Moolman, *Women Aloft*, p. 18.

5. Ibid., p. 18.

6. "Miss Scott Makes Bow," p. 1.

7. Ibid., pp. 1, 6.

8. Kenneth B. Keller, "Nation's First Aviatrix Earned Her Wings Here!" p. 1E.

9. Moolman, *Women Aloft*, p. 18.

10. "Blanche Scott obituary," p. 40.

CHAPTER 24: FIRST LADY OF FITNESS

1. Mrs. S. T. Rorer, "What Nervous People Should Eat," *The Ladies' Home Journal* 26 (February 1909): 40.

2. Annie Payson Call, "Why Fuss So Much About What I Eat?", *Ladies' Home Journal* (January 1909), p. 22.

3. Lulu Hunt Peters, *Diet and Health with Key to the Calories*, p. 13.

4. Ibid., p. 107.

5. Ibid., p. 109.

6. Ibid., p. 110.

7. Ibid., p. 100.

8. Ibid., p. 59.

9. Ibid., p. 13.

CHAPTER 25: MADAME CHAIRMAN

1. *Dictionary of American Biography,* p. 145.

2. T. H. Caraway obituary, *The Nation,* November 18, 1931, p. 531.

3. James T. Edwards, ed., *Notable American Women,* p. 285.

4. *Dictionary of American Biography,* p. 145.

5. Hermann B. Deutsch, "Hattie and Huey," *Saturday Evening Post,* October 15, 1932, p. 7.

6. *Dictionary of American Biography,* p. 144.

7. Deutsch, "Hattie and Huey," p. 7.

8. Ibid., p. 88.

9. Ibid., pp. 88–89.

10. Edwards, *Notable American Women,* p. 285.

11. Ibid., p. 286.

Sources

American Mutoscope v. Edison Mfg. Co., Circuit Court D., New Jersey, May 6, 1905.

Andrews, Matthew Page. *The Founding of Maryland.* Baltimore: Williams & Wilkins; New York: Appleton-Century, 1933.

Arber, Edward. *The Story of the Pilgrim Fathers,*A.D. 1606– 1623; *As Told by Themselves, Their Friends, and Their Enemies.* Boston: Houghton, Mifflin, 1897.

Archer, Gleason L. *With Axe and Musket at Plymouth.* New York: American Historical Society, 1936.

Archives of Maryland (Baltimore: Maryland Historical Society, 1891).

Banning, William. *Six Horses.* New York: Century, 1930.

Barnes, Joseph W. "Rochester and the Automobile Industry." *Rochester History* 43 (April and July 1981).

Blanche Scott obituary. *The New York Times,* January 13, 1970, p. 40.

Bowen, Richard LeBaron. *Early Rehoboth.* 2 vols. Concord, N.H.: Rumford, 1950.

Bradford, Governor William. *Of Plymouth Plantation, 1620–1647.* New York: Knopf, 1976.

Bradstreet, Anne. *The Tenth Muse Lately Sprung Up in America.* London, 1650.

Bradstreet, Anne. *Several Poems.* Boston, 1678.

Brady, William A. "Showman." *Saturday Evening Post,* January 11, 1936, p. 22; January 25, 1936, p. 23; February 8, 1936, p. 74; February 22, 1936, p. 76; March 7, 1936, p. 77; March 21, 1936, p. 80; April 4, 1936, p. 81.

Brody, Jane. *Jane Brody's Nutrition Book.* New York: Norton, 1981.

Brown, Martha C. "Of Pearl Ash, Emptins, and Tree Sweetin." *American Heritage,* August/September 1981, pp. 104–107.

Bryan, George S. *Edison: The Man and His Work.* Garden City, N.Y.: Garden City Publishing, 1926.

Burns, Robert Daniel. "Semi-Centennial of Selden's 'Gas Buggy.' " *Rochester Democrat,* May 5, 1929.

Burr, George Lincoln, ed. *Narratives of the Witchcraft Cases, 1648–1706.* New York: Barnes & Noble, 1914. Reprint. 1945.

Bush, Frank Summer. *History of Huntington County, Indiana.* Chicago: Lewis, 1914.

Caffrey, Kate. *The Mayflower.* New York: Stein & Day, 1974.

Call, A. P. "Why Fuss So Much About What I Eat?" *Ladies' Home Journal* 26 (January 1909); 22.

Chilton, W. B. "The Brent Family." *Virginia Magazine of History and Biography,* April 1905 and January, April, and July 1908.

Collections of the Maine Historical Society. Sec. 1 Vol. 5. (Portland, Maine: Brown, Thurston, Printer, 1857).

Commager, Henry Steele. *Documents of American History.* 8th ed. New York: Appleton, 1968.

Converse, Margaret. "George Selden and His Road Engine." *Rochester Democrat and Chronicle,* August 22, 1971.

Cooley, Timothy Mather. *Sketches of the Life and Character of the Reverend Lemuel Haynes, A.M.* New York: Harper & Bros., 1837.

Creel, George. "The Woman Who Holds Her Tongue." *Collier's Magazine,* September 18, 1937, pp. 22, 25.

Davis, Maxine. "Five Democratic Women." *Ladies' Home Journal,* May 1933.

Demos, John Putnam. *Entertaining Satan: Witchcraft and the Culture of Early New England.* New York: Oxford University Press, 1982.

Deutsch, Hermann B. "Hattie and Huey." *Saturday Evening Post,* October 15, 1932.

Dictionary of American Biography. Edited by Dumas Malone. New York: Scribners, 1935. (Copyright renewed 1963.)

Dillon, Francis. *The Pilgrims.* Garden City, N.Y.: Doubleday, 1975.

Dow, George Francis. *The Pirates of the New England Coast, 1630–1730.* Salem, Mass.: Marine Research Society, 1923.

Doyle, Kathleen. "Louis Prang: Father of the American Christmas Card." *American History Illustrated,* December 1988.

Drayton, John, ed. Letter from Major Andrew Williamson to the President of South Carolina, August 4, 1776. In *Memoirs of the American Revolution, from Its Commencement to the Year 1776, Inclusive; as Relating to the States of North-Carolina and Georgia.* Charleston, 1821; Reprinted as Drayton, John, ed. *Memoirs of the American Revolution as Relating to the State of South Carolina.* New York: The New York Times and Arno Press, 1969.

Dunham Public Library, Whitesboro, New York.

Edison American Mutoscope Co. Circuit Court of Appeals, Second Circuit, March 10, 1902.

Edison American Mutoscope (Biograph) Co. Circuit Court S.D., New York, July 15, 1901.

Egan, Pierce. *Boxiana: Sketches of Ancient and Modern Pugilism.* Introduction by Dennis Prestidge. Facsimile ed. July 1812. Reprint. Leicester, England: Vance Harvey Publishing, August 1971. Printed by Unwin Brothers Ltd., Old Woking, Surrey, England.

"Explosion of a Fundamental Fallacy in Diet." *Current Literature* 6 (September 1907): 327–328.

"The Fallacy of the Fuel Units (or Calories) of Foods." *Contemporary Review* 118 (December 1920): 816–822.

Farish, Thomas Edwin. *The Gold Hunters of California.* Chicago: Donahue, 1904.

Fell, John L. *Film Before Griffith.* Berkeley: University of California Press, 1983.

General Court of Trial, Newport County, Rhode Island (1671–1724). Record I.

Germantown Historical Society Collections.

Gilbert, Miriam. *Henry Ford: Maker of the Model T.* Boston: Houghton Mifflin, 1962.

Gill, Crispin. *Mayflower Remembered.* New York: Taplinger, 1970.

Gillespie, C. Bancroft. *Portland Past and Present.* Portland, Maine: Evening Express Publishing, 1899.

Glenn, Horton B. *How to Get Thinner Once and for All.* New York: Dutton, 1965.

Goodwin, John A. *The Pilgrim Republic.* Boston: Houghton Mifflin, 1920.

Gorn, Elliott J. *The Manly Art: Bare-Knuckle Prize Fighting in America.* Ithaca, N.Y.: Cornell University Press, 1986.

Grayston, Florence L. "Lambdin P. Milligan: A Knight of the Golden Circle." *Indiana Magazine of History* 43 (December 1947): 379–391.

Gutheim, Frederick. *The Potomac.* New York: Rinehart, 1949.

Hamilton, Edward P. *Chocolate Village.* Milton, Mass.: Milton Public Library Collections and Milton Historical Society Collections, 1966.

Hamilton, Edward P. *A History of Milton.* Milton, Mass.: Milton Historical Society, 1957.

Hampton, Benjamin Bowles. *A History of the Movies.* 1931. Reprint. New York: Arno Press, 1970.

Hanks, Charles Stedman. *Our Plymouth Forefathers.* Boston: Authors' Publishing, 1907.

Harris, Sherwood. *The First to Fly: Aviation's Pioneers.* New York: Simon & Schuster, 1970.

Harrison, E. S. *History of Santa Cruz County.* San Francisco: Pacific Press, 1892.

Hill, Ralph Nading. *Contrary Country: A Chronicle of Vermont.* New York: Rinehart, 1950.

Hodge, Harriet Woodbury. *Mayflower Families in Progress: John Billington of the Mayflower and His Descendants for Five Generations.* Plymouth, Mass.: General Society of Mayflower Descendants, 1988.

Hodges, Margaret. *Hopkins of the Mayflower.* New York: Farrar, Straus & Giroux, 1972.

Hosmer, James Kendall, ed. *Winthrop's Journal.* Vols. 1 and 2, *History of New England 1630–1649.* New York: Scribners, 1908; New York: Barnes & Noble, 1959.

Houghton Library Collections, Harvard University.

Hutchinson, Robert, ed. *Poems of Anne Bradstreet.* New York: Dover, 1969.

Ives, J. Moss. *The Ark and the Dove: The Beginning of Civil and Religious Liberties in America.* London: Longmans, Green, 1936.

James, Edward T., ed. *Notable American Women, 1607–1950:*

A Biographical Dictionary. 3 vols. Cambridge, Mass.: Belknap/ Harvard University Press, 1971.

Janeway, Elizabeth. *The Early Days of Automobiles.* New York: Random House, 1956.

"John B. Curtis Obituary." *Daily Eastern Argus,* June 14, 1897.

"Kalorie Kids." *Ladies' Home Journal* 40 (January 1923): 91.

Kaplan, Sidney, and Emma Nogrady Kaplan. Rev. ed. *The Black Presence in the Era of the American Revolution.* Amherst: University of Massachusetts Press, 1989.

Karlsen, Carol F. *The Devil in the Shape of a Woman: Witchcraft in Colonial New England.* New York: Norton, 1987.

Keller, Kenneth B. "Nation's First Aviatrix Earned Her Wings Here!" *Indiana Journal-Gazette,* December 20, 1964.

Kelley, Darwin, ed. "Lambdin P. Milligan's Appeal for States' Rights and Constitutional Liberty During the Civil War." *Indiana Magazine of History* V, 46, no. 3: 263–283.

King, Jonathan. *The Mayflower Miracle.* London: David & Charles, 1987.

Klaus, Samuel, ed. *The Milligan Case.* New York: Knopf, 1929.

Knight, Arthur. *The Liveliest Art.* New York: Macmillan, 1957.

Kuykendall, Ralph S. *The Hawaiian Kingdom.* 2nd ed. Vol. 2, 1854–1874, *Twenty Critical Years.* Honolulu: University of Hawaii Press, 1966.

Land, Aubrey C. *Colonial Maryland: A History.* Millwood, N.Y.: KTO Press, 1981.

Lately, Thomas. *The First President Johnson: The Three Lives of the Seventeenth President of the United States of America.* New York: Morrow, 1968.

Lesh, U. S. "A Knight of the Golden Circle." *The Michigan Alumnus.* July 26, 1947; Fort Wayne: Public Library of Fort Wayne and Allen County, 1956. Reprinted with special permission of the author and of the publisher of the *Michigan Alumnus.*

Library of Congress Collections.

Longwell, Marjorie. *America and Women*. Philadelphia: Dorrance, 1962.

Lord, John. *The Life of Emma Willard*. New York: Appleton, 1873.

Lutz, Alma. *Emma Willard: Pioneer Educator of American Women*. 1964. Reprint. Westport, Conn.: Greenwood, 1983.

MacGowan, Kenneth. *Behind the Screen*. New York: Delacorte, 1965.

McClain, Jim. *A Brief Account of the Wicked Doings of Dixie Bull*. (pamphlet). 1st ed. printed by Court Printers, N.Y., 1980.

Maine Archives, Augusta.

Massachusetts Archives, Dorchester.

Massachusetts Historical Society Collections, Boston.

Mason, Julian D., ed. *The Poems of Phillis Wheatley. Rev. and enlarged ed*. Chapel Hill: University of North Carolina Press, 1989.

Mast, Gerald. *A Short History of the Movies*. New York: Pegasus, 1971.

McCullough, Edo. *Good Old Coney Island: A Sentimental Journey into the Past*. New York: Scribners, 1957.

Mellen, Kathleen Dickinson. *The Gods Depart: A Saga of the Hawaiian Kingdom 1832–1873*. New York: Hastings House, 1956.

Memorial History of Boston. Edited by Justin Winsor. 4 vols. Boston: Osgood, 1881.

Minkin, Gabe. *Getting Thin*. Boston: Little, Brown, 1983.

"Miss Scott Makes Bow to Public." *Indiana Journal-Gazette*, October 24, 1910, p. 1.

Moody, Ralph. *Stagecoach West*. New York: Crowell, 1967.

Moolman, Valerie. *Women Aloft*. Alexandria, Va.: Time-Life Books, 1981.

Morrison, Olin Dee. *Indiana at Civil War Time*. Athens, Ohio, 1961. Published by author.

Myers, Albert Cook, ed. *Narratives of Early Pennsylvania, West New Jersey, and Delaware, 1630–1707*. New York: Scribners, 1912.

The National Encyclopedia of American Biography. 62 vols. New York: James T. White & Company, 1898, p. 384. (Rev. ed., 1979).

The New York Times. "Jeffries and Sharkey Here," November 3, 1899, p. 5; "Jeffries Won the Fight," "The Fight By Rounds," November 4, 1899, p. 3; "Biograph Fight Pictures," November 21, 1899, p. 4. "Our First Royal Visitor," August 9, 1866, p. 1; "Thirty Years in Disguise," January 9, 1880, p. 2.

Nolan, Alan T. "Ex Parte Milligan: A Curb of Executive and Military Power." In *We the People: Indiana and the United States Constitution, Lectures in Observance of the Bicentennial of the Constitution*. Indianapolis: Indiana Historical Society, 1987.

North, Joseph, *The Early Development of the Motion Picture*. New York: Arno, 1973.

Orcutt, William Dana. *Good Old Dorchester, 1630–1893: A Narrative History of the Town*. 2nd ed. Cambridge, Mass.: University Press, 1908.

Pennypacker, Samuel Whitaker. *The Settlement of Philadelphia, Pennsylvania*. Philadelphia: William V. Campbell, 1899.

"Perils of a Simple Diet". *Current Literature* (February 1909): 215.

Pert, P. L., Jr. "Maine Spruce Gum Tycoon Unnoticed During Lifetime." *Maine Sunday Telegram*, June 27, 1965, p. 2.

Peters, Lulu Hunt. *Diet and Health with Key to the Calories*. Chicago: Reilly and Lee, 1918.

Peters, Lulu Hunt. *Diet for Children and Adults and the Kalorie Kids.* New York: Dodd, Mead, 1924.

Peters, Lulu Hunt. "Vittles and Vitality." *Collier's Mazagine,* June 12, 1926, pp. 8–9.

Peters, Dr. Lulu Hunt. "Watch Your Weight!" *American Magazine* 93 (March 1922): 56–57.

Piercy, Josephine K. *Anne Bradstreet.* New York: Twayne, 1965.

"Plaque Commemorates First Vote Cast by a Woman." *San Francisco Chronicle,* June 17, 1940.

Ploski, Harry A., and James Williams, comps. and eds. *The Negro Almanac: A Reference Work on the African American.* 5th ed. Detroit: Gale Research, 1989.

Portland, Maine, Public Library Collections.

Potter, Kate Berry. "Passages in the Life of the Author of Aunt Maguire's (sic) Letters, Bedott Papers, etc." *Godey's Lady's Book,* July and August 1853.

Ramey, Mary E. W. *Chronicles of Mistress Margaret Brent.* 1915.

Rehoboth (Massachusetts) Antiquarian Society.

Richeson, Cena Golder. "The Woman in Charles Parkhurst," *True West,* August 1983, pp. 39–40.

Rhode, Eric, *A History of the Cinema: From Its Origins to 1970.* London: Penguin Books, 1976.

Rhode Island Historical Society, Providence.

Roberts, Dana. "Two Letters in Old Desk Sketch Inventor's Trials." *Rochester Times,* May 8, 1929.

Robinson, William H. *Phillis Wheatley and Her Writings.* New York: Garland, 1984.

Rorer, Mrs. S. T. "What Nervous People Should Eat." *Ladies' Home Journal* 26 (February 1909): 40.

Ross, John, "Was This a Conspirator's House?" *Indianapolis Star Magazine,* April 28, 1947, p. 14.

Rudolph, Jack. "Tom Molyneaux—America's 'Almost' Champion." *American History Illustrated,* August 1979, pp. 8–10, 12–14.

Sassaman, Richard. "Pssst! Didja Know That Tom Edison Staged Illegal Fights for Flicks?" *Sports Illustrated,* July 12, 1982.

Sayers, Edwin. "George Had the Idea First." *Rochester Democrat and Chronicle Upstate Magazine,* May 6, 1979.

Schappes, Morris, ed. *A Documentary History of the Jews in the United States 1654–1875.* 2nd ed., rev. New York: Citadel, 1952.

Scott, Kenneth. *Counterfeiting in Colonial America.* New York: Oxford University Press, 1957.

Scott, Robert. "I Invented the Automobile." *Automobile Quarterly* (Winter 1966).

Selden, George D. "Horses Hated Rochester Alumnus, Pioneer, Inventor of Automobile." *Rochester Alumni-Alumnae Review,* February/March 1940.

Selections From the Fancy; or, True Sportsman's Guide by an Operator. Barre, Mass.: Imprint Society, 1972.

Shamburger, Page, and Joe Christy. *Command the Horizon.* New York: Barnes, 1968.

Sharkey, Tom, with Morrow Mayo. "Fighting the Champions." *Saturday Evening Post,* September 12, 1936.

Shields, John C., ed. *The Collected Works of Phillis Wheatley.* New York: Oxford University Press, 1988.

Sifakis, Carl. *The Encyclopedia of American Crime.* New York: Facts On File, 1982.

Sievers, Harry J. "The Trial of Lambdin P. Milligan." Fort Wayne: Public Library of Fort Wayne and Allen County, 1964. (Pamphlet is a reproduction of Slovers, *Benjamin Harrison: Hoosier Statesman,* vol. 2, pp. 35–45.)

Simmons, Amelia. *American Cookery.* Rev. ed Hartford: Hudson & Goodwin, 1796.

Simonhoff, Harry. *Jewish Notables in America 1765–1865: Links of an Endless Chain.* New York: Greenberg, 1956.

Snow, Edward Rowe. *Pirates and Buccaneers of the Atlantic Coast.* Boston: Yankee Publishing, 1944.

Spruill, Julia Cherry. "Mistress Margaret Brent." *Maryland History Magazine,* December 1934.

Stevens Memorial Library Collections, North Andover, Massachusetts.

Stimpson, George. *A Book About a Thousand Things.* New York: Harper, 1946.

Stimpson, George. *Information Roundup.* New York: Harper, 1948.

Strong, Sydney, ed. *Roger Clap's Memoirs.* Seattle: Pigott-Washington, 1929.

Tait, Samuel W., Jr. "Legal Case of Civil War Days Paralleled in Recent Ruling." *Fort Wayne News Sentinel.* 1942.

Taylor, Clarence G. "The Strange Story of 'Cockeyed Charley.' " *Argonaut,* December 23, 1955, p. 8.

Taylor, Mary K. "America's First Cookbook." *Early American Life,* February 1991, pp. 40–43.

Watkins, Howard. "One-Eyed Charlie's Secret." *Westways,* October 1960, pp. 24–25.

Weitenkampf, Frank. *American Graphic Art.* New ed., rev. and enl. New York: Macmillan.

Wheatley, Phillis. *Poems on Various Subjects Religious and Moral.* (Published according to Act of Parliament, Sept. 1, 1773, by Arch.d Bell, Bookseller No. 8 near the Saracens Head, Aldgate.)

Whitcher, Frances Miriam Berry. *The Widow Bedott Papers.* Introduction by Alice B. Neal. New York: J. C. Derby; Boston: Phillips, Sampson; Cincinnati: H. W. Derby, 1856.

Whitcher, M. L. *Widow Spriggins, Mary Elmer, and Other Sketches.* 1867.

White, Elizabeth Wade. *Anne Bradstreet: The Tenth Muse.* New York: Oxford University Press, 1971.

Who's Who in America, 1908–1909.

Who Was Who Among North American Authors.

Who Was Who in America, vol. 1.

Wildes, Henry Emerson. *William Penn.* New York: Macmillan, 1974.

Williams, Selma. *Riding the Nightmare: Women & Witchcraft.* New York: Atheneum, 1978.

Williams, T. Harry. *Huey Long.* New York: Knopf, 1969.

Willison, George F. *The Pilgrim Reader: The Story of the Pilgrims as Told by Themselves & Their Contemporaries Friendly and Unfriendly.* Garden City, N.Y.: Doubleday, 1953.

Willison, George F. *Saints and Strangers.* New York: Reynal & Hitchcock, 1945.

Wilson, Mary Tolford. "Amelia Simmons Fills a Need: American Cookery, 1796." *William and Mary Quarterly* 14 (January 1957): 16–30.

Wilstach, Paul. *Tidewater Maryland.* 1931. Reprint. New York: Tudor, 1945.

Wilstach, Paul. *Potomac Landings.* 4th ed. New York: Tudor, 1937.

Winther, Oscar Osburn. *Via Western Express and Stagecoach.* Palo Alto, Calif.: Stanford University Press, 1945.

Wolfe, Gerald R. "The Selden Patent." *Antique Automobile,* part 1, May/June 1982, and part 2, July/August 1982.

Woody, Thomas. *A History of Women's Education in the*

United States. 1929. Reprint. New York: Octagon, 1966. (1929).

Young, Alexander. *Chronicles of the Pilgrim Fathers of the Colony of Plymouth, 1620–1625.* New York: Da Capo, 1971.

Young, John V. "Ghost Towns of the Santa Cruz Mountains." *San Jose Mercury Herald,* June 24, 1934, p. 17.

Index